Dive Ontario!

Also by Cris Kohl:

DIVE SOUTHWESTERN ONTARIO!

SHIPWRECK TALES: The St. Clair River (to 1900)

DIVE ONTARIO TWO! More Ontario Shipwreck Stories

DIVE

ONTARIO!

The Guide to Shipwrecks and Scuba Diving

by Cris Kohl

**ILLUSTRATED WITH PHOTOGRAPHS,
MAPS, AND DRAWINGS**

INCLUDING ARTWORK by ADAM HENLEY

Published by
Cris Kohl,
16 Stanley Avenue,
Chatham, Ontario, Canada N7M 3J2
Telephone: (519) 351-1966
Fax: (519) 351-1753

Nautical chart portions are reproduced by permission of the Canadian Hydrographic Service, Ottawa. The chart portions reproduced in this book are not for use in navigation. The Charts and Publications Regulations of the Canada Shipping Act require vessels operating in Canadian waters to carry the latest, best scale, corrected CHS charts. The diagrams and chart portions in this book do not meet the requirements of the Act.

For further information, or to order charts, contact: Chart Distribution Office, Canadian Hydrographic Service, Department of Fisheries and Oceans, P.O. Box 8080, 1675 Russell Road, OTTAWA, Ontario, Canada K1G 3H6, telephone (613) 998-4931, fax (613) 998-1217.

NOTE: photo credits are shown in terms of the author's source for the photograph rather than a specific photographer who might have taken it, except where the photographer is known and specifically named.

The author thanks the talented Great Lakes marine artist, Robert McGreevy, for producing the drawing that is embossed onto the hardcover of this book. This graphic art, modified by Mr. McGreevy from one of his earlier sketches, depicts some of the components of our Great Lakes maritime heritage: historical research, underwater exploration, and photography.

First Edition: December, 1990
Revised and Enlarged Edition: November, 1995

iv

*This book is dedicated to all who dive Ontario waters---
past, present, and future*

Disclaimer

The author of *Dive Ontario! The Guide to Shipwrecks and Scuba Diving* has made every effort to assure the accuracy of the contents of this book. However, no warranty or guarantee is expressed or implied that the information contained in *Dive Ontario! The Guide to Shipwrecks and Scuba Diving* is accurate or correct, or may not contain errors. The author shall in no way be responsible for any consequential, incidental, or exemplary loss or damage resulting from the use of any of the graphics or printed information contained in *Dive Ontario! The Guide to Shipwrecks and Scuba Diving*. The author disclaims any liability for omissions, errors, alterations, and misprints, and here gives further notice that *Dive Ontario! The Guide to Shipwrecks and Scuba Diving* is not to be used for navigation. An explanation: the expressions, "scrounge dive" and "scavenger dive" refer to a) locating, viewing, and photographing heritage material underwater without disturbing it, and/or b) bringing up only modern items such as lures, sinkers, other fishing equipment, golf balls, lighters, random bottles not in a garbage dump site, metal cans, and other items regularly collected by divers doing environmental clean-up dives. All heritage sites must remain undisturbed by scuba divers.

ACKNOWLEDGEMENTS

To the First Edition: The author sincerely thanks the following individuals, listed alphabetically, for information that led to the completion of this book: Gilles Beaulieu, Ottawa; Louise Begin and Jim Sauberli of the Wet Owls Scuba Club, Ottawa; Bob Day, Superintendent, Fathom Five National Marine Park, Tobermory; Don Edwards of Thunder Bay, Northwest Director of the Ontario Underwater Council; Peter Engelbert, shipwreck expert with the Ontario Ministry of Culture and Communications; Ed Fabok and Art Vermette of the South Shore Scuba Club, Leamington; Alan Given of Wiarton; Fred Gregory, Executive Director, Save Ontario Shipwrecks; Charles Guibord, Ottawa; Joyce Hayward, President, Ohio chapter, Save Ontario Shipwrecks; Doug Jackson of the Sarnia Underwater Club; John Karry, President, Windsor chapter, Save Ontario Shipwrecks; Gary Kennedy of Chatham; Ryan LeBlanc, President, Lake Superior chapter, Save Ontario Shipwrecks; Scott McWilliam, of Brantford, for valuable information on Lake Superior's north shore shipwrecks; David Monahan, Director, Marine Cartography, and Ron Lemieux, both of the Canadian Hydrographic Service, Ottawa; Stan McClellan, Marine Advisor, Fathom Five National Marine Park; Roy Pickering, President, Kent Divers Association, Chatham; Gary Porcaro of the Seaway Divers, Welland; Mary Lynn Prince of Ottawa; Tim Rees, President, Bluewater Scuba Club, Port Elgin; Karen Ridding of the Ontario Underwater Council; Douglas Rosser, Executive Director (1978-1990), Ontario Underwater Council; Rod Stevens of Kingston; Frank and Sharon Troxell of the Great Lakes Aquanauts of Greater Detroit; Bessel J. VandenHazel; John Varney, President, Sudbury chapter, Save Ontario Shipwrecks; and Peter White, President, Ontario Underwater Council. For anyone I may have inadvertently overlooked, please forgive me; I do thank you for your assistance.

The generous co-operation of the following institutions and their helpful staffs is also gratefully acknowledged: the Ontario Underwater Council; Save Ontario Shipwrecks; the Province of Ontario Archives, Toronto; the Public Archives of Canada, Ottawa; the Canadian Hydrographic Service, Ottawa; Fathom Five National Marine Park, Tobermory; the Great Lakes Historical Society, Vermilion, Ohio; the Institute for Great Lakes Research (Bowling Green State University), Perrysburg, Ohio; the Chatham Public Library, Chatham, Ontario; the St. Marys District Museum, St. Marys, Ontario.

The author thanks Andrew Van Zelst, Mercury Press, Chatham, Ron Paine and Cam Gregory, Bookshelf Bindery, Ridgetown, and Keith Dawson, Instant Print Shoppe, Chatham, for their advice and work in the printing of this book.

Lastly, the author sincerely thanks all his relatives and other friends for their encouragement, support, and help that led to the completion of this project, and for tolerating the many hours of travel, patience, seclusion, and absence necessitated by the research, field work, photography, and writing of the text.

Additions to the Revised Edition: Lou Bumbala of Sea N' Sky Dive Shop, Prescott, diver Joe Drummond of Wheatley, diver Kathy Everson, Trenton journalist, Adam Henley, talented Toronto-area artist, diver Kathy Hoey from Simcoe, diver Pat Kelly of Ajax, diver Shari Lynn Müller from Wallaceburg, Picton diver Doug Pettingill, diver Tim Philp of Brantford, Toronto-area diver Peter Ridjniks, commercial diver James Taylor of Picton, diver Hugh Wyatt of Sault Ste. Marie, Susan Yankoo and George Wheeler of the Ducks Dive Shop, Point Traverse, the Great Lakes Marine Collection of the Milwaukee Public Library, the Metropolitan Toronto Public Library, and the Lake Carriers Association, Cleveland, Ohio.

CONTENTS

INTRODUCTION

The rapidly-growing interest in scuba diving as a recreational sport, especially in these health-minded late 1900's, has produced large numbers of scuba-certified people searching, with eager curiosity, for dive sites. Ontario certainly has many locations that will delight and thrill sub-aqua explorers for a long time. This book describes 250 dive sites and gives the reader scuba-related information on topics such as safety and emergencies, diveshops, boat charters, clubs, the Ontario Underwater Council, Save Ontario Shipwrecks, fish, etc.

Ontario, the second-largest province in the second largest nation on the face of this earth, is an underwater explorer's paradise. Thousands of established and potential dive sites exist within Ontario's range of 1,000 miles (1,600 kms.) in an east-to-west direction, and 1,050 miles (1,680 kms.) from north to south.

We are blessed with an official count of 226,918 lakes in Ontario, or about 400,000 if one includes all the water holes that are minimal in size (Source: Fisheries Branch, Ministry of Natural Resources, publication: "Counts and Measurements of Ontario Lakes -- 1978"); these bodies of water measure 44,762,966 acres (approximately 18,000,000 hectares), covering 16.6% of the province's area. Ontario also has 20,000 miles (32,186 kilometres) of rivers.

Ontario's freshwater shoreline extends 2,362 miles (3,801 kilometres) along the Great Lakes, of which the lion's share is in Ontario. Lakes Superior, Huron (including all of Georgian Bay and the North Channel), St. Clair, Erie, and Ontario lie along the southern border of Ontario.

Ontario's saltwater shoreline (you didn't know we had one, did you!) extends 680 miles (1,094 kilometres) along the James and Hudson Bays on the northern edge of the province. This saltwater underwater realm remains totally unexplored.

This book offers suggestions and descriptions of where to dive in Ontario. This book will not tell you where to go camping, or motelling, or where to do your conventional siteseeing, or where to launch your boat. This book doesn't even give you a map of Ontario! You can pick up that information free of charge from the provincial government tourist bureaus scattered around the province. I felt no need to make the book larger, and thus charge you more than the small fortune you're already paying, for information available for free. For free copies of the province's annual booklets on "Camping," "Accommodations," and "Marinas," or a free roadmap of the province, write to Ministry of Tourism and Recreation, Province of Ontario, Queen's Park, Toronto, Ontario, M7A 2E5.

Since no book is perfect, the author welcomes your comments, corrections, additions, and suggestions. Please write to him at 16 Stanley Ave., Chatham, Ontario, Canada, N7M 3J2, or telephone him at (519) 351-1966.

I hope this book brings people (back) into diving.

Cris Kohl,
Chatham, Ontario, Canada

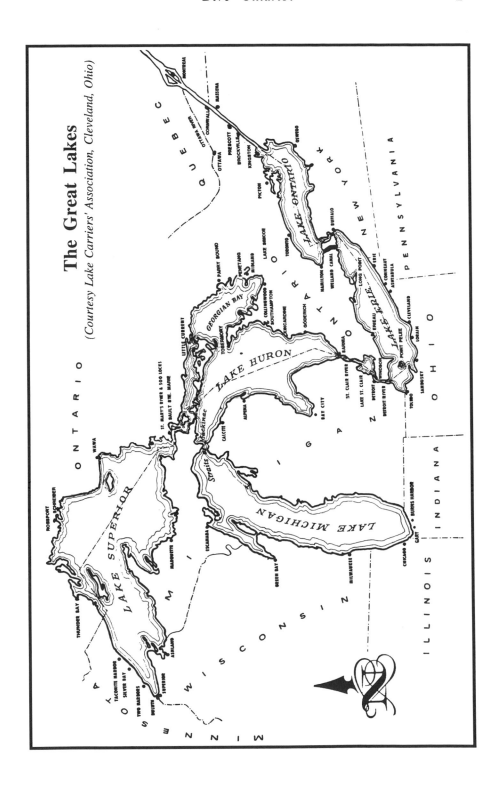

The Great Lakes

(Courtesy Lake Carriers' Association, Cleveland, Ohio)

Some Notes on
Scuba Diving Safety

WARNING

Diving is a potentially dangerous activity. The author does not endorse or encourage specific practices, nor is this book meant as a substitute for proper training, education, and personal dive site and self-skills evaluation. The author accepts no liability for the scuba diving practices or judgments of his readers. You're on your own.

This is not a "how to" book on scuba diving; it is a "where to" guide to dive sites in Ontario.

Regarding scuba safety, let me offer the following somewhat consoling statistics: in the U. S. for the year 1987, the following activities had these death rates per 100,000 people -- mountain climbing, 599; hang gliding, 114; parachuting, 24; snowmobiling, 13; mountain hiking, 6.4; scuba diving, 2.9.

Yes, scuba diving is one of the safest activities a human being can enjoy.

I have identified each of the dive sites as suitable for novice, intermediate, or advanced divers, or midway points in between each of these designations. I thank Joyce Hayward and the Bay Area Divers of Ohio for their assistance:

A novice dive: a) is less than 60' (18 metres) in depth.
b) is suitable for a newly-certified diver or infrequent diver.
c) has no or very little current.
d) has good visibility.
e) may include wreck diving with no penetration.

An intermediate dive: a) is suitable for more experienced divers.
b) may reach depths between 60' and 100' (18 to 30 metres).
c) may include wreck diving with no penetration.
d) may involve waves or some current.
e) may involve open water sites with boat entries.
f) has good to moderate visibility.
g) may have other conditions which may warrant more experience.

An advanced dive: a) may reach depths between 100' and 130' (30 to 39 metres).
b) is suitable for very experienced divers (may prefer specialty certification).
c) may involve wreck penetration, swift or variable current diving. cold water, or ice diving.
d) may have extremely limited or zero visibility.
e) may require special skills such as navigation, rescue, cave or cavern diving training, or special equipment.

Regarding safety during scuba diving: use common sense and neither forget nor neglect nor ignore your training.

When using a diveboat, keep a lookout aboard at all times. Fly both the swallow tail, blue-and-white alpha flag and the red-and-white divers down flag from a boat when divers are actually in the water. The passing boater who may fail to recognize one flag may respond the other.

It is not yet the law in Ontario (except in Fathom Five National Marine Park at Tobermory) that the red-and-white divers down flag must be flown whenever divers are in the water, but it would be foolhardy to dive without it.

Never dive with the diveboat unattended. Should an emergency occur below, or should the exhausted divers be unable to get back on board the boat, an assistant who stays on the boat is always helpful. In my neophyte diving days, we drift-dove down the Snye River, a branch of the St. Clair River in the Flats area, holding on to a line attached to an unattended boat; fortunately the worst thing that happened was that a passing powerboater pilfered my dive flag!

An obvious bit of advice, yet on occasion ignored, is to avoid diving in front of freighters that require great distances to make even slight turns. If you do end up with one passing immediately over you, hug the bottom of the river or lake. If necessary, sink your knife into the bottom to act as a holding post. Don't do anything that may force you to make an emergency ascent. While you're flat on the bottom, with the water, sand, and silt swirling madly all around you from the freighter's propeller, ask yourself how you got into that situation in the first place. Then, don't do it again.

Current diving requires special training and practice; start with a slow current before you attempt to go diving on the *Monarch* or the *Eastcliffe Hall* .

Make sure that you have a sharp dive knife with you in case you get caught in some of the old fishing nets on shipwrecks or in the miles of monofilament fishing lines around docks and in river debris. Also, never, ever dive alone.

Beware of concrete buoy anchors and submerged piles (or "spiles" or "posts" or whatever you prefer to call them) suddenly appearing from the edge of visibility. They could frighten a novice diver moving quickly downstream. Obviously, divers should not hit these obstructions or snag dive gear on them.

Don't scuba dive in or near canals. Lockmasters and boaters would find divers a potentially dangerous (mostly to the person of the divers) nuisance.

Scuba diving is a lot like riding a motorcycle; once you lose respect for it, it will kill you.

I think we all agree that we want neither more scuba deaths, nor government legislation that will restrict our diving or our dive sites. The Ontario Underwater Council (O.U.C.) is the liaison, or buffer, between the sport diving community and government. Support the Council, not only by joining it as a member, but also by diving safely and not becoming a fatality statistic or the cause of an inquest that will put our sport on trial. Since 1979, the O.U.C. has published an annual scuba accidents and fatalities report. We can't bring back the dead, but we can learn from their mistakes and become better divers. For information on these reports, call (416) 426-7033, fax (416) 426-7336, or write to the Ontario Underwater Council, 1185 Eglinton Ave. East, NORTH YORK, Ontario M3C 3C6.

Lastly, don't forget that there is a list of emergency telephone numbers on the last page of this book.

The Ottawa River Area

Site 1: The Mint Site

Location: The Ottawa River, in downtown Ottawa, just behind and a
bit downstream from the Royal Canadian mint. Head out of
Ottawa on Sussex Drive. Just past the mint, turn left at the
first set of lights. This is Lady Grey Drive. From the parking
lot just off Sussex, when you are facing the river, turn left
down a short, rough road (or park in the lot and carry your gear
down.)

Access: Shore. There is a public floating dock you can use.

Skill Level: Intermediate - advanced.

Depth: 0 - 60 feet (0 - 18 metres).

Visibility: 4 - 10 feet (1.2 - 3 metres).

Description: With a name like "the mint site," one conjures up all
sorts of things: is this where the old mint dies were dumped
when the coins for any given year had been stamped? Is this
where they dumped all the coins that had horrible errors, such
as double-strikes, that kept them out of circulation?
Unfortunately, nothing as sensational as that awaits the diver
here. This is a scavenger dive; in the past, old bottles, such as
blob-top torpedoes, and clay pipes were the rewards of patient
searching, but most of those have been removed. There is also a
huge sturgeon, about 7' (2 metres) in length, which suddenly
startles unsuspecting divers who think he is a log -- until he
swims away. His name is Oliver. Don't hurt him.

Hazards: The water is the typical-northern-Ontario-lake-and-river
coffee colour (with no milk added), and the deeper you dive, the
darker it gets, even at high noon. Underwater lights don't go
far, and it is too easy to lose one's dive buddy. There are many
submerged logs on which the diver must avoid getting
snagged. There is also the typical one to one-and-a-half knot
Ottawa River current running at this site. Boating traffic can
also be heavy at times, so fly a divers down flag.

Diving in the Ottawa River has its advantages and disadvantages. The poor visibility in dark water full of sunken logs indicates barriers that hide old bottles, such as these divers' tokens of accomplishment. The site is close to downtown Ottawa, near the mint, and the divers are members of the Wet Owls Underwater Club of Ottawa. (Photos by Cris Kohl.)

Site 2: The Wreck of the *Bruce*

Location:	The Ottawa River, at the site of the rowing club, just off Sussex Drive near downtown Ottawa.
Access:	Shore.
Skill Level:	Intermediate.
Depth:	20 - 30 feet (6 - 9 metres).
Visibility:	3 - 10 feet (1 - 3 metres).

Directions: Take Sussex Drive away from downtown Ottawa until, just past the mint, you get to Lady Grey Drive. Turn left onto this street and drive a short distance to the parking lot. This is virtually the same location as "the mint site," but for the latter, you turn down the left road as you face the river. For the *Bruce,* you turn down the right road to the water's edge at the Rideau Rowing Club.

Background: The 87-ton, 100-foot-long (30-metre) wooden paddlewheel steamer, *Bruce,* built at Goderich, Ontario in 1862, changed hands a number of times in her 13-year career. Purchased by Brockville residents in 1873, the *Bruce* operated on the Rideau as a passenger and freight boat. Sold to Ottawa Valley interests in the autumn of 1873 and renamed the *Seaman,* her first voyage in the new 1874 season proved to be too much, when her fully-loaded cargo holds started leaking. The vessel was purposely run ashore near East Templeton, and later taken to Hull for repairs. In March of 1875, the *Bruce,* still tied up at Hull, mysteriously burned to the water's edge. Concerns were expressed that the still-floating hull would become a menace to navigation, so apparently the remains of the *Bruce* were towed across the river to Ottawa and allowed to sink in 20' - 30' (6 - 9 metres) of water in Entrance Bay, at the foot of the Rideau Canal locks.

In 1980, a man named Frank Martin started the Santa Maria Society, which attempted to place a number of local shipwrecks into a small, easily-accessible underwater area to be known as the Santa Maria Underwater Park Area. Working with about 42 volunteers interested in nautical archaeology, the *Bruce* was raised and carefully moved the short distance to her present location, where she reportedly lies close to two other wrecks that sank there, the *Ivy* and the *William King.* Careful records were kept describing each artifact and its original location. The item providing the greatest interest was a 39" (one-metre) brass telescope, which was almost fully functional. This item was placed on exhibit in a local dive shop "to permit everyone to gain some sense of the history of the Ottawa River." This item's present location is unknown.

Description: The superstructure of the *Bruce* burned off, so there is no penetration diving on this wreck. She lies in 20 to 30 feet (6 to 9 metres), not far from the shore and the dock. The is sometimes a rope, attached to the dock, that leads to the wreck site . There is a definite hull shape and ribbing that can be viewed by the curious diver at this site. There is reportedly an old stationwagon and much modern garbage around the *Bruce* site.

Hazards: Boating traffic is heavy, especially on weekends and evenings, so use of a dive flag is wise. The one-and-a-half-knot current is not usually a problem for a diver with some river experience. In poor visibility, which occurs frequently since the water is naturally coffee-coloured, diver disorientation can occur. Entanglement in old, snagged fishing line is also a possibility, so carry a knife. Beware of sunken logs and modern debris on which a diver's scuba gear could become caught or entangled.

Site 3: Lemieux Island, Ottawa River

Location: Take the Ottawa River Parkway, direction west, away from downtown Ottawa. Upstream from the Chaudiere Bridge is a series of islands in the Ottawa River, the largest of which is Lemieux Island.

Access: Shore or boat.

Skill Level: Intermediate

Depth: 0 - 50 feet (0 - 15 metres)

Visibility: 6 - 12 feet. (1.8 - 3.6 metres)

Description: This site is actually a large area consisting of several sites, all of which fit the same description. The biggest problem is finding a place to park your vehicle. It seems that half the time, the bridge to the island is closed due to construction or maintenance, and there is absolutely no parking along the Parkway side of the river. The bottom is a series of rock ledges that run deeper and deeper into the river. This is also a scavenger dive, so be prepared to find a vast array of modern garbage as well as the occasional old bottle that will be considered a "keeper."

Hazards: The current is a bit faster here than downstream, so more skill in swiftwater diving is required. The dark-coloured water limits visibility, even with a dive light, as one goes deeper. Because of boaters, carry a dive flag/float with you.

Site 4: Braeside; Sand Point Lighthouse

Location: About 40 miles (65 kms.) west of Ottawa. From the town of Arnprior, one must follow the river road through Braeside to Sand Point right on the Ottawa River.

Access: Shore.

Skill Level: Intermediate.

Depth: 0 - 60 feet (0 - 18 metres).

Visibility: 4 - 10 feet (1.2 - 3 metres).

Description: The old ferry used to run from here across the river to Norway Bay, Quebec. The ferry's last wharf, built in 1910, is the base of the Sand Point lighthouse. About 300' (90 metres) downstream are the submerged remains of an older wharf which runs out from the shore. Old bottles are commonly found at these sites.

Hazards: Some current exists, and a light is necessary to locate anything in this dark water. Boating traffic also exists, so fly a divers down flag. Be considerate of people fishing, too.

The Sand Point Lighthouse is used both as a diver's exit and entry point, as well as a fishing platform for bubble-watchers. (Photo by Cris Kohl.)

Site 5: Calabogie, Black Donald Lake

Location:	About 70 miles (110 kms.) west of Ottawa.
Access:	Shore or boat.
Skill Level:	Intermediate.
Depth:	To 30 feet (9 metres), excluding the mine.
Visibility:	5 - 8 feet (1.5 - 2.4 metres).

Directions: Take road #508 southwest from highway 17 just west of Arnprior. Once you get to Calabogie, go straight through and follow the signs to Black Donald Lake (usually there are signs directing the visitor to the Black Donald Mine historic marker at Graphite Bay. The site is 200 feet, or 60 metres, beyond that marker.) The Graphite Bay Campground no longer exists, but the lady that lives in the house at the far end of the small bay from the historic marker will likely, for a small fee, allow you to park on her property and dive from there (her late husband did that in the past).

Background: From 1896 until 1954, the town of Black Donald was the site of Ontario's richest graphite deposit. This small community sprang up around the extracting and milling operations. Since part of the original mine extended under the lake waters (known then as Whitefish Lake), flooding was a constant threat, and indeed, it did occur in 1904 and 1950. In 1967, it flooded again, this time on purpose. Ontario Hydro had built a dam on the Madawaska River for the production of hydroelectricity; after buying out the townspeople, the company burned down the houses right to their foundations, and removed all trees and brush to below the water level, before flooding the area.

Description: This is an unusual divesite. The foundations of about a dozen houses exist in the small bay area. There is also an old Packard automobile that was left behind. Snails abound at this location, including many that are a considerable size! If you follow the submerged roadway far enough, you will see the white highway posts on either side. The mine shaft is located on the other side of the submerged road from the former townsite, but diving the mine itself is not recommended.

Hazards: Boating traffic is slow and light in the small bay area, but picks up somewhat as you venture out into the lake, so use a divers down flag. If you stay off the bottom, the visibility will remain good. In fact, the vis can be as good as 20' (6 metres) on some days for divers who can control their buoyancy and their natural urges to grovel in the muck. Also please respect the rights of nearby property owners; we are guests in their domain.

Two such warning signs (above) at Black Donald Lake appear to be a threat to divers, but they are simply a warning not to venture into the dangerous and deep mine area. The small bay area holds the main objects of interest, the house foundations and the remains of an old car. (Photos by Cris Kohl.)

Site 6: The Wreck of the *Mayflower*

Location:	Lake Kamaniskeg, near Barry's Bay, Ontario.
Access:	Boat.
Skill Level:	Novice - intermediate.
Depth:	20 feet (6 metres).
Visibility:	10 - 20 feet (3 - 6 metres).

Directions: Highway 60 from the west, 62 from the south, and 60/62 from the east will bring you to Barry's Bay. The wreck lies about 500' (150 metres) off the eastern shore of Lake Kamaniskeg. There is a public boat launch at Combermere. A compass bearing of 040 degrees magnetic to the southern end of Mayflower Island (beware of submerged rocks!) and a bearing of 135 degrees magnetic to Sand Beach will pinpoint the wreck site.

Background: The wooden sternwheeler, *Mayflower,* measuring 77' x 18' x 4' (23.1 x 5.4 x 1.2 metres) sank in a storm on November 12, 1912, while underway with 12 people and a corpse in a coffin from Barry's Bay to Combermere. The floating coffin saved three people, but the other nine died.

Description: On the lake's sandy bottom, the *Mayflower's* hull, boiler, engine, and paddle wheel, as well as resident bass and sunfish, may be seen. Save Ontario Shipwrecks has surveyed and put a plaque on this wreck.

Hazards: Use a dive flag to signal your presence. Don't miss your diveboat, as it is a long swim back to shore. Respect the rights of cottage-owners.

The 59-ton sternwheeler, Mayflower, *was built at Combermere in 1904 and sank in 20' (6 metres) of water in 1912.* (Photo: Public Archives of Canada.)

The *Mayflower* Site in Lake Kamaniskeg

Artwork by Adam Henley

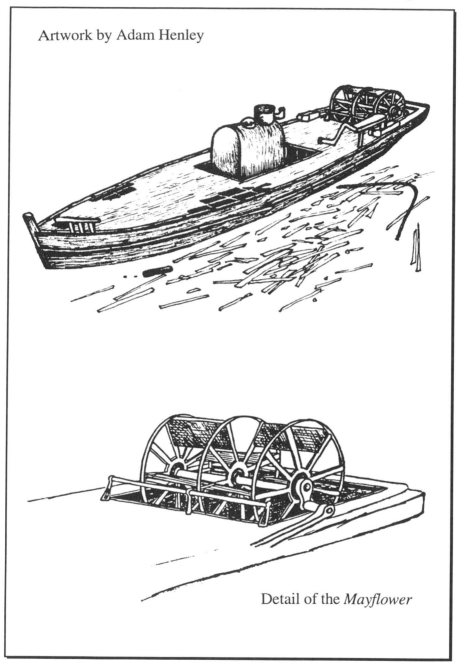

Detail of the *Mayflower*

Site 7: Driftwood Provincial Park

Location:	About 22 miles (35 kms.) west of Deep River, along the south shore of the Ottawa River.
Access:	Shore.
Skill Level:	Novice - intermediate.
Depth:	To 40 feet (12 metres).
Visibility:	4 - 8 feet (1.2 - 2.4 metres).
Description:	Exploring tea-coloured water once again requires the use of lights. Natural elements, as well as modern, man-made debris, can be found.
Hazards:	There is some current that could pose difficulties for the inexperienced diver. Be on the lookout for submerged logs, trees, and driftwood (that's why this park has that name!)

Worth Checking Out?

Barry's Bay, Bridge Ruins

This site on the Madawaska River has been explored by divers and is of interest because of scenic submerged cribs. Shore markers for the old bridge are visible as one enters the water at Bark Lake. The depth goes to 35' (10.5 metres) with good visibility.

Barry's Bay, Bark Lake Cliffs

This site, since it involves depths of 50' - 90' (15 - 27 metres), is not for novice divers. Lights are necessary for the deeper end of the scale. The cliffs are to the left of the Bark Lake entrance point.

Warning:

Avoid diving the Bytown locks wrecks, the *Otter* and the *Resolute* because it is too dangerous due to the boating traffic and the operation of the locks. Also, Pink's Lake, in Québec, near Ottawa, is now closed to diving.

Some Popular Québec Sites near Ottawa:

a) Lac Simon is deep (300'+, or 90+ metres), although there is the wreck of a small boat in about 40' (12 metres) of very clear water.

b) Back mine is just north of Buckingham. Since this mine descends to over 150' (45 metres) and is considered cavern diving, it is for very advanced, specially-trained divers only. There are no fish, no growth, just rock formations.

c) A tug rests in a bay in 20' - 25' near the town of Chénéville, Québec.

Site 8: Bon Echo Provincial Park

Location: About 20 miles (32 kms.) north of Kaladar on Highway 41, about 70 miles (110 kms.) northwest of Kingston, and about 100 miles (160 kms.) from Ottawa.

Access: Shore or boat.

Skill Level: Intermediate - advanced.

Depth: Variable; from 0 to very deep.

Visibility: 20 - 30 feet (6 - 9 metres) usually.

Directions: Once in Bon Echo Provincial park, drive to the large parking lot used for the Visitor Centre. From here, it is a brief hike to "The Narrows," a popular area for diving. Arrange diving activity in the park in advance with the park officials. On occasion, the local pontoon boat ferry has been hired to take scuba divers to the cliff face just to the northwest of "The Narrows."

Description: This is considered to be the best wall dive in Ontario. Cascading rocks and jagged cliffs slope down the rock face to a depth of about 50' (15 metres). Beyond that depth is a sheer, straight wall of rock which plunges into the black abyss. Mazinaw Lake is the deepest lake in southern Ontario, with a depth of about 473' (142 metres) and impressive cliffs rising 373' (112 metres) above the lake. There is considerable fish life to appreciate.

Hazards: There is occasional boating traffic and a bit of a current in "The Narrows". The big potential danger at this site is diving too deep. Plan your maximum depth in advance and watch your depth gauge continuously.

Mazinaw Lake cliffs, Bon Echo Provincial Park, at sunset (Photo by Cris Kohl.)

The St. Lawrence River

Site 9: The *Fred Mercur* Wreck

Location:	Off Stanley Island, St. Lawrence River.
Co-ordinates:	N 45 02' 03", W 74 37' 18".
Access:	Boat.
Skill Level:	Novice - intermediate.
Depth:	2 - 45 feet (0.6 - 13.5 metres).
Visibility:	Variable, to 30 feet (9 metres).

Background: The wooden propeller, *Fred Mercur,* built at Buffalo, New York in 1882, was 232 feet (69.4 metres) long with a beam of 35' 5" (10.7 metres), a draft of 18' 2" (5.5 metres) and a gross tonnage of 1,224.37. From 1882 until 1919, the vessel sailed under U. S. registry, which changed when Canadian interests purchased her in 1919. The vessel burned to a total loss after she was beached in a bed of rushes on the west side of Stanley Island in the St. Lawrence River near Cornwall on July 3, 1925. Six round-trips by a nearby cottager in his rowboat saved the entire crew.

Directions: A boat is best launched from the mainland northeast of Cornwall, Ontario, to get the divers to the west side of Stanley Island. The bow of the wreck, which comes very close to the surface of the water, is usually marked with a jug by local divers. On some occasions, the water level is so low that the wreck's bow can be a boating hazard, so approach with caution!

Description: This fish-rich site has a moderate current flowing over the stone and sand bottom (although some silt has settled around the hull itself). The wreck can be explored descending from the shallow bow, or a descent/ascent can be made along an anchor line. Swarms of American eels, some over six feet (two metres) in length, have made this site home. The hull of the wreck is intact, still containing the coal cargo, with the rudder and propeller of particular note, in spite of the 1984 damage done to the stern when a freighter dragging its anchor hit the wreck. The portion of the forward superstructure which did not burn completely lies upside-down just downstream from the hull. A tractor which went through the ice sits in about 25' (7.5 metres) just off the bow.

Hazards: As mentioned, there is a moderate current which could be a bit of a nuisance, the bow of the wreck comes close to the surface of the water, thus creating a potential boating danger, and visibility on the site can be significantly impaired if a careless or inconsiderate diver starts stirring up the silt along the hull.

The Fred Mercur, *built by the Union Dry Dock Company, Buffalo, New York, in 1882, was destroyed by flames in 1925.* (Photo: author's collection.)

The Mille Roche Power House

Artwork by Adam Henley

Site 10: Mille Roche Power House

Location:	Lake St. Lawrence, west of Cornwall.
Access:	Boat.
Skill Level:	Intermediate - advanced.
Depth:	35', 55', and 75' (10.5, 16.5, 22.5 metres).
Visibility:	6 - 20 feet (1.8 - 6 metres).

Background: The Mille Roches Power House, constructed by the St. Lawrence Power Company in 1900-1901, could generate up to 3,000 horsepower from its location near the Cornwall Canal at the former town (now submerged) of Mille Roches. The plant operated until 1955 under various owners, and in 1958, the building itself was demolished in preparation for the St. Lawrence Seaway flooding.

Directions: From Highway 401, it is best to proceed to the Moulinette Road exit, number 778, about seven miles (11 kms.) southeast of Cornwall, which leads into Long Sault. There, head east towards Cornwall for three miles (4.8 kms.) until you arrive at Guindon Park. Besides offering a public boat launch, the park also provides change and washroom facilities, as well as picnic tables for post-diving festivities. Normally during the dive season, the site is buoyed, and can be reached by taking a boat on a heading of 183 degrees magnetic for a distance of 0.5 miles (0.8 km.).

Description: The brick building and generators were removed from the site before flooding, but two 35-inch Samson water turbines remain intact, as well as the intake gate mechanisms, a wheel chamber, exciter reservoirs, water release pits, and the tailrace. The intake gate mechanisms lie at a depth of 35' (10.5 metres), while the power house floor is situated at 55' (16.5 metres) and the water release pits and tailrace at 75' (22.5 metres). Bring a dive light for viewing the deepest remains.

Hazards: Boating traffic can be a problem, especially on weekends, so use of a dive flag is wise. The one-to-two-knot current will not usually present a difficulty, and this current is noticeable only during the descent and ascent. On the deepest level, one's bottom time must be carefully gauged to avoid decompression.

NOTE: Save Ontario Shipwrecks offers an excellent brochure, with superb drawings by Nick Baets, for this dive site. For further information about this and other items, write to Save Ontario Shipwrecks, 2175 Sheppard Avenue East, Suite 310, WILLOWDALE, Ontario, Canada M2J 1W8.

Site 11: Lock 21

Location:	Macdonell Island, near Ingleside, Ontario.
Access:	Shore.
Skill Level:	Advanced.
Depth:	40 - 60 feet (12 - 18 metres).
Visibility:	6 - 20 feet (1.8 - 6 metres).

Background: Constructed in 1885-86 as part of the second enlargement of the canal system, Lock 21 is 270' (81 metres) long between the gates, 45' (13.5 metres) wide, and has 14' (4.2 metres) of clearance over the sill. The lock operated under various agencies (the Department of Railways and Canals until 1936, the Department of Transport from 1936 to 1958) until the area was flooded as part of the St. Lawrence Seaway construction and the hydro dam at Cornwell.

Directions: Take Highway 401 as far as the exits to either Ingleside or Long Sault. From there, take Highway 2 to the Long Sault Parkway (entrance fee is about $6.00 per vehicle) to Macdonell Island. The fee is charged by the St. Lawrence Parks Commission to maintain its excellent washrooms, snackbars, picnic sites, nature trails, and camping facilities along this Parkway. At the southwestern end of Macdonell Island, ropes run to the site, with the upstream rope taking the diver to the site and the downstream one leading back to shore. Sometimes there is an historic plaque at the site of the roped entry point, but don't count on it.

Description: The upstream rope leads the diver into a strong 2 - 3 knot current which exists throughout the dive. This rope leads to the weir and sluice gates, and concrete walkways, a bollard, and chain-wells can also be explored. Divers have placed lines from various points to aid in exploration, but neither Save Ontario Shipwrecks nor the author accepts any responsibility or liability for these lines and their use while diving. Once again, you're on your own.

Hazards: The current is fairly strong, the visibility can be low, and the bottom of the site is deep (lock bottom is at 60', or 18 metres). Other than that, the only other point of potential irritation is the enormous and omnipresent Canada goose droppings at the entrance and exit junctures. In fact, these beautiful but poorly-toilet-trained birds are so predominant in this park that their natural calling cards are virtually everywhere. Watch where you step!

NOTE: Save Ontario Shipwrecks offers an excellent brochure, again with pre-eminent drawings by Nick Baets, as well as a plastic field guide for this dive site. For information on both, write to Save Ontario Shipwrecks, 2175 Sheppard Ave. E., Suite 310, WILLOWDALE, Ontario, Canada M2J 1W8.

Site 12: Chrysler Park Wreck

Location:	Northeast of Morrisburg, Ontario.
Co-ordinates:	N 44 56' 03", W 75 03' 43".
Access:	Boat.
Skill Level:	Advanced.
Depth:	65 feet (19.5 metres).
Visibility:	6 - 20 feet (1.8 - 6 metres).

Background: This small wooden propeller is a mystery wreck. Rumour has it that she might be the wreck of the *Chippewa,* which sank in this area on August 12, 1920.

Directions: A few miles of travel northeast from Morrisburg, Ontario, brings the avid diver to Chrysler Memorial Park right on the shores of the St. Lawrence River. From there, one can look out across the open water to Wilson Hill Island, which is part of the United States of America. Between those two points and just inside the international boundary (on the Canadian side) is the location of this wreck site.

Description: Little is known about this wreck except that she is a small (approximately 65 feet, or 19.5 metres, in length) wooden propeller, sitting in about 65 feet (19.5 metres) of water and rising roughly 18 feet (5.4 metres) from the bottom, so it is about 47 feet (14.1 metres) to the top of the wreck from the surface.

Hazards: Boating traffic is heavy since this site lies right in the middle of the main shipping channel, and that means huge freighters plow back and forth across these waters. The current is very strong here as well, further detracting from the ease of this dive site. For these reasons, this site is not very popular and very little identification work has been able to be done on this shipwreck.

Worth Checking Out?

Unidentified Wrecks at Ile Simard:

Close to the northwest end of Ile Simard, near the Quebec side of the channel, lie the remains of two unidentified hulls, probably schooner-barges abandoned for age. These wrecks, lying in the shallows, are better suited for snorkel explorations, but strapping on a tank is also possible here.

Site 13: The *Eastcliffe Hall* Wreck

Location:	Near Morrisburg, Ont., St. Lawrence River.
Co-ordinates:	N 44 55' 29", W 75 06' 04".
Access:	Boat.
Skill Level:	Advanced.
Depth:	40 - 65 feet (12 - 19.5 metres).
Visibility:	8 - 30 feet (2.4 - 9 metres).

Background: The bulk freight motor vessel, *Eastcliffe Hall,* originally built to a length of 253' 4" (76 metres) when constructed by Canadian Vickers Shipyards, Ltd., in Montreal in 1954, was lengthened in size to make her more commercially competitive when the St. Lawrence Seaway opened in 1959. She was one of only three canal-sized ships that was lengthened because of the Seaway. Exactly 90' (27 metres) of steel sheeting were welded onto her length by her original builder. Her beam remained the same at 43' 8" (13 metres), giving her a singularly long-and-narrow appearance. Her draft increased from 19' (5.7 metres) to 22' 8" (6.8 metres), while her gross tonnage expanded from 2,140 to 3,335.

   The *Eastcliffe Hall* was upbound from Sorel, Quebec, for Cleveland, Ohio, with about 4,000 tons (compare that to her gross tonnage!) of pig-iron when, at about three o'clock in the morning on July 14, 1970, she struck a shoal near Chrysler Shoal, although she kept moving slowly. About three-quarters of an hour later, the ship slammed into the 300-ton concrete buoy abutment at Chrysler Shoal and sank within three minutes. Nine lives were lost in this tragic mishap.

Directions: Take the Highway 401 exit to Upper Canada Village. Turn east briefly on Highway 2 until you arrive at the entrance to the Chrysler Marina about 1,200' (360 metres) on your right. You can launch your boat from here. There is usually no marker on this wreck, since she lies very close to the regular Seaway ship channel just within the Canadian border, so once near the site, you will have to watch for her on your depth recorder. Anchor downstream from the wreck; the swim back, after your dive, will be easier!

   For those boaters with no Loran C on board, find the point that will give you bearings of 265 degrees magnetic with buoy #75 that has a flashing green light (to the west), 095 degrees magnetic with the flashing green light on the north tip of Bradford Island, and 035 degrees magnetic with the entrance to Marina Harbour back on the Canadian mainland. The approximate location of the *Eastcliffe Hall* is marked on Canadian Hydrographic Service chart number 1415. Anchor next to the wreck, not on it, as anchors in the past have done damage to shipwrecks.

Description: The bow of the wreck points into the current. The superstructure of the *Eastcliffe Hall* has been dynamited to remove her threat to the navigation safety of other vessels, so much tangled steel wreckage is found, especially at her stern, an area that should be avoided by divers. Besides, the most interesting characteristic of the stern, namely the vessel's two propellers (she carried twin, four-cylinder, diesel engines), were removed shortly after the sinking. The wreck was partially salvaged, which would explain the presence of pieces of her pig iron ingots scattered about on her deck (sloppy salvaging!) Her six holds are open and of interest to scuba divers, but penetration of this wreck is for the ultra-experienced only! The bow offers passages and cabins which can be explored, but only by those experienced divers who have made complete penetration preparations! This is no place to lose track of direction!

Hazards: Since this is again the middle of the shipping channel of the St. Lawrence River, boating traffic, including that of huge freighters, is heavy. The variable three-to-six-knot current can pose problems until the diver is protected by portions of the wreck. The fast current swirls the sand on the bottom around to reduce visibility to about four to ten feet (1.2 to 3 metres). In poor visibility, diver disorientation can occur, especially suddenly inside a shipwreck. Definitely use an anchor line for the descent and ascent portions of the dive, and be certain that you can find your way back to that line for the ascent, or you may find yourself reaching the surface on a free ascent a substantial distance downstream from your diveboat!

The Eastcliffe Hall *wreck is an advanced divesite.* (Photo: author's collection.)

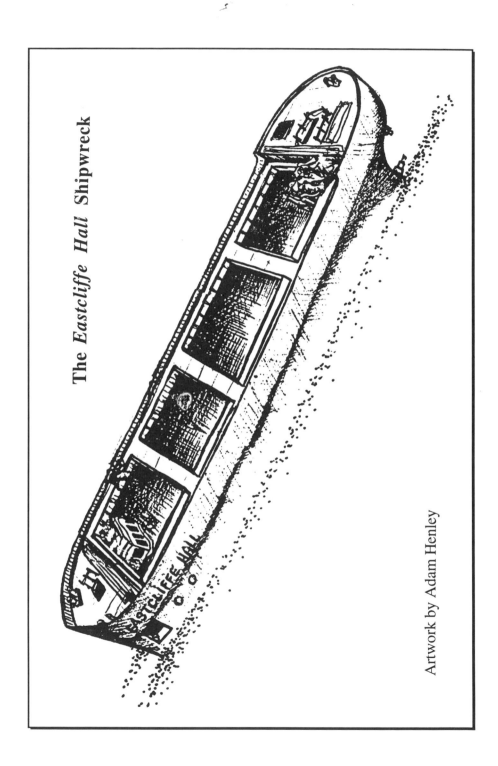

The *Eastcliffe Hall* Shipwreck

Artwork by Adam Henley

Site 14: The Wreck of the *Conestoga*

Location:	Off Cardinal, Ontario, St. Lawrence River.
Co-ordinates:	Not necessary to locate this site, but here they are anyway: N 44 46' 46", W 75 23' 36".
Access:	Shore or boat.
Skill Level:	Novice - intermediate.
Depth:	28 feet (8.4 metres).
Visibility:	7 - 30 feet (2.1 - 9 metres).

Background: The wooden combination passenger and package steam freighter, *Conestoga,* measuring 253' (75.9 metres) length by 36' (10.8 metres) beam by 16' 3" (4.7 metres) draft, was built by Thomas Quayle and Sons, Cleveland, Ohio, and launched on July 6, 1878, at an enormous, for then, cost of $90,000. On December 31, 1919, she was sold to Canadian interests and given Canadian registry. While downbound with 30,000 bushels of wheat (much of which was later salvaged), the *Conestoga* caught fire and sank on May 22, 1922, outside Lock 28 of the old Galop Canal, about one mile (1.6 km.) east of the town of Cardinal.

Directions: From the intersection of Highway 2 and Road No. 22 in Cardinal, Ontario, proceed along Road No. 22 towards the river. At the bottom of the hill, you will see a Legion building. Turning to the right of that structure, take the unserviced, i.e. bumpy, dirt road along the causeway for about 0.6 miles (0.9 km.). The large upper portion of the vessel's 1878 Cuyahoga Iron Works steeple compound engine seems intent on exhibitionism as it flashes out and reveals the sleeping quarters of this ship about 80' (24 metres) from shore. There is a small, narrow parking area at the site.

Description: The wooden hull of the *Conestoga,* lying with the bow pointing upstream, is still in very good condition, although fire and ice damage have taken their toll of the superstructure. An unsuccessful salvage venture broke off one blade from the 14-foot (4.2-metre) propeller. A windlass and anchor chain adorn the bow, with a Dake steam winch nearby. The S.O.S. plaque just up from the boiler keeps going astray. The rudder lies flat off the stern. *Conestoga's* anchor graces the lawn of a motel in Ogdensburg, New York.

Hazards: The current is usually mild, but is stronger at the bow. Boaters zoom by on occasion, so be sure to fly the divers down flag.

NOTE: Save Ontario Shipwrecks offers an excellent brochure, plus a plastic field guide for this dive site. Contact them at 2175 Sheppard Ave. E., Suite 310, WILLOWDALE, Ontario, Canada M2J 1W8.

The Conestoga *is probably the most popular scuba dive site in the St. Lawrence River because of her interesting artifacts and her shallow position close to a mainland shore.* (Photo: Great Lakes Historical Society, Vermilion, Ohio.)

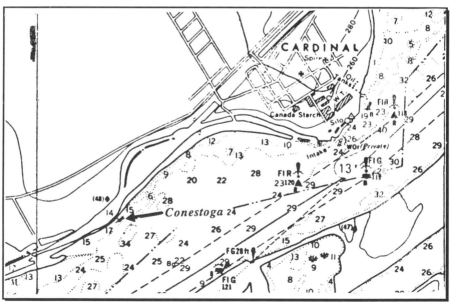

The Charts and Publications Regulations of the Canada Shipping Act require vessels operating in Canadian waters to carry the latest, best scale, corrected Canadian Hydrographic Service (CHS) charts. This document does not meet the requirements of the Act. (Portion of CHS chart 1416.)

The steeple compound engine of the Conestoga *is an unfailing, obvious clue guiding divers to the vessel's remains.* (Photo by Cris Kohl.)

The Conestoga's *bow anchor chain links are measured by a diver utilizing his dive knife.* (Photo by Cris Kohl.)

STEAMER BURNS NEAR CARDINAL

Conestoga, Grain Laden For Montreal, Totally Destroyed on Sunday.

Prescott, May 22.—The steamer Conestoga, loaded with

The Conestoga's *obituary headlines in* The Daily British Whig (Kingston) *newspaper on Monday, May 22, 1922, were to-the-point.*

Diver Shari Müller explores the huge, four-bladed propeller on the wreck of the Conestoga. *Visibility in the St. Lawrence River has improved immensely in recent years due to the zebra mussels filtering water.* (Photo by Cris Kohl.)

Site 15: The Wreck of the *Rothesay*

Location:	Just off the west side of Prescott, Ontario.
Co-ordinates:	N 44 41' 58", W 75 31' 40"
Access:	Shore or boat.
Skill Level:	Intermediate.
Depth:	20 - 30 feet (6 - 9 metres).
Visibility:	8 - 30 feet (2.4 - 9 metres).

Background: Launched in 1868 at St. John, New Brunswick, the 193' (57.9-metre) by 28.8' (8.6 metres) by 7.9' (2.3 m.) wooden side wheeler *Rothesay* sank in a collision with the tug *Myra,* on Sept. 12, 1889, killing two of the latter's crew. The wreck was found on Sept. 25, 1964 by Ottawa divers.

Directions: An historic marker commemorating Loyalist Justus Sherwood is posted just southwest of the town of Prescott along Highway 2 at Riverview Heights. Park your car on the grass strip there and suit up.

Description: Best vis can be had in the spring or fall. Two buoys mark the route to the wreck, one about 100' (30 metres) offshore, and the other on the wreck 300' (90 metres) out. A line on the bottom between the markers can be used as a guideline. Sights include the smokestack, boilers, walking beam, paddlewheels, and rudder. (See the S.O.S. brochure and plastic field guide: Save Ontario Shipwrecks, 2175 Sheppard Ave. E., Suite 310, WILLOWDALE, Ontario, Canada M2J 1W8.)

Hazards: The mild surface current dissipates at depth. The wreck was dynamited in mid-ship in 1901 for practice, so little remains intact of that part.

The wooden sidewheeler Rothesay. (Photo: The Great Lakes Marine Collection of the Milwaukee Public Library)

The lengthy underwater trail from shore makes it easy for visiting divers not to get lost and miss the Rothesay. *Heavy concrete blocks serve as anchors for the guidlines* (above). *Zebra mussels are beginning their infestation of this shipwreck, but much wood, such as the planking around this missing porthole, is still recognizable* (below). (Photos by Cris Kohl).

Site 16: Prescott, Fort Wellington

Location:	Just east of Prescott, Ontario.
Access:	Shore or boat.
Skill Level:	Novice - Intermediate.
Depth:	0 - 30 feet (0 - 9 metres).
Visibility:	8 - 20 feet (2.4 - 6 metres).

Background: The original fort was first constructed on this site in 1813 to protect the St. Lawrence waterway during the War of 1812 with the United States. The fort has been restored to its 1840 era style by Parks Canada.

Description: Underwater exploring of the old pilings, all that remain of the former dock, in front of Fort Wellington has brought to light some old bottles, dishes, and clay pipes.

Hazards: Boating traffic includes water-skiers and fisherpersons, so utilize a dive flag, and the current can run fairly fast on some days.

Site 17: Prescott, the Windmill Site

Location:	Just east of Prescott, Ontario.
Access:	Shore or boat.
Skill Level:	Novice - intermediate.
Depth:	0 - 30 feet. (0 - 9 metres).
Visibility:	8 - 20 feet (2.4 - 6 metres).

Background: In 1838, shortly after the Upper Canada Rebellion, a group of Canadian refugees and American sympathizers launched an attack from the U. S. on the town of Prescott. Their ship went aground at the site of this windmill, and, following a seven-day fiasco, the entire invasion force of almost 300 men was captured.

Description: Dive directly below the Windmill. To the left (east) of the Windmill, a set of wooden stairs and a path lead to a picnic table positioned on a flat rock at the water's edge. It's a perfect place to suit up. Enjoy the sights of American eels, rubble from the old mill, and possible cannon balls, etc.

Hazards: The current can be fast. Fly a divers down flag to ward off the waterskiers and the people fishing from boats.

Worth Checking Out?

The *Fleur Marie* **Wreck Site:** The remains of this scuttled vessel were located off Prescott, Ontario, in late June, 1995, just within U.S. waters, but only a few minutes boat-ride from Prescott's marina. The old schooner, *Fleur Marie,* also known as *Fleur de Marie,* had lain abandoned at Prescott for years when, in October, 1884, a tug finally towed her unsightly remains out into the river and sank her in about 48' (14.4 metres) of water. The clear water moves fast over this intermediate-advanced divesite, but there is lots to see, such as the centreboard box, transom, hull, ribbing, and vast numbers of fish.

Site 18: The *John B. King* Wreck

Location:	Near Brockville, Ontario.
Co-ordinates:	N 43 33' 46", W 75 42' 43".
Access:	Boat.
Skill Level:	Very advanced.
Depth:	90 feet (27 metres).
Visibility:	6 - 30 feet (1.8 - 6 metres).

Background: One of the most severe loss-of-life marine accidents occurred off the northeast point of Cockburn Island in the St. Lawrence River near Brockville, Ontario on June 26, 1930. The 140' (42-metre) long drill scow, *John B. King,* with a huge crew of 41 on board, was busily placing underwater charges while at anchor in the main shipping channel. A sudden summer thunderstorm brewed, and lightning struck just as the vessel was pulling away from the dynamite-laden site. All the submerged charges, as well as the dynamite still on board, detonated. The massive explosion rocketed wreckage a couple of hundred feet into the air, and a few seconds later, when the immense cloud of smoke cleared, the ship was gone, along with 30 of the crew. A U.S. Coast Guard cutter about a kilometre upstream responded immediately to the frightening sound and was able to rescue eleven survivors at the tragic site.

Directions: A boat can be launched at Brockville, Ontario. The wreck rests about 80' (24 metres) downstream from number "143 A" flashing green light buoy, just west of Cockburn Island.

Description: The wreck site consists of heavily twisted metal lying scattered on the bottom.

Hazards: This is a very dangerous dive. The St. Lawrence River currents are strong at this point, and the depth of 90' (27 metres) makes this a deep, dark dive. It is difficult to secure an anchor in the wreckage because of the current, and, once done, it could be difficult to retrieve your anchor if it gets snagged in the twisted metal wreckage.

Site 19: The *Robert Gaskin* Wreck

Location:	Off the pier at Brockville, Ontario.
Access:	Boat.
Skill Level:	Intermediate - advanced.
Depth:	60 feet (18 metres).
Visibility:	8 - 30 feet (2.4 - 9 metres).

Background: The *Robert Gaskin,* originally a triple-masted, iron-rigged, wooden barque but later altered to a work barge, was strongly built to Lloyd's specifications for trans-Atlantic travel. With iron knees connecting her deck and hull and fastened with treenails throughout her construction, she was prepared to weather any ocean conditions. However, her destiny was to transport grain and stone cargoes between Milwaukee, Wisconsin, and Prescott, Ontario. This 132' 6" (39.7-metre) by 26' 3" (7.9-metre) by 11' 3" (3.4-metre) vessel, launched at Kingston, Ontario, on April 21, 1863, boasted a carrying capacity of 20,000 bushels.

In late 1889, this vessel met its ultimate fate by sinking not once, but a total of three times while attempting to salvage the train ferry propeller *William Armstrong,* which had sunk on June 30, 1889 after a portion of her stern dropped out. A salvage pontoon broke loose from the wreck site of the *Armstrong* on September 18, 1889, and smashed into the starboard bow of the *Gaskin,* sinking her virtually on top of the *Armstrong.* The salvage vessel was in need of salvage, and on November 11, 1889, the *Gaskin* was raised nearly to the surface when a hose coupling on the pontoon detached and dropped the vessel to the bottom again. Twelve days later, the *Gaskin's* masts towered high above the water as she was raised and towed about 600' (180 metres) away from the *Armstrong.* Unfortunately, a rear pontoon which happened to be chained to the keelson tore the *Robert Gaskin's* stern away, and she sank for the third and final time at the site she presently occupies.

Incidentally, the *William Armstrong* was eventually salvaged the following year (1890), taken to Ogdensburg, New York, for repairs, and returned to ferry service, surviving well into the 1920's under the name *Mons Meg.*

The site of the *Robert Gaskin* was discovered by divers in 1980.

Directions: From Highway 401, follow the signs to the Brockville Museum and head down to the wharf in town. A yellow buoy marks the site, and it is easy to locate about 1,500' (450 metres) by boat off the Marine Park in Brockville.

The Wreck of the *Robert Gaskin*

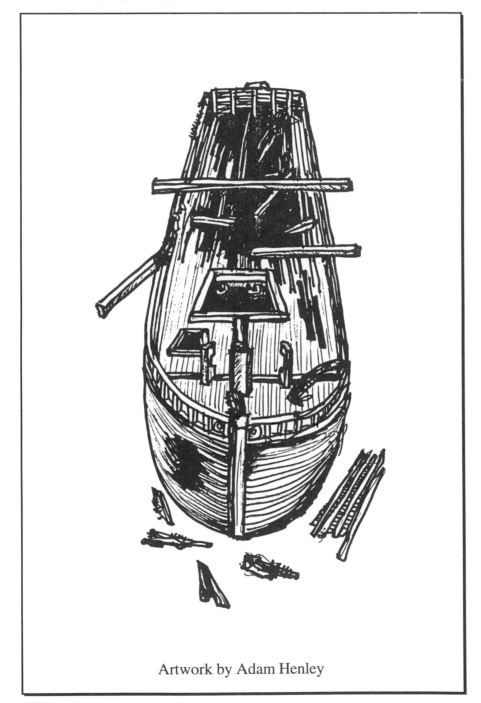

Artwork by Adam Henley

Description: The slight current should be no problem as the divers head down the line to the wreck, sitting in 60' (18 metres) of water. The vessel lies with the bow facing downriver, parallel to the shore. The first item the divers will notice is the large kingpost erect on the forward starboard side, near the large hole that formed when the pontoon struck the vessel causing her to sink the first time. A huge timber beam about 14" (35 centimetres) square lies across the deck and about seven feet (two metres) beyond. Other planking and rusty chain clutters the deck. The bow is flat and blunt. Two cargo holds can be cautiously penetrated (bring lights), with one containing two steel barrels full of rivets and chain links. The torn-away stern portion of the wreck is broken and scattered.

Hazards: Boating traffic can be heavy on some days, so definitely fly a divers down flag. Because the wreck sits in 60' (18 metres) of water, and divers will likely attain that depth when they study the hole in the starboard bow, this is considered a deep dive, and due preparations must be made. If the divers cautiously penetrate a cargo hold, they must be especially careful not to stir up the silt so that they can find their way out again easily enough.

Site 20: MacDonald's Point

Location:	Southwest of Brockville, Ontario.
Access:	Boat. Launch at Brockville.
Skill Level:	Intermediate - advanced.
Depth:	30 - 100 feet (9 - 30 metres).
Visibility:	6 - 20 feet (1.8 - 6 metres).

Description: An old dump site is located about 200' (60 metres) west of the end of MacDonald's Point, right against the shore. This shore drops off steeply, with depths of 30' (9 metres) about 10' (3 metres) offshore, 60 ' (18-metre) depths about 20' (6 metres) offshore, and 100' (30 metres) about 30' (9 metres) out from shore. Old bottles and even a model T automobile can be seen. Boat access is necessary since MacDonald's Point offers no parking amidst numerous private cottages and a sign on the roadway indicating "Dead end. Local traffic only, please."

Hazards: Be cautious with depth and the rather strong current. Consider drifting this site rather than trying to fight the current. If done properly, the current will carry the divers around the point into calm water, but if they attempt to surface earlier, they will likely encounter a strong downdraft current from the slight whirlpool effect at the end of the point. This can be a frightening encounter if unprepared for it. Save plenty of air for surfacing.

Site 21: The Battersby Island Wreck

Location:	Just southwest of Brockville, Ontario.
Co-ordinates:	N 44 33' 11", W 75 43' 34".
Access:	Boat.
Skill Level:	Advanced, with swiftwater diving training.
Depth:	15 - 20 feet (4.5 - 6 metres).
Visibility:	6 - 15 feet (1.8 - 4.5 metres).

Background: This unidentified wooden vessel is truly a mystery, but her construction suggests that she was built in the early-to-mid-19th century.

Directions: A boat is necessary to get divers to the site at the southwest end of Battersby Island. It could be difficult positioning an anchor in the wreck, so an optional approach would be to land the divers on the island itself and proceed with a shore dive, pulling oneself hand over hand along the rocks until the wreck is reached.

Description: The wreck lies, for the most part, buried under debris that drifted down from the dynamiting that took place upstream when the channel was deepened..

Hazards: The fast current and low visibility are the major drawbacks to this dive. Since this wreck lies in a particularly strong current area, only specially-trained divers with great stamina should attempt to dive this site. They should also take along underwater lights.

Site 22: The *Lillie Parsons* Wreck

Location:	Sparrow Island, s.w. of Brockville, Ontario.
Co-ordinates:	N 43 33' 23", W 75 43' 09".
Access:	Boat.
Skill Level:	Intermediate - advanced.
Depth:	42 - 83 feet (12.6 - 24.9 metres).
Visibility:	8 - 30 feet (2.4 - 9 metres).

Background: Launched on Sept. 5, 1868 at Tonawanda, New York, the two-masted, fore-and-after, centreboard schooner, *Lillie Parsons,* measured 131' (39.3 metres) in length, 26' (7.8 metres) in beam, and 10' (3 metres) in draft. The vessel was loaded with 500 tons of coal, heading from Black Rock, N. Y., to Brockville, Ontario, on August 5, 1877, when a sudden squall heeled her onto her beam ends and shifted her cargo. The crew escaped to safety, and shortly thereafter, the vessel struck a rock, filled with water, and sank on a relatively shallow shoal. The swift current in the treacherous Brockville Narrows gradually worked the *Lillie Parsons* into deeper water.

Directions: The shipwreck lies just off the northwest corner of Sparrow Island, which is about two miles (three kilometres) southwest of Brockville, Ontario. A boat can be launched at Brockville. The Brockville Parks Department operates the island's facilities; with prior permission and fee payment, one may camp on the island, which offers docks, outhouses, picnic tables, and firewood.

Description: The anchor and chain from the *Lillie Parsons* are on land display on Sparrow Island, with the anchor chain trailing down into the water and extending to the wreck location, thus making it easy to locate the site. This chain ends at the intact hull, which lies upside-down, enabling divers to explore the hull and keel areas. Other interesting parts of this wreck are the stern, transom, rudder, centreboard trunk, beam shelf, after deck with the rudderhead, stern deadwood, and the keelson with stanchions attached. Save Ontario Shipwrecks offers an excellent brochure on this dive site.

Hazards: The ever-present and variable current runs between 2.3 and 3.6 knots, so this site is recommended for only very experienced swiftwater divers. Penetration is possible, although not recommended because of the potential difficulties or problems. Cave or ice diving techniques prevail when shipwreck penetration is done. There is boating traffic above, so the use of a divers down flag is recommended. The wreck is slowly slipping off the ledge where she currently rests, so make certain that you are not inside or under her when she finally does slide off.

Site 23: The Grenadier Island Wrecks

Location:	Grenadier Island, near Mallorytown, Ontario.
Co-ordinates:	N 44 24' 14", W 75 53' 13".
Access:	Boat.
Skill Level:	Novice - intermediate.
Depth:	18 feet (5.4 metres).
Visibility:	6 - 15 feet (1.8 - 4.5 metres).

Background: This unidentified wooden wreck was likely abandoned for age at a spot along Grenadier Island where it would be out of the way and not interfere with navigation. Two other shallower and less interesting wrecks lie at N 44 24' 57", W 75 51' 00".

Directions: The locations of these shipwrecks are marked on Canadian Hydrographic Service chart #1418 off the southeast part of Grenadier Island.

Description: This unidentified wreck lies broken up and scattered on a sandy bottom in about 18' (5.4 metres) of water. This protected area offers a refuge for fish, which can be found in large numbers at this site.

Hazards: There are virtually no hazards. There is little or no current, the depth is shallow, and there is no penetration for which to prepare. The occasional bit of boating traffic would be the only concern to divers about to surface.

The burbot, also known as ling, ling cod, and "lawyerfish" (presumably because of its ugliness) is found on many Great Lakes shipwrecks. (Photo: Cris Kohl)

Site 24: The *Henry C. Daryaw* Wreck

Location:	West of Brockville, Ontario, at Buoy Shoal.
Co-ordinates:	N 44 31' 34", W 75 45' 50".
Access:	Boat.
Skill Level:	Advanced.
Depth:	55 - 85 feet (16.5 - 25.5 metres).
Visibility:	8 - 30 feet. (2.4 - 9 metres).

Background: The steel freighter *Henry C. Daryaw* tore a huge gash in her starboard side when she ran aground in dense fog near Brockville on Nov. 21, 1941 with the loss of one life. Built in France in 1919, the ship measured 219' 2" (65.9 metres) by 35' (10.5 metres) by 13' 2" (4 metres).

Directions: The wreck appears on chart #1418, about six miles (9.5 kms.) west of Brockville, and about one-quarter mile (400 metres) offshore.

Description: The hull lies upside down in 55' - 85' (16.5 - 25.5 metres) of water. The bow is aimed into the current, while the stern is wedged against a bank. Bow anchors and the hull gash that caused her sinking can be seen.

Hazards: There is a strong current, so use of an anchor line for the descent and ascent is recommended. The current poses another problem as there are no handholds on the smooth hull. It gets dark beyond the bow, so bring a light. Avoid getting wedged between the bank and the ship's stern.

The Henry C. Daryaw *sank with a cargo of coal.* (Photo: author's collection.)

The Wreck of the *Henry C. Daryaw*

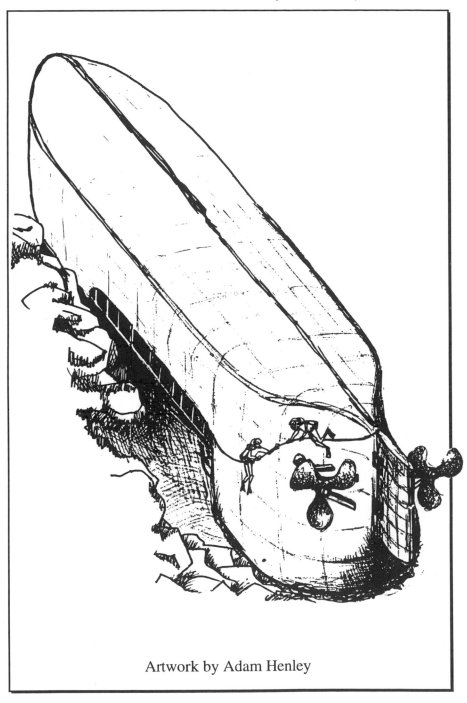

Artwork by Adam Henley

Site 25: The Wreck of the *Keystorm*

Location:	East of Mallorytown, Ontario.
Co-ordinates:	N 44 25' 48", W 75 49' 20".
Access:	Boat.
Skill Level:	Advanced.
Depth:	30 - 100 feet (9 - 30 metres).
Visibility:	1 - 10 feet (0.3 - 3 metres).

Background: This steel canaller, built in England in 1910, sank two years later on Oct. 26, 1912, when she ran aground at Scow Island Shoal, Chippewa Point, St. Lawrence River. Her crew escaped and, after five hours aground, she slid off into deeper water. Her coal cargo was salvaged in 1919.

Directions: It is best to launch a boat at Mallorytown Landing, Ontario.

Description: The *Keystorm's* bow rests in 30' (9 metres) of water, while the stern sits in 100' (30 metres). Access to two of her holds in possible, but penetration is not recommended due to the site's hazards.

Hazards: Boating traffic can be heavy , so take a dive flag with you. The wreck, although in good condition, lies in an area of strong current and decreased visibility, especially beyond the 50' (15-metre) depth. Solid experience and extreme caution are advised when diving this site.

The steel propeller, Keystorm, *measured 250' (75 metres) in length, 42' 5" (12.7 metres) in beam, and 17' 5" (5.3 metres) in draft.* (Photo: B. Smith.)

The Wreck of the *Keystorm*

Artwork by Adam Henley

Site 26: The Rockport Wall

Location:	Off Rockport, Ontario.
Co-ordinates:	Not necessary to locate this site.
Access:	Shore.
Skill Level:	Intermediate - advanced.
Depth:	To 80 feet (24 metres).
Visibility:	10 - 30 feet (3 - 9 metres).

Directions: At the town of Rockport on the St. Lawrence River, proceed to the restaurant along the river and ask permission to dive from their huge dock. Just to the east of the dock (downstream) is a large rock. It has been the custom of divers to suit up at the dock, swim over to the rock, and make their descent there. This is the wall dive area. Dine at the restaurant later.

Description: The wall dive is a popular checkout site for advanced courses because of its shore proximity and good visibility. As an aside, there is reportedly the wreck of a small Prohibition rumrunner in about 75' (22.5 metres) 200' (60 metres) out from the southwest corner of the dock at an angle of about 45 degrees. This would be at the opposite end of the dock from the huge rock. The story exists that an Ottawa diver found intact bottles of illicit elixir there. Unfortunately, the bottles had been sealed with screw cap lids, which had rusted, and the booze had gone bad. Corked bottles would still be good, but it is not known if any such sealers were used on the contents of this wreck. Be cautious; you're on your own on this one, too!

Hazards: Boating traffic can be heavy here, so take a divers down flag with you. Go only as deep at this site as your experience will allow. Don't forget to account for some current.

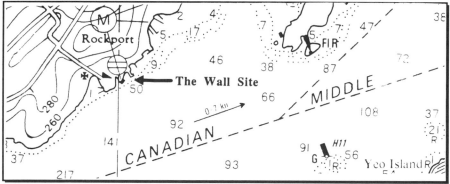

The Charts and Publications Regulations of the Canada Shipping Act require vessels operating in Canadian waters to carry the latest, best scale, corrected Canadian Hydrographic Service (CHS) charts. This document does not meet the requirements of the Act. (Portion of CHS chart 1419.)

Site 27: The Bateau Channel Wreck

Location:	At Howe Island, St. Lawrence River, Ont.
Co-ordinates:	N 44 15' 53", W 76 20' 23".
Access:	Boat (shore access from Howe Island).
Skill Level:	Novice.
Depth:	15 feet (4.5 metres).
Visibility:	8 - 20 feet (2.4 - 6 metres).

Directions: One needs a boat for transportation from the mainland to Howe Island across the Bateau Channel, which runs about halfway between Gananoque and Kingston, Ontario. The bow of the wreck is above the water.

Description: This shipwreck, which seems likely to be the ferry vessel, *Amherst Islander I,* is about 60' (18 metres) long. The maximum depth at this site is about 18' (5.4 metres). As is the case with most shallow shipwrecks, there is abundant fish life at this site. The visibility is generally good and the mild current poses no problems.

Hazards: No evident hazards exist other than summer or weekend boaters that come by to inspect the wreckage.

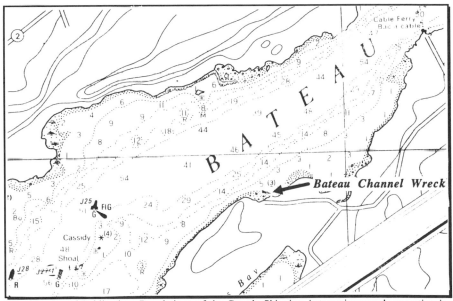

The Charts and Publications Regulations of the Canada Shipping Act require vessels operating in Canadian waters to carry the latest, best scale, corrected Canadian Hydrographic Service (CHS) charts. This document does not meet the requirements of the Act. (Portion of CHS chart 1419.)

Site 28: Holliday Point Wreck

Location:	Holliday Point on Wolfe Island, Ontario.
Access:	Boat.
Skill Level:	Novice - intermediate.
Depth:	17 - 46 feet (5.2 - 13.6 metres).
Visibility:	12 - 24 feet (3.6 - 7.2 metres).

Background: This unidentified wooden sailing vessel has left us no evidence of her name or background.

Directions: Take a boat to the north side of Wolfe Island, across from Howe Island, to Holliday Point, which is clearly marked on chart #1420.

Description: This shipwreck lies in approximately 17' - 46' (5.2 - 13.6 metres) of water. Unfortunately, because of her position in the shallows, the vessel is broken up except for her bow portion, which remains relatively intact.

Hazards: Boating traffic may be the only potential problem, so take a divers down flag with you and fly it. With such little current and such good visibility, a diver should have no difficulties enjoying the wreck remains and the bountiful numbers of fish at this site.

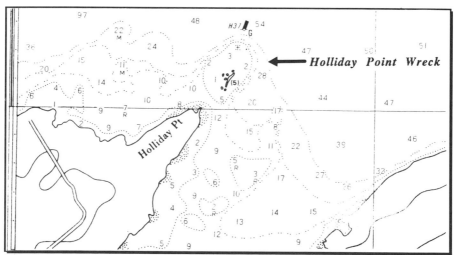

The Charts and Publications Regulations of the Canada Shipping Act require vessels operating in Canadian waters to carry the latest, best scale, corrected Canadian Hydrographic Service (CHS) charts. This document does not meet the requirements of the Act. (Portion of CHS chart 1439.)

Kingston and Lake Ontario

Kingston, Ontario, nestled nicely in the northeast corner of Lake Ontario at the point where the lake empties into the St. Lawrence River, is rich in history, particularly maritime history. The Kingston site is the location that was chosen by the explorer LaSalle for an important meeting between the Governor of New France, Frontenac, and the Iroquois chiefs in 1673. To impress the Indians, Frontenac constructed a stockaded fort there; it was also used to tap the fur trade in the Lake Ontario region. In 1675, LaSalle rebuilt the fort with stone bastions and named it Fort Frontenac. In the 1700's, the site served as a defended port of trans-shipment, handling supplies heading to the western forts and furs brought up in canoes and lake schooners from the frontier regions. In 1783, the site was settled by United Empire Loyalists from New York State, who renamed it Kingston in honour of King George III. By 1793, Kingston was chosen as the chief naval base for Lake Ontario, the establishment of which was crucial later during the War of 1812 with the United States. The Kingston dockyard became furiously engaged in a shipbuilding race with the American Lake Ontario base at Sackets Harbor. Ships the size of those that were sailing across the oceans of the world at that time were constructed at Kingston. The fort that had been built at Point Henry during the war to protect the dockyard was rebuilt on a larger scale in 1832-36 (this is the present Fort Henry which serves as a public attraction). Shipping traffic from the west increased steadily, and the harbour at Kingston enjoyed boom times until the rise of the railways. The last regularly-scheduled passenger steamer called at Kingston in 1951.

What does all that mean to the average scuba diver? It means that this area has a high concentration of shipwrecks! In fact, most modern analysts view Kingston as the second most popular area (after Tobermory), in terms of shipwrecks, for divers to enjoy scuba diving in the province of Ontario. The wrecks range from sailing vessels to sidewheelers, from war of 1812 naval ships to 20th century ferryboats.

Non-shipwreck shore dives can also be done; years ago, we explored the area just behind the Marine Museum of the Upper Great Lakes, and found charred remains of a ship, chain twisted by the flames' heat, old embossed bottles located beyond elbow depth in the muck, and a lawn chair (in superb condition!)

The area around old Fort Henry still, on occasion, yields items of historical interest, and in late November, 1985, two divers doing routine maintenance on the 139-year-old Martello tower in Kingston's Confederation Basin found fifteen 32-pound (14.5 kilogram) cannonballs, which Parks Canada refurbished for display at historic sites across Canada.

Sites not described in this book, but which may be worth checking out, are the Amherst Island wrecks at the southeast end of that island (both are wooden propellers in 65', or 19.5 metres, of water) and the wrecks abandoned around that famous shipbuilding site, Garden Island.

In the interests of safety, no site that is deeper than 130' (39 metres), which is the recognized sport diving limit, is described in this book. Hence, the *Lyman M. Davis* off Toronto harbour is omitted, as well as such sites in Lake Superior as the *Judge Hart* and the *Gunilda*. It's been said that you've got to be a real "whackadoodle" to dive those truly deep sites; this book will not encourage anyone to be a "whackadoodle!"

Site 29: Deadman Bay,
Prince Regent and *Psyche*

Location:	Deadman Bay, east of Fort Henry, Kingston.
Access:	Shore or boat.
Skill Level:	Novice - intermediate.
Depth:	12 - 25 feet (3.6 - 7.5 metres).
Visibility:	8 - 15 feet (2.4 - 4.5 metres).

Background: The War of 1812 provided impetus for major naval ship construction at Kingston. The *Prince Regent,* built completely at Kingston, was a 1,294-ton warship carrying approximately 58 cannons in all. Launched in April, 1814, she became heavily involved with the fighting at Oswego, New York, the next month. After the war, she was kept in reserve with many other vessels, finally sinking in Navy Bay after a few years of inactivity. Raised and towed to Deadman Bay, she again found her way to the bottom, this time with finality. The *Psyche* was transported in pieces from England and assembled at the Kingston dockyard. However, the war ended before she could be used, and she was eventually abandoned in the bay.

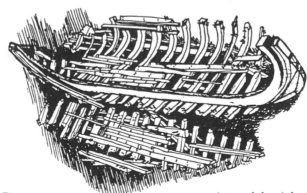

The *Prince Regent*   Artwork by Adam Henley

Directions: The *Prince Regent* is situated in about 20' to 25' (6 to 7.5 metres) of water about 300 feet (90 metres) from the shore opposite Cartright Point. The *Psyche* remains are located in shallower water (about 12 feet, or 3.6 metres) at the end, or head, of the bay. The wrecks can be done as a shore dive from Arrowhead Point.

Description: The keel and ribs are virtually all that remain of these two ancient shipwrecks. As part of their on-going 1987 "Deadman Bay Project," Preserve Our Wrecks (P.O.W.) of Kingston has measured, numbered, and tagged the frames, as well as photographed and videotaped these wrecks.

Hazards: These wrecks lie in a shallow, sand-and-silt-bottom bay, with the diver not having to feel any concerns about current or lack of light. The occasional boater can be a problem unless you are flying a divers down flag.

Site 30: The *St. Lawrence* Wreck

Location:	East of the penitentiary, Kingston, Ontario.
Access:	Shore.
Skill Level:	Intermediate.
Depth:	5 - 10 feet (1.5 - 3 metres).
Visibility:	2 - 5 feet (0.6 - 1.5 metres).

Background: The *St. Lawrence* is considered the mightiest sailing war vessel ever seen on the Great Lakes. Constructed at Kingston for use in the War of 1812, the ship ironically took most of the war to construct. When she finally did sail across Lake Ontario to Niagara, no enemy ship was even sighted, let alone confronted! Pierre Berton described the *St. Lawrence* as a ship "too precious to be risked in battle and too grand to be used as [a] transport." The war ended two months after the *St. Lawrence's* "maiden voyage," and this 2,304-ton vessel was stripped of her cannons and masts and towed to Morton's distillery, where her broken remains lie to this day.

Directions: The *St. Lawrence* is marked on Canadian Hydrographic Service chart #1459 as lying just east of the Kingston Penitentiary, in a little manmade bay at the foot of Morton Street. A city-owned park area is adjacent to this site, and divers can get suited up and wade in there.

Description: The few remaining planks of the *St. Lawrence* are scattered along the bottom of this shallow bay quite close to shore. There is no need to worry about any current, as there is none. This, however, is not good for the visibility, since silt is easily stirred up and visibility is usually poor. Members of Preserve Our Wrecks, Kingston, have examined, measured, photographed, and videotaped these remaining frames of this once-mighty vessel.

Hazards: The poor visibility and the occasional bit of boating traffic would be a diver's main safety concerns at this site.

Site 31: The *Wolfe Islander II*

Location:	3 miles (4.8 kms.) east of Kingston, Ont.
Co-ordinates:	N 44 13' 55", W 76 24' 98".
Access:	Boat.
Skill Level:	Intermediate - advanced.
Depth:	45 - 80 feet (13.5 - 24 metres).
Visibility:	8 - 30 feet (2.4 - 9 metres).

Background: Built in Collingwood, Ont., in 1946, the 164' (49.2 metre) *Wolfe Islander II* ferry plied the waters between Wolfe Island and Kingston for almost 30 years, carrying tourists, cars, trucks, and future divebook writers. She was purposely scuttled as a dive site on Sept. 21, 1985.

Directions: The vessel was sunk in a protected "all-weather" bay about three miles (4.8 kms.) east of Kingston. The *Wolfe Islander II* is probably the most dived shipwreck in the Kingston area, so just follow the charter boats.

Description: The ship sits upright in 80' (24 metres) of water, and visiting divers can explore her open deck area, complete with davits, bollards, dorades, smokestack, railings galore, and many other items too numerous to mention. The more experienced divers can also explore her interior.

Hazards: Don't get lost below deck! The doors and hatches have all been removed, but she's a big ship. Keep track of your depth and bottom time, since a diver can get carried away while exploring the many delightful sites.

Diver Sherrill Lynn, gliding past the superstructure of the Wolfe Islander II, *pauses to inspect one of the ship's overhead lights.* (Photo by Cris Kohl.)

The *Wolfe Islander II*

Artwork by Adam Henley

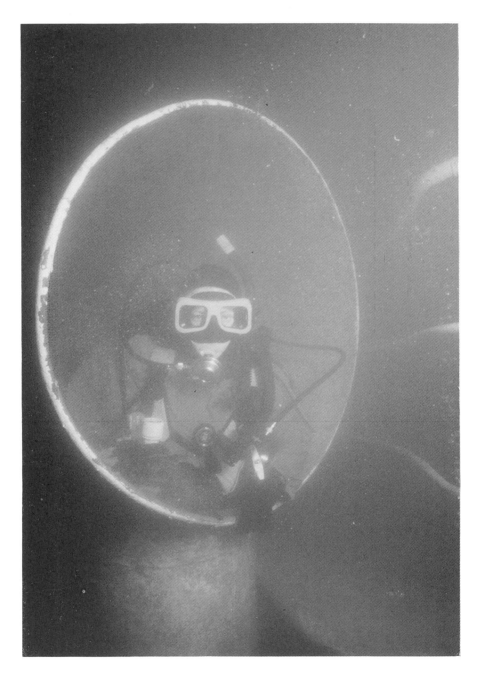

The dorades, or air vents, of the Wolfe Islander II *make excellent underwater photography props --- and a diver, in this case, Sherrill Lynn, willing to climb into one also helps!* (Photo by Cris Kohl.)

Site 32: The "K.P.H." Wreck

Location: This unknown wreck is located off Olympic Harbour, in front of the Kingston Psychiatric Hospital. In fact, that's what the letters K.P.H. stand for! This site is usually buoyed.

Access: Boat.

Skill Level: Intermediate - advanced.

Depth: 65 feet (19.5 metres) maximum.

Visibility: 8 - 20 feet (2.4 - 6 metres).

Description: This unidentified flat barge, about 100' (30 metres) long, is steel-framed, wood-sheathed, wood-decked, and has 6' - 8' (1.8 - 2.4 metres) of height when exploring below deck (use caution!) There are two boilers inside this wreck, as well as other numerous internal details like coal chutes, piping, and machinery. The stern in completely broken open, with loose boards littering the area. Steel beams supporting the decking make penetration diving safer than one might expect it to be. The rudder seems to be missing, but a four-bladed propeller is still intact. Right at the stern, a large funnel or smokestack stands upright off the bottom.

Hazards: The current is usually mild and the visibility is usually good, but use caution if penetrating this wreck. The open hold at the bow can be penetrated, but silt is all-too-easily stirred up, ruining visibility not only for oneself and buddy, but also for the other divers that may be following.

The Psychiatric Barge

Artwork by Adam Henley

Site 33: The Nicknamed *"Titanic"*

Location: Near Kingston, Ontario.
Access: Boat.
Skill Level: Intermediate - advanced.
Depth: 75 feet (22.5 metres).
Visibility: 8 - 30 feet (2.4 - 9 metres).
Description: This unidentified vessel is a huge, intact barge with two large boilers and enormous anchor chain. This wreck may be penetrated by more experienced divers. The site is usually buoyed by local divers in the spring.
Hazards: Divers must certainly consider the depth, and be watchful of their bottom time. Penetration of this wreck could prove dangerous, depending upon dive conditions and level of diver experience.

Site 34: The *Horace L. Taber* Wreck

Location: This shipwreck site is situated to the west of Four Mile Point, on the north side of Simcoe Island
Access: Boat.
Skill Level: Novice - intermediate.
Depth: 5 - 20 feet (1.5 - 6 metres).
Visibility: 6 - 20 feet (1.5 - 6 metres).
Description: Originally launched at St. Clair, Michigan, in 1867 as a two-masted schooner named the *Amoskeag,* the vessel was rebuilt in 1883 as a three-masted schooner renamed the *Horace L. Taber.* She was a very old vessel when, on Nov. 26, 1922, with a cargo of coal, she ran aground in a snowstorm. The coal was later salvaged, but the entire crew was lost. The wreck is now badly broken up and scattered, with her donkey boiler being the predominant feature of this site.
Hazards: This site is usually calm, with negligible current flowing over the sand bottom. Beware of boating traffic in the area.

The beautiful lines of the three-masted schooner, Horace L. Taber, *can be appreciated in this scene of her at dock. She measured 135' (40.5 metres) by 26' (7.8 metres) by 10' 3" (3 metres).* (Photo: The Great Lakes Marine Collection of the Milwaukee Public Library.)

Site 35: The Wreck of the *Aloha*

Location:	Off Nine Mile Point, Simcoe Island.
Access:	Boat.
Skill Level:	Novice - intermediate.
Depth:	55 feet (16.5 metres).
Visibility:	8 - 30 feet (2.4 - 9 metres).

Background: This schooner-barge, built by William Dulac at Mt. Clemens, Michigan, in 1888, measured 173' (51.9 metres) in length, 32' 5" (9.7 metres) in beam, and 12' (3.6 metres) in draft. On Oct. 29, 1917, while in tow of the steamer *C. W. Chamberlain* bound for Kingston with a load of coal, the *Aloha* began to leak in a gale and, several hours later, foundered. The steamer managed to rescue everyone except the captain.

Directions: This site is buoyed and can be found abreast of Nine Mile Point, Simcoe Island.

Description: Most of the hull is intact, although she was picked clean of most of her artifacts years ago. Anchor chain sits on the bow attached to a windlass. Divers can penetrate the holds and see the original coal cargo. At the stern, in the sand, can be seen a capstan, steering quadrant, and rudder post. The Roman numeral depth markings are interesting to study closely.

Hazards: Be aware of occasional boating traffic in this area.

The schooner-barge Aloha *sank in a gale on Oct. 28, 1917, with the loss of her captain.* (Photo: Institute for Great Lakes Research, Perrysburg, Ohio.)

Chain extends straight down from the Aloha's *starboard bow hawser pipe to the anchor sitting in the sand. (above.). In 1982, Jacques Cousteau condemned the Great Lakes as being "void of life," but had he been exploring the* Aloha, *his opinion might not have been so pessimistic. Schools of fish abound at this site! (below)* (Photos by Cris Kohl.)

Site 36: The Wreck of the *Comet*

Location:	Two miles (3 kms.) off Nine Mile Point.
Co-ordinates:	N 44 08' 34", W 76 35' 15".
Access:	Boat.
Skill Level:	Intermediate - advanced.
Depth:	85 feet (25.5 metres).
Visibility:	8 - 15 feet (2.4 - 4.5 metres).

Background: The elegant, graceful sidewheel steamer, *Comet,* was built by George N. Ault at Portsmouth (Kingston), Ontario, in 1848. She measured 174' (52.2 metres) in length, 24' (7.2 metres) in beam, and 10' (3 metres) in draft, with a gross tonnage of 337. The *Comet* underwent a name change in 1854, and for the next six years, she was known as the *Mayflower.* The year before she sank, her original name was restored. On April 20, 1851, the *Comet's* boiler exploded as she was leaving Oswego, New York, killing eight persons. The hull was later raised and rebuilt, but she was no longer considered a lucky ship.

On May 15, 1861, the captain of the *Comet,* amidst storm signals and rolling squalls, decided to take his vessel out of the safety of the harbour. Simultaneously, the American schooner, *Exchange,* was frantically running before the storm in quest of a safe harbour. In the obscured visibility produced by the foul weather, the bow of the *Exchange* sliced deeply into the hull of the *Comet.* It soon became apparent that the sidewheeler was destined to sink, and crew and passengers were ordered to abandon ship. Three lives were lost as the *Comet* plummeted to the depths of Lake Ontario with her cargo of farm implements. Six scuba divers from Kingston located the wreck of the *Comet* in her deep, watery grave in October, 1967.

Directions: The *Comet* lies about two miles (3.2 kms.) southwest of Nine Mile Point near Kingston. She is buoyed by local divers every spring.

Description: The vessel's bow and stern have collapsed, but her distinctive sidewheels are still intact and tower about 25' (7.5 metres) off the lake bed. The rocker arms and walking beams are also clearly visible. Remnants of her railing, doors, and smokestacks can be seen along the east side, and portions of her farm implements cargo are scattered around the wreck site.

Hazards: The wreck lies in deep water, so being constantly conscious of bottom time is essential. Since the slight current is negligible, silt has built up on the wreck, and it is very easy for careless or thoughtless divers to stir up the silt and reduce the visibility for the others. It gets dark down there at that depth, so take a dive light. The wreck is not intact, and therefore there is no penetration, but a light will reveal details of the scattered artifacts.

For a drawing of the paddlewheeler, *Comet,* please turn to page 98 of this book.

The sidewheel steamer Comet *(above): built 1848, sank 1861.* (Photo: Bill Humphries.) *The axle of one of the* Comet's *huge paddlewheels is plain to see and appreciate at this site (below).* (Photo by Cris Kohl.)

Site 37: The *George A. Marsh* Wreck

Location:	Three miles (4.8 kms.) off Nine Mile Point.
Co-ordinates:	N 44 07' 69", W 76 36' 26".
Access:	Boat.
Skill Level:	Intermediate - advanced.
Depth:	70 - 85 feet (21 - 25.5 metres).
Visibility:	8 - 30 feet (2.4 - 9 metres).

Background: Built in 1882 at Muskegon, Michigan by William Footlander, the three-masted schooner, *George A. Marsh,* named after a lumber magnate, could claim the final measurements (after a couple of rebuilds) of 135' (40.5 metres) by 27' (8.1 metres) by 9' 3" (2.8 metres), with 220 gross tons. This sleek vessel was built to haul lumber products for the Marsh company and had a capacity of 300,000 board feet of lumber. However, towards the end of her career, she was moving coal cargoes to ports along Lake Ontario and the St. Lawrence River.

On August 8, 1917, loaded with coal from Oswego, New York, to Kingston, the *George A. Marsh* encountered a furious summer storm in the middle of the night and, after a several-hour struggle to make a protected bay, sank with the loss of 12 of the 14 people on board, including the captain's wife and five of their children.

Directions: This site is located about three miles (4.8 kms.) off Nine Mile Point, to the southwest of Kingston, Ontario. Local divers buoy it.

Description: This shipwreck is almost 100% intact. Besides the many deadeyes, blocks, and belaying pins, there is the ship's wheel and a stove on the deck, complete with cooking utensils. Also look at and appreciate her rigging, lifeboat, bowsprit, and pottery artifacts. It is easy to see why Kingston area divers are proud and protective of this wreck. Anyone caught desecrating this site would likely have a long swim back to shore -- before being tarred and feathered!

Hazards: The wreck sits deep and in silt that is easily disturbed. Be aware of both your bottom time and the fact that there may be divers coming down the line not too far behind you, and they will want to be impressed by this beautiful shipwreck site, too. Don't muck it up for them.

The schooner George A. Marsh *was 35 years old when she foundered with the loss of 12 lives.* (Photo: Institute for Great Lakes Research, Perrysburg, Ohio.)

The George Marsh *proudly displayed her name on a transom board* (Photo: The Great Lakes Marine Collection of the Milwaukee Public Library.)

Photographs of the *George Marsh's* masts protruding above water at the wreck site were published in *The Daily British Whig* (Kingston) on Saturday, August 25, 1917, with the heading and cutline, "A Tragedy of Lake Ontario. The picture shows all that remains of the schooner *George Marsh,* which was lost in a storm near Kingston, with twelve of those on board."

The *George A. Marsh* Shipwreck

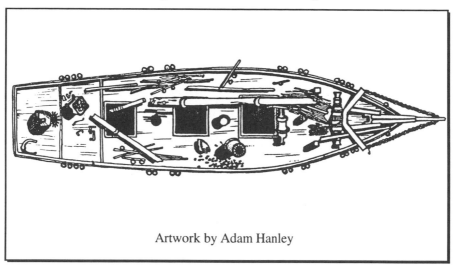

Artwork by Adam Hanley

The ship's wheel on the George A. Marsh *attracts much attention from visiting divers, in this case, commercial diver James Taylor.* (Photo by Cris Kohl).

Site 38: *City of Sheboygan* Wreck

Location: Southwest of Amherst Island, near Nut Island.
Access: Boat.
Skill Level: Advanced.
Depth: 104 feet (31.3 metres).
Visibility: 8 - 30 feet (2.4 - 9 metres).
Description: This three-masted schooner, built by Fred Hamilton at Sheboygan, Wisconsin and launched on July 5, 1871, enjoyed a career that spanned almost 45 years on the Great Lakes. She foundered in a violent storm on September 25, 1915. Helpless Amherst Island fishermen gazed in silent horror as the captain and the crew of four drowned. The wreck is deep, and hence well-preserved. For that reason, local divers have kept her location quite a secret. The ship's wheel and an anchor are the only items that were removed (and are now in a museum) from this otherwise intact shipwreck. Her masts, rigging, and most other items, including deadeyes, are present.
Hazards: The depth of this wreck is an inhibiting factor. The site is cold and dark (lights are required), but the slight current is negligible.

SCHOONER WENT DOWN

CITY OF CHEYBOYGAN SANK ON SUNDAY MORNING

Near Amherst Island—It Left Kingston on Saturday With Feldspar For Buffalo.
On Sunday morning about 11 o'clock the schooner City of Cheyboygan, loaded with feldspar from

Kingston newspaper headlines on Wednesday, May 16, 1923, reported the tragic loss of the schooner, *City of Sheboygan. (The Daily British Whig).*

The City of Sheboygan, *used mainly in the lumber trade, served the Great Lakes for almost 45 years before her tragic sinking on September 25, 1915, with the loss of five lives.* (Photo: Institute for Great Lakes Research, Perrysburg, Ohio.)

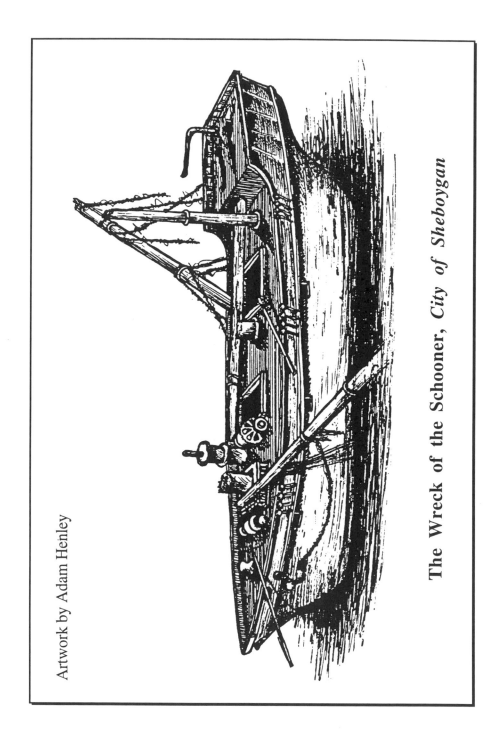

Artwork by Adam Henley

The Wreck of the Schooner, *City of Sheboygan*

Diver Doug Pettingill studies one of several deadeyes on the starboard railing of the schooner, City of Sheboygan (Photo by Cris Kohl).

Site 39: The *William Jamieson* Wreck

Location:	Off the north shore of Amherst Island.
Access:	Boat.
Skill Level:	Intermediate - advanced.
Depth:	80 feet. (24 metres).
Visibility:	10 - 30 feet (3 - 9 metres).

Background: This schooner, built by William Jamieson at Mill Point (Deseronto), Ontario, immodestly named after himself, and launched on July 3, 1878, measured 100' (30 metres) in length, 25' 4" (7.6 metres) in beam, 8' 6" (2.5 metres) in draft, and had a gross tonnage of 143. On May 15, 1923, the 45-year-old vessel showed her age when she opened her seams during a severe storm. The crew abandoned ship and the vessel hit the bottom with her hard coal cargo.

Directions: The wreck lies near the north side of Amherst Island, west of Emerald.

Description: Much silt rests on this site, but the visibility usually remains quite good. The wreck is intact with some of her rigging and bow pumps still in their original positions.

Hazards: This is a deep dive, so more-than-usual caution should be exercised, especially if silt is kicked up and the visibility is disturbed.

The schooner William Jamieson *sank with a load of anthracite coal on May 15, 1923.* (Photo: Institute for Great Lakes Research, Perrysburg, Ohio.)

The schooner, William Jamieson, *underway.* (Photo: author's collection.)

Site 40: The Wreck of the *Quinte*

Location:	Southwest of Deseronto.
Co-ordinates:	N 44 10' 35", W 77 02' 30".
Access:	Shore or boat.
Skill Level:	Novice - intermediate.
Depth:	5 - 10 feet (1.5 - 3 metres).
Visibility:	5 - 12 feet (1.5 - 3.6 metres).

Background: Built by Iubin Chabot at Montreal in 1871 and launched as the *Beauharnois,* the sidewheel steamer, *Quinte,* became the flagship of the Deseronto Navigation Company and measured 138' (41.4 metres) by 22' 5" (6.7 metres) by 7' 5" (2.2 metres). Her name was changed to *Quinte* in 1882. On October 23, 1889, the vessel, with 24 passengers on board, caught fire just off Grassy Point, three miles (4.8 kms.) from Deseronto. She was fully ablaze by the time she was grounded, and five people died.

Description: Only that portion of the vessel below the waterline exists in about 5' - 10' (1.5 - 3 metres) of water. There is a sandy bottom with negligible current, so the visibility is usually good. Coins have been located here by youngsters using the remains as a swimming spot.

Hazards: Boating traffic can get heavy, so fly a divers down flag.

The sidewheeler Quinte *with a full load of passengers.* (Photo: Public Archives.)

Site 41: The Wreck of the *Echo*

Location:	One-half mile (0.8 kilometre) off Gull Bar near False Duck Island.
Access:	Boat.
Skill Level:	Novice - intermediate.
Depth:	22 feet (6.6 metres).
Visibility:	4 - 12 feet (1.2 - 3.6 metres).
Description:	This "fore-and-after" (meaning it was a two-masted schooner; a "three-and-after" was marine slang for a three-masted schooner) sank on October 12, 1861, while enroute from Toronto laden with barley. The entire crew was saved. This wreck was located on Sept. 17, 1967 by members of the Quinte Aqua Divers, Belleville, Ontario.
Hazards:	The occasional boating traffic could be menacing.

Site 42: The Wreck of the *Banshee*

Location:	Between Timber Island and the Duck Islands.
Co-ordinates:	Approximately N 43 56', W 76 51'.
Access:	Boat.
Skill Level:	Novice - intermediate.
Depth:	18 feet (5.4 metres).
Visibility:	4 - 12 feet (1.2 - 3.6 metres).
Description:	The propeller *Banshee,* measuring 119' (35.7 metres) by 18' (5.4 metres) by 8' (2.4 metres), carried a cargo of 6,000 bushels of wheat, 250 barrels of flour, and 300 kegs of butter from Port Stanley, on Lake Erie, towards Montreal, when she sank in a nefarious storm after her engine expired and she drifted into the shallow waters of Gull Shoal. One life was lost; ten survived. Members of the Quinte Aqua Divers, Belleville, Ontario, located these wreck remains, which they believe to be those of the *Banshee,* in late 1967.
Hazards:	The wreck is badly broken up, so disorientation is possible while exploring this site.

Site 43: The *Annie Falconer* Wreck

Location:	1.5 miles north, False Duck I. Lighthouse.
Access:	Boat.
Skill Level:	Intermediate - advanced.
Depth:	80 feet (24 metres).
Visibility:	8 - 30 feet (2.4 - 9 metres).

Background: Measuring 108' (32.4 metres) by 24' (7.2 metres) by 9' (2.7 metres), the twin-masted schooner, *Annie Falconer,* was built at Kingston by George Thurston and launched on May 22, 1867. By 1875, the Annie Falconer was valued at only $8,000; in 1882, $6,000; by 1890, only $4,500.

The *Annie Falconer* carried many cargoes during her long life on the Great Lakes: lumber, ice, coal, shingles, staves, salt, and grain.

This vessel foundered in a violent storm on November 12, 1904, while underway with a cargo of soft coal for A. W. Hepburn from Sodus Point, New York to Picton, Ontario. The crew of seven reached Amherst Island in the ship's yawl boat "after hours of suffering and hardship" (*The Daily British Whig,* Monday, November 14, 1904), but the first mate, James Sullivan, died of exposure shortly thereafter when he wandered away from the rest of the crew. The vessel was owned and sailed by Capt. Murney Ackerman, of Picton, Ontario, which was the home town of the entire crew. The estimated value of this old vessel was only $1,000, while the coal cargo was valued at $1,500.

The *Annie Falconer* was found by divers Barbara Carson and Doug Pettingill in 1975. Many of the vessel's artifacts were raised and donated to the local museum at South Bay, where they are on exhibit.

Directions: The vessel sank off South Bay Point in the vicinity of False Duck Island and Timber Island.

Description: The *Annie Falconer* sits upright in about 80' (24 metres) of mud. She is well-preserved, with deadeyes, anchors, ship's wheel, blocks, and chain on display. Her stern is broken off, but it lies within visible range at an angle to the main hull.

Hazards: The 80' depth makes this a deep dive, so caution must be used.

The *Annie Falconer,* from a painting by Gibbons.

The Annie Falconer *was named after the first owner's wife, who had died seven years before her namesake vessel was built!.*(Photo: author's collection).

The Schooner, *Annie Falconer*

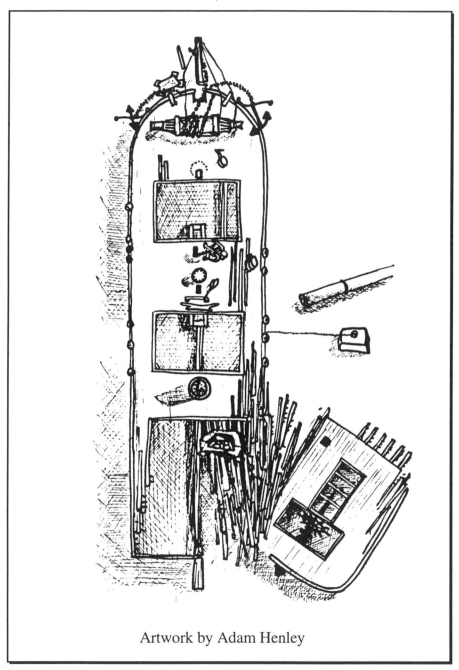

Artwork by Adam Henley

The collapsed bowsprit, studied by diver Pat Kelly, signals Mother Nature's course on the schooner, Annie Falconer *(above.). The ship's wheel is the usual focal point. The absence of a silty patina on the wooden handles of the wheel indicates that many visiting divers have taken turns steering the "Annie." (below)* (Photos by Cris Kohl.)

Site 44: The *John Randall* Shipwreck

Location:	School House Bay, Main Duck Island.
Access:	Boat.
Skill Level:	Novice - intermediate.
Depth:	To 20 feet (6 metres).
Visibility:	10 - 30 feet (3 - 9 metres).

Background: This wooden propeller, built in 1905 by the Shelby and Youlden
Company of Kingston, Ontario, and measuring 116' (34.8 metres) by 22' 5"
(6.7 metres) by 11' 4" (3.4 metres), carried a coal cargo from Oswego, New
York towards Belleville, Ontario, when she encountered a severe storm on
Nov. 16, 1920, off Main Duck Island. Captain Harry Randall steamed the
vessel towards shelter in School House Bay. There, the ship leaked and
sank, with only the wheelhouse above water. With the lifeboats washed
away, the life-jacketted crew abandoned ship on a hatch cover and made the
safety of the island, where they remained the guests of the lighthousekeeper
for nine days. Captain Randall's father, meanwhile, had enlisted the aid of a
spiritualist, who informed the worried captain that his son and crew were
safe and happy, but that their ship had sunk near an island. How right she
was, and how joyful the father must have been when his son returned alive!
Unfortunately, exactly a year later, Captain Harry Randall perished when the
ill-fated steamer *City of New York* sank on L. Ontario with all eight hands.

Description: The vessel remains lie flattened in the waters of the bay.

Hazards: Since the wreck is scattered, disorientation is possible at this site.

Headline on page one of *The Daily British Whig* (Kingston), Nov. 26, 1920.

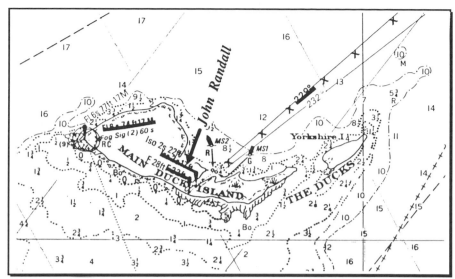

The Charts and Publications Regulations of the Canada Shipping Act require vessels operating in Canadian waters to carry the latest, best scale, corrected Canadian Hydrographic Service (CHS) charts. This document does not meet the requirements of the Act. (Port from CHS chart 2064).

The John Randall, *built in 1905, wrecked in 1920.* (Photo: author's collection).

The John Randall's *bow remained above water for a short period of time after the vessel sank, but ice, wind, and wave action soon flattened the remains* (above; photo: author's collection.). *Underwater videographer, Jim Stayer, captures the* Randall's *flattened remains on tape.* (below) (Photo by Cris Kohl.)

Site 45: Wreck of the *C. Hickox*

Location:	Off Main Duck Island, Lake Ontario.
Access:	Boat.
Skill Level:	Novice.
Depth:	5 - 20 feet (1.5 - 6 metres).
Visibility:	5 - 12 feet. (1.5 - 3.6 metres).

Background: Built by the Henry D. Root Shipyard at Lorain, Ohio, in 1873, the wooden bulk freight steamer *C. Hickox* measured 140' (42 metres) in length, 24' 10" (7.5 metres) in beam, and 9' (2.7 metres) in draft. Having departed Little Sodus, New York, loaded with coal, the *C. Hickox* ran aground at the head end of Main Duck Island, where she mysteriously caught fire and burned to the water line on December 2, 1906.

Directions: Her boilers, which are still visible, mark the wreck site off Main Duck Island.

Description: What little remains of this wreck is scattered and buried in the sand bottom off Main Duck Island.

Hazards: The current here is negligible, and the shallow depths should make this a safe and interesting site.

The steamer, C. Hickox, *is seen in winter lay-up.* (Photo: author's collection.)

Site 46: The *Olive Branch* Wreck

Location:	Near False Duck Island.
Access:	Boat.
Skill Level:	Advanced.
Depth:	98 feet (29.4 metres).
Visibility:	6 - 20 feet (1.8 - 6 metres).

Background: This uninsured (her insurance had expired on Sept. 15, two weeks earlier!) two-masted schooner, measuring 92' (27.6 metres) in length, 22' (6.6 metres) in beam, and 8' (2.4 metres) in draft, had been built in Picton, Ont., in 1871 by Messrs. Redman. Operating as a barley carrier, she sank in a storm on Sept. 30, 1880 off False Duck I., near one of the Pennicons. All lives were lost: Captain Ault of Kingston, Mrs. Minnie Jarvis of Belleville, the cook, two French sailors and one from Oswego.

The first inkling of disaster was reported on September 30, 1880; the *Chicago Inter Ocean,* for example, reported that

> **Captains of schooners arriving from the West to-day report a schooner capsized near the Ducks. She was light, with a capacity of about 10,000 bushels, and apparently bound from Oswego for this port [Kingston]. Owing to the heavy southeast gale which has been blowing all day, they could render no assistance.**

That same newspaper reported on October 9, 1880 that

> **Captain Dix, of the White Oak, enroute to this port [Kingston], lowered a boat and approached the mast of the sunken vessel at the Ducks. The fly was secured and brought to this city, and brought to the inspection of Mrs. Captain McKee, who made it. She believes it belonged to the Olive Branch. The suspicions have thus been confirmed beyond a doubt. Captain Dix says the vessel lies about two miles from Timber Island, in about 70 feet of water. Her bow is about eight or ten feet higher than her stern. She is on a sloping shoal. All hands must have been on deck at the time of the disaster.**

Description: This wreck is intact, resting upright at the base of a shoal down which she seems to have slid (the original account put the wreck in 70 feet; she is now in 98 feet). Most of her original equipment remains on board, including a windlass, ship's wheel, deadeyes, blocks, a standing capstan, a pump, hinged catheads (the starboard one with a steel-stock fluke anchor), a Quebec stove, a fallen mast with wire rigging, and a collapsed bowsprit.

Hazards: The depth and occasional low visibility make this an advanced dive.

The Schooner, *Olive Branch*

Artwork by Adam Henley

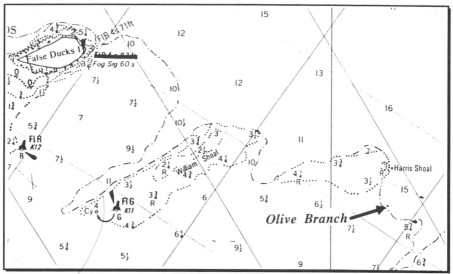

The Charts and Publications Regulations of the Canada Shipping Act require vessels operating in Canadian waters to carry the latest, best scale, corrected Canadian Hydrographic Service (CHS) charts. This document does not meet the requirements of the Act. (Port from CHS chart 2064).

A deadeye (part of the standing rigging) along the starboard railing of the schooner, Olive Branch, *waits unamused as half a dozen zebra mussels begin their infestation of the artifacts on this shipwreck.* (Photo by Cris Kohl).

The wooden handles of the Olive Branch's *metal wheel have surprisingly deteriorated* (above.). *A leather shoe sole is a grim reminder that all on board this vessel died when their ship went down.* (below) (Photos by Cris Kohl.)

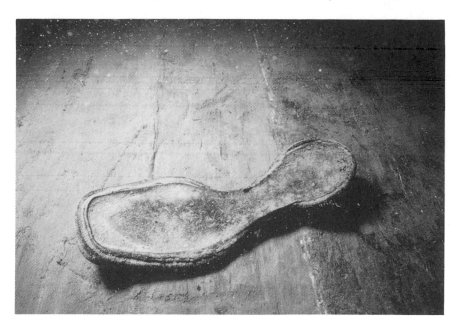

Site 47: The Wreck of the *Fabiola*

Location:	Off the southeast corner of False Duck Island, just west of the False Duck Light.
Access:	Definitely a boat dive!
Skill Level:	Novice - intermediate.
Depth:	55 feet (16.5 metres).
Visibility:	8 - 20 feet (2.4 - 6 metres).
Description:	This two-masted schooner, carrying dimensions of 95' (28.5 metres) by 22. 4" (6.7 metres) by 9' (2.7 metres), was launched at Oakville, Ont., under the name *Red Oak* in 1852 (her name change to *Fabiola* occurred in 1876). She was an old, twice-rebuilt vessel when she was lost south of False Duck Island on Oct. 23, 1900, downbound from Oswego, New York with a cargo of coal. The bow, with its windlass and capstan, is quite intact, but the stern has collapsed.
Hazards:	The dive conditions are usually quite favourable, with good visibility, no current, and sand bottom.

Fish such as bass are often found, individually or schooling, on shipwrecks in Lake Ontario, this case being on the Fabiola. *Freshwater sponges grow on the wooden railing in the background.* (Photo by Cris Kohl).

Diver Doug Pettingill explores the intact windlass at the bow of the schooner Fabiola. *A windlass was a cylindrical, horizontal, chain-hauling, ratchet device used to raise anchors.* (Photo by Cris Kohl.)

Site 48: The *Florence* Shipwreck

Location: About 300' (90 metres) off Timber I., Point Traverse.
Access: Boat.
Skill Level: Novice - intermediate.
Depth: 40 - 50 feet (12 - 15 metres); rock bottom.
Visibility: 8 - 20 feet (2.4 - 6 metres).
Description: The wooden tug, *Florence,* measuring 91' (27.3
                     metres) x 19' 8" (5.9 metres) x 9' (2.7 metres), and built by
                     the Maritime and Industrial Company at Lévis, Québec in
                     1885, worked in Québec, Amherstburg, Ont. (1903-1908),
                     New Brunswick, Windsor, Ont. (1927-1932) before springing
                     a leak and sinking at this site on Nov. 14, 1933 with no loss
                     of life. Salvage attempts moved her from her original depth of
                     80' (24 metres) to shallower water, and her engine and screw
                     are missing. The bow and boiler, plus a hatch ladder, are intact.
Hazards: There is usually good visibility and no current.

The tugboat, Florence, *plied Great Lakes waters for almost half a century.*
(Photo: The Great Lakes Marine Collection of the Milwaukee Public Library.)

Kathy Eveson investigates chain and the upper portion of the steam engine on the Florence *(above.). Salvage work and shallow water conditions have broken up most of this still-interesting shipwreck* (below) (Photos by Cris Kohl.)

Site 49: The *Belle Sheridan* Wreck

Location:	Weller's Bay, south of Trenton, near Beecroft Point.
Access:	Shore or boat.
Skill Level:	Novice - intermediate.
Depth:	12 feet (3.6 metres).
Visibility:	6 - 10 feet (1.8 - 3 metres).
Hazards:	This wreck lies badly broken up, scattered, and often buried in sand. As a result, diver disorientation is possible. Be aware of boating traffic.

Background: The two-masted schooner, *Belle Sheridan,* built at Oswego, New York by Andrew Miller in 1852, measured 123' (36.9 metres) in length, 22' 8" (6.8 metres) in beam, and 10' 2" (3 metres) in draft, with a gross tonnage of 265. Coal-laden while enroute from Charlotte to Toronto, she ran aground near Beecroft Point during the Great Gale of November, 1880, dragging her anchors, with disastrous results.

The press (*Chicago Inter Ocean,* November 9, 1880) reported:

A private dispatch states that the schooner Belle Sheridan is a total wreck at Weller's Bay, and that six of the crew -- probably all hands -- are lost. The victims are Captain McSherry, Mate McSherry, two seamen named McSherry, and two seamen whose names are not known. The male members of the McSherry family, who hail from Toronto, are all lost by this disaster. Captain McSherry was the father of the three other men of that name. The Sheridan...was owned by Captain McSherry, rated B1, and was valued at $6,000. Whether insured is not known.

Other sources indicate that the First Mate on the *Belle Sheridan* was an experienced sailor named John Hamilton, and the Second Mate was a powerful giant named Samuel Boyd. Four of Captain McSherry's sons were working on board: John, 21 years old, James, 18, Thomas, 17, and Edward, 13. Although the ship was grounded only a hundred yards from shore, and hundreds of people gathered in an effort to assist the stricken crew, James was the sole survivor. Holding tightly to a huge timber, he jumped overboard and swam madly for shore, arriving more dead than alive before being transported to a nearby farmhouse for warmth and food.

Captain McSherry had purchased the *Belle Sheridan* in 1878 for $3,600 where she lay sunk at her Toronto dock at the foot of Church Street; he raised her, rebuilt her, and turned her into a family business, tragically.

In 1933, portions of the *Belle Sheridan's* deck and ribbing were raised and returned to Toronto.

On November 7, 1928, the Toronto Telegram *printed a commemorative, 40th anniversary story on the* Belle Sheridan. *The above drawing of the vessel, and the map below indicating where she first dropped anchor to ride out the storm, and where the ship grounded and broke up, are from that source.*

WHERE THE "BELLE SHERIDAN" POUNDED TO PIECES

Site 50: *John A. MacDonald* Wreck

Location: Off east shore, mouth of Presqu'ile Bay, Ontario.
Co-ordinates: N 44 00' 36", W 77 40' 30".
Access: Boat.
Skill Level: Novice.
Depth: 6 - 8 feet (1.5-2.4 metres). Usually marked by a jug.
Visibility: 4 - 8 feet (1.2 - 2.4 metres).
Description: The two-masted schooner, *John A. MacDonald,* was
    originally launched as the *John A. Torrance* in 1841 at
    Burlington, Ontario. Measuring 112' (33.6 metres) in length,
    19' 9" (5.9 metres) in beam, and 9' (2.7 metres) in draft, she
    received her name change in 1860. On Nov. 17, 1872, she
    began taking on water while enroute from Hamilton to
    Kingston with a coal cargo, and was run ashore at the mouth
    of Presqu'ile Bay, where she broke up. No lives were lost.
    While most of this wreck is broken up and buried in the sand,
    decking, with its planking and spikes, is visible.
Hazards: Boating traffic in and out of the bay should be noted,
    and a divers down flag should be flown.

Site 51: Wreck of the *Ida Walker*

Location: At the mouth of Weller's Bay, near Presqu'ile Point.
Co-ordinates: N 44 00' 57", W 77 36' 22".
Access: Shore or boat.
Skill Level: Novice.
Depth: 10 - 12 feet (3-3.6 metres). Usually marked by a jug.
Visibility: 6 - 10 feet (1.8 - 3 metres).
Description: The two-masted schooner, *Ida Walker,* sought storm
    shelter on Nov. 19, 1886, while loading at the nearby
    unprotected port of Wellington. The sweeping seas forced her,
    half-loaded with barley and dragging her anchor, onto the shoal
    at the mouth of Weller's Bay. The nearby Wellington
    lifesaving station rescued the entire crew before the vessel
    broke up. Today, she lies broken and scattered and partially
    buried in the sand at a depth of about 12' (3.6 metres) of water.
Hazards: Boating traffic is a concern in the warm months.

Site 52: Presqu'ile Provincial Park

The Annual O.U.C. Treasure Hunt Dive

Background: In the 1970's, the Ontario Underwater Council, with assistance from local scuba clubs, began the tradition of sponsoring and organizing a "Treasure Hunt" weekend, offering opportunities for divers and their families to enjoy camping and socializing with other divers and their families, and possibly winning a big, donated prize (or one of the many smaller ones!).

Directions: The town of Brighton is reached by taking Highway 401 exit #509 onto Highway 30 south. From Brighton, travel a bit west and south to Presqu'ile Provincial Park; numerous signs point out the route. Divers' signs lead the way to the Treasure Hunt site within the park itself. The park is about 90 miles (145 kilometres) east of Toronto.

Description: Usually over 400 paired-up scuba divers and snorklers splash through the shallow water (max. depth: 13', or 3.9 metres) just offshore to locate one of the hundreds of markers, or "flags," that are planted by organizers from boats that morning. Volleyball, tugs-of-war, kids' events, a campfire singalong, pancake breakfast, etc. are also planned for the weekend.

Hazards: Since this usually takes place on the third weekend in June, divers overheating while waiting for the start is possible. Once divers are in the water, reduced visibility could occur. Fast-moving, groping divers with occasionally flailing appendages may pose a hazard. But all in all, it's a fun time! Contact the O.U.C. at (416) 426-7033 for further information.

Hundreds of divers prepare to race to the water in the annual Ontario Underwater Council Treasure Hunt at Presqu'ile Provincial Park. (Photo by Cris Kohl.)

Site 53: The Wreck of the *Juno*

Location:	Just off shore, north of Bowmanville, Ont.
Co-ordinates:	N 43 53' 01", W 78 80' 02".
Access:	Shore or boat.
Skill Level:	Novice.
Depth:	6 - 12 feet (1.8 - 3.6 metres).
Visibility:	4 - 10 feet (1.2 - 3 metres). Best if wind is offshore.

Background: Built at the Adam McDonald Shipyard in Wallaceburg, Ontario in 1885, lengthened at the same place in 1898, and finally converted to a self-unloader at Port Dalhousie, Ont., in 1913, the oak-hulled propeller, *Juno,* was stripped of her machinery in 1914 and she was removed from service to be utilized as a breakwall and loading pier (a fate similar to the *Gladstone's* at Point Edward near Sarnia) for a shoreline quarry. A few years later, her hull broke up and her usefulness was terminated.

Directions: Lying about 200' (60 metres) from shore, the wreck site is 42 miles (68 kilometres) east of Toronto, south of Highway 401, near Waverly Road. The site is usually marked with jugs early in the season.

Description: The badly broken-up bow, with a half-buried windlass, rests in the shallows; the slightly deeper stern offers the 8' upright propeller.

Hazards: The wreck sits on a hard sand bottom in a current-free location. Passing boaters can pose a problem, so always use a divers down flag.

The propeller, Juno, *worked on the great Lakes for 29 years.* (Photo: The Great Lakes Marine Collection of the Milwaukee Public Library.)

Site 54: The *Julia B. Merrill*

Location:	Lake Ontario, near the Humber River.
Co-ordinates:	N 43 37' 05", W 79 26' 80".
Access:	Boat.
Skill Level:	Intermediate - advanced.
Depth:	60 feet. (18 metres).
Visibility:	4 - 10 feet (1.2 - 3 metres).

Background: A mob's Viking-funeral-like fondness allowed the classic schooner, *Julia B. Merrill,* to be purposely engulfed by flames for sheer public spectacle at Sunnyside Park in Toronto in July, 1931. Built in 1872 at Wenona, Michigan, by F. A. Carpenter, and rebuilt in Canada in 1910, this vessel's final measurements were 125' 5" (37.6 metres) by 26' 5" (7.9 metres) by 8' 2" (2.5 metres). Unlike the vast majority of the sailing vessels on the lakes, the *Merrill* was not converted to a tow-barge, but maintained her original purpose, working under sail, until her demise.

Description: The superstructure of this shipwreck is totally burned away, but her keel, rudder, and posts are still intact.

Hazards: Lying as she does near the wreck of the *Sligo,* the visibility here is also poor, with an overwhelming silt presence that clouds the site quickly.

The Julia B. Merrill *under full sail near Kingston, Ontario, in 1926.* (Photo: The Great Lakes Marine Collection of the Milwaukee Public Library.)

Site 55: The *Alexandria* Shipwreck

Location:	Below Scarborough Bluffs, Markham Rd.
Access:	Boat.
Skill Level:	Intermediate.
Depth:	5 - 10 feet (1.5 - 3 metres).
Visibility:	1 - 3 feet (0.3 - 0.9 metres).
WARNING:	Divers require permission to dive in this area from the Metropolitan Toronto Police Marine Unit. Divers must also sign liability release forms.

Background: The *Alexandria,* a sidewheel steamer measuring 161' 7" (48.5 metres) in length, by 25' 2" (7.5 metres) in beam, and 8' 1" (2.4 metres) in draft, was built in Montreal in 1866 by Auguste Cantin. Originally named the *Alexandra,* the additional letter "i" was added in 1883. A rebuild at Picton, Ontario, enlarged her dimensions to 173' (51.9 metres) by 30' 6" (9.1 metres) by 8' 11" (2.7 metres).and her gross tonnage from 350 to 863.

On August 3, 1915, bound from Port Hope to Toronto with a partial cargo of general merchandise, mostly pickles, potatoes, and sugar, the *Alexandria* encountered severe weather, became stranded near the Scarborough Bluffs, and broke up from the severe pounding just off the beach. All on board were rescued by the crowd of people that gathered on shore and managed to get a lifeline to the stricken vessel.

After the storm, the collapsed vessel remained an interesting local site, lying on her port side, helplessly embedded in the bottom, proclaiming her anguish with the loud presence of her huge boiler, iron girders, and oak timbers. Before long, every valve, nut, and bolt was removed by local swimmers desiring a souvenir. Rumour has it that many cellars were well-stocked with vinegar containers and canned goods from the *Alexandria,* while many of her huge timbers, useless as part of a shipwreck back in those unappreciative days, were retrieved for shed construction.

Directions: The site is located at the base of the Scarborough Bluffs, opposite Markham Road.

Description: The *Alexandria* is totally broken up and scattered on a combination sand and silt bottom in shallow (average 7', or 2.1 metres) water. Her boiler is still visible from the surface.

Hazards: Boating traffic can be heavy and the underwater visibility is very poor, so take a dive flag with you and make great effort to keep track of where you are in relation to the shore, the wreck, and your dive boat.

The Alexandria *in a St. Lawrence River canal, 1914, above.* (Photo: Ontario Public Archives.) *A year later, the vessel lay wrecked at the base of the Scarborough Bluffs. The shipwreck lies broken and scattered in the shallow water, and the poor visibility detracts from this site's popularity.* (Photo: author's collection.)

Site 56: The Wreck of the *Sligo*

Location:	Lake Ontario, near the Humber River.
Co-ordinates:	N 43 36' 64", W 79 27' 27.5"
Access:	Boat.
Skill Level:	Advanced.
Depth:	67 feet (20.1 metres).
Visibility:	3 - 10 feet (0.9 - 3 metres).

Background: The long life of the *Sligo* saw many changes in her. Launched as the three-masted bark, *Prince of Wales,* she was built at the famous yard of Louis Shickluna at St. Catharines in 1860. As such, the vessel made several trans-Atlantic crossings before being converted to a schooner-barge at her original shipyard in 1863. She was rebuilt, renamed the *Sligo,* and registered as a new vessel at St. Catharines on April 11, 1874, measuring 138' (41.2 metres) in length, 23' (6.9 metres) in beam, and 11' 8" (3.5 metres) in draft, with 284 net tons. Finally, in 1893, the conversion to a bulk-freight schooner-barge occurred at the James Simpson Shipyard, Port McNicoll, Ontario.

A fierce gale parted the towline between the *Sligo* and the towing tug *New York* on September 5, 1918. Loaded with 90 tons of limestone, the *Sligo* foundered.

Description: When Toronto diver, Don Macintyre, located the resting place of the *Sligo,* he tried hard to keep it a secret for fear of wreckstrippers tearing it apart. In spite of his efforts, some irresponsible divers managed to find it, and by early 1986, the wreck was half-stripped, with most of the cutlery, dishes, deadeyes, tools and personal belongings of the crew having disappeared. S.O.S. Toronto realized that in order to save the rest of the wreck, they had to open it up to the diving community, thereby making almost every area diver familiar with what was at the site. Anybody stripping the wreck after that would face the diving community's resentment and a greater risk of getting caught. Divers were locating artifacts from outside the ship's hull and placing them on the wreck where they could be seen and appreciated by everyone diving there. The anchor, wheel, and windlass are still intact. This site is usually buoyed.

Hazards: The poor visibility in this part of the lake creates hazardous diving conditions. Always concentrate on your position in relationship to the rest of the shipwreck, the line to the surface, and the dive boat.

The schooner-barge Sligo *in Kincardine, Ontario, harbour* (Photo: Institute for Great Lakes Research, Perrysburg, Ohio.)

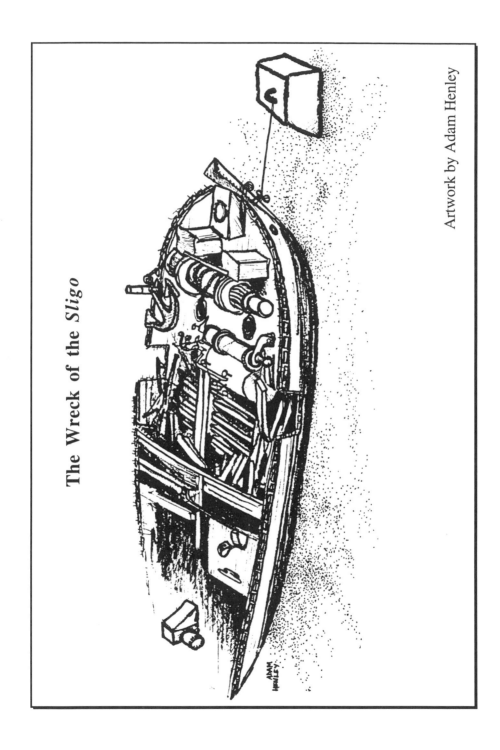

The Wreck of the *Sligo*

Artwork by Adam Henley

The Niagara River

Site 57: Chippawa Creek

Location: Chippawa Creek, near the town of Chippawa, Ont.
Access: Shore or boat (bottom drift from a line).
Skill Level: Intermediate - advanced.
Depth: to 35 feet (10.5 metres).
Visibility: 4 - 12 feet (1.2 - 3.6 metres).
Description: Chippawa Creek's relatively short length offers numerous entry and exit points, but the general consensus is that diving at the town of Chippawa itself is your best bet for finding old bottles. The drop-off point (where it gets deep) is right near shore, and the sides of the drop-off are rocky. The creek bottom is a mixture of rock, sand, and clay.
Hazards: There is a very strong current here, so this is not the place to try out a drysuit for the first time! Swiftwater diving is something that is best learned by gradually building up to a stronger current. There is usually not too much boating traffic, but do your creek-bottom exploration with a dive flag anyway, just in case.

Site 58: Frenchman's Creek

Location: Frenchman's Creek is about one-third of the way from Fort Erie to Chippawa.
Access: Shore or boat.
Skill Level: Intermediate - advanced.
Depth: to 30 feet (9 metres) maximum.
Visibility: 4 - 12 feet (1.2 - 3.6 metres).
Description: Dive in the Niagara River where this creek enters. You can do a long drift dive (not too long, or you'll end up over the falls), or stay put and dig in a small, limited area.
Hazards: With the strong current here, it is recommended that you do not dive deeper than 20' (6 metres), where the current is still managable. Beware of boaters and fly a divers down flag.

Site 59: Black Rock Creek

Location: Black Rock Creek is about two-thirds of the way down from Fort Erie to Chippawa. Look for Netherby Road and the Niagara Parkway.

Access: Shore or boat.

Skill Level: Intermediate - advanced.

Depth: To 30 feet (9 metres).

Visibility: 4 - 12 feet (1.2 - 3.6 metres).

Description: As with the previous site, dive in the Niagara River rather than the small creek itself. Once again, old bottles and other items reflecting this area's rich history can be seen.

Hazards: Because the current is quite strong here, it is recommended that you do not dive too deep (beyond 20', or 6 metres) so that you can stay in the managable portion of the river. Use of a dive flag is wise.

Worth Checking Out?

Port Colborne Breakwall

The breakwall at Port Colborne is also an interesting location, with its many fish, anchors, and bottles. The visibility is usually good, namely about 15' - 20' (4.5 - 6 metres), with a maximum depth of about 40' (12 metres). Beware of boating traffic here; always use a dive flag to warn boaters of your presence.

From the "Better-Late-Than-Never" Department:

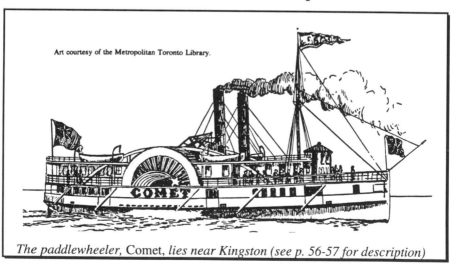

Art courtesy of the Metropolitan Toronto Library.

The paddlewheeler, Comet, *lies near Kingston (see p. 56-57 for description)*

Lake Erie

Site 60: The Wreck of the *Raleigh*

Location:	Lake Erie, near Sherkston, Ontario.
Access:	Boat.
Skill Level:	Novice - intermediate.
Depth:	35 feet (10.5 metres).
Visibility:	10 - 20 feet (3 - 6 metres).

Directions: Launch your boat at Port Colborne, to the west of this site. The wreck site is about three-quarters of a mile (1.2 kms.) offshore and is usually marked with a jug. If it's not marked, line up two shore ranges: a large cottage with the Port Colborne smokestack to the northwest, and a row of telephone poles between two clumps of trees to the northeast.

Background: This wooden freighter, built at the Quayle & Martin Shipyard in Cleveland, Ohio, in 1871, measured 235' (70.5 metres) in length, 34' (10.2 metres) in beam, and 23' 9" (7.1 metres) in draft. On November 30, 1911, the *Raleigh* damaged her rudder in severe winds while four miles east of Port Colborne, ran aground, and foundered in the heavy seas.

Description: The ship's boiler, engine room machinery, propeller, rudder, bow winch and anchor chains remain at the site.

Hazards: Boating traffic must be considered in summer and warm weekends. Since the site is offshore, all boat dive precautions must be taken.

The smoke-belching steamer Raleigh *underway.* (Photo: author's collection.)

Four Quarries Near Lake Erie

Site 61: Hagersville Quarry

Location: About 1.5 miles (2.4 kilometres) out of Hagersville.
Access: Shore.
Skill Level: Novice - intermediate.
Depth: 20' - 25' (6 - 7.5 metres) average. Maximum 80' (24 metres).
Visibility: 10 - 25 feet (3 - 7.5 metres).
Description: This old quarry flooded many years ago, and the day-use recreational area built up around it is named "Sunspot Quarry." This spring-fed quarry contains a total of 55 acres of water surface area. There are numerous cars in this quarry, with usually good visibility averaging 15' (4.5 metres). There is one 80' (24-metre) hole which has had a 30' (9-metre) sailboat placed in it, but this location is for advanced divers only. Steep rock cliffs edge most of the quarry, but near the parking lot, there are plenty of places where one can enter and exit the water. There is a fee to enter this park, and there are also picnic areas, washrooms, and a concession stand in operation.
Hazards: The one deep (80', or 24-metre) hole is for advanced divers using caution. Other than that, the only other possible hazard is bumping into the many summer swimmers and people floating on plastic or rubber floats dotting the water surface. I have seen inexperienced divers doing giant stride entries from the top of one of the lower cliffs, only to have half their gear come off and sink to the bottom of the quarry once they hit the water.

Site 62: Elora Gorge Quarry

Location:	Between Fergus and Elora, Ontario.
Access:	Shore.
Skill Level:	Novice - Intermediate.
Depth:	To 30 feet (9 metres).
Visibility:	6 - 15 feet (1.8 - 4.5 metres).

Directions: This day-use recreational quarry is located on the northeasterly outskirts of the town of Elora on County Road 18, (the Fergus-Elora Road).

Background: In the early 1900's, the Whitestone Lime Company established nine lime kilns, a stone crusher, and a railroad siding at this site (many of the building ruins can be seen today). About 1930, the company abandoned the quarry when black streaks appeared in the limestone.

Description: Although the entire recreational area comprises 43 acres (17 hectares), only two acres are water. Cliffs, rocks, and fish can be seen here. Aquatic growth gets thick by the end of the summer. Cliffs rising to 40' (12 metres) surround most of the quarry. There is a sandy beach area, washrooms, concession stand on weekends, nature trails, drinking water, and picnic areas. The site is available for scuba diving only during limited hours (weekday mornings for two hours, and only if prearranged. Check with the park for hours and permission). For information, call (519) 846-9742, or write Elora Gorge Conservation Area, P.O.Box 356, Elora, Ont., N0B 1S0.

The Elora Gorge Conservation Area quarry near Fergus. (Photo by Cris Kohl.)

Site 63: Innerkip Quarry

Location:	Near Woodstock, Ontario.
Access:	Shore.
Skill Level:	Novice - Intermediate.
Depth:	To 28 feet (8.4 metres).
	Mine shaft: to 54' (16.2 metres).
Visibility:	4 - 18 feet (1.2 - 5.4 metres).

Directions: From Highway 401 from the west, take exit #238 (Highway 2) towards Woodstock for one mile (1.6 km.), turn right onto Oxford County Rd. 4 for 4.7 miles (7.7 kms.) At the village of Innerkip, turn right on George St. From Highway 401 from the east, take exit #250 west into Innerkip, drive through the town, and turn left onto George Street.

Background: Established in 1928, this quarry supplied railroad trackbed ballast until 1937 when it flooded. Purchased by private interests in 1957, the area was turned into a recreation centre.

Description: The quarry contains the fuselages of two small airplanes (a Cessna and a W.W.II Harvard trainer), a car, schoolbus, and two old boats, plus some original foundations and two mine shafts. There are picnic areas, camping, a concession stand, washrooms, and airfill station. Contact Trout Lake Recreation Park, (its technical name), P.O.Box 57, Innerkip, Ont., N0J 1M0, telephone summer, (519) 469-3363, winter, (519) 469-3431.

Hazards: The mine shafts silt rapidly, with loss of visibility and orientation. Beware of multitudinous swimmers/high-board divers on summer weekends.

This rare photograph shows Innerkip Quarry during the 1930's, with the mine shaft at lower right. (Photo: Woodstock Public Library.)

The quarry at Innerkip, Ontario, known formally as the Trout Lake Recreation Park, caters to campers, swimmers, sun-lovers, fun-lovers, and scuba-divers. (Photo by Cris Kohl.) *The fuselage of a World War II Harvard trainer was in the quarry for years before being raised, sandblasted, painted and repositioned in 1984. Barry Barton, Kim Barton, and the author pose with the beautified wreck before it was returned to the 25' (7.5-metre) depths.* (Photo by Rose Kohl).

Site 64: St. Marys Quarry

Location:	Just south of St. Marys, Ontario.
Access:	Shore.
Skill Level:	Novice - intermediate.
Depth:	To 60 feet (18 metres).
Visibility:	5 - 18 feet (1.5 - 5.4 metres).

Directions: This bisected quarry lies on the southern edge of the town of St. Marys, Ontario, along both sides of Water Street South. There is parking.

Background: This limestone quarry was mentionned as early as 1846 in the Canadian Gazetteer. The "wild" section of the quarry, between the C.P.R. tracks and Water Street South, was originally three separate quarries, but by 1910, all were operated by one businessman. The supervised swimming area has been a park since the early 1960's, open from the long weekend in May until Labour Day weekend. There is an admission fee to the park.

Description: The eastern side, or east quarry, is about 60' (18 metres) deep at its maximum point. A tunnel runs under the roadway connecting the two quarries, and old railroad tracks run through this tunnel, but they are mostly under sludge. There is also reportedly a crane that was left on the bottom.

Hazards: Since the depth can reach 60', use caution and watch your bottom time. Be careful when exploring the tunnel between the two quarry sections.

The old Thames Quarry at St. Marys was named so because the Thames River flows by only a short distance to one side. (Photo: St. Marys District Museum.)

The quarry at St. Marys is today used almost exclusively by swimmers and picnickers, although scuba divers occasionally explore its 60' (18-metre) depths in hopes of finding quarry artifacts, such as rails and trucks, that were supposedly left behind. There is a tunnel under the road that connects the supervised section of the quarry (above) *with the "wild" part* (below). (Photos by Cris Kohl.)

Site 65: The Coal Schooner Wreck

Location:	In Lake Erie, off Port Stanley, Ontario.
Loran Co-ordinates:	44269.2/57975.8
Access:	Boat.
Skill Level:	Intermediate - advanced.
Depth:	72 feet (21.6 metres).
Visibility:	6 - 20 feet (1.8 - 6 metres).

Background: This unidentified wooden schooner loaded with a cargo of small coal (probably for household use) was located by fishermen in 1987 when their nets caught on the wreckage 13.6 miles (20 kms.) off Port Stanley.

Description: This virgin wreck is still intact and upright, complete with all its cargo, fittings, etc. A diver can penetrate the wreck at the bow and swim virtually the entire 188' (56.4-metre) length below deck to the stern, since there is about 4' (1.2 metre) of space between the coal cargo and the beams of the decking (much of which is missing). Steel strappings heavily reinforced the hull, a shipbuilding technique used in the late 1800's. However, there is a large hole on the wreck's port side, indicating both the failure of this method as a defensive technique and the possibility of a collision with another vessel. Items of interest are the enormous amount of chain at the bow, one of the anchors partially buried in the sand off the starboard bow, huge wooden blocks lying on the deck, a distinctive bilge pump at midship, an impressive ship's wheel [which was removed in the early autumn of 1987, but returned to the shipwreck on June 16, 1988 as part of a Save Ontario Shipwrecks (St. Thomas chapter) project with this vessel], a large rudder post sticking up through the deck and resembling a mast (the masts themselves have broken off over the years), a rudder that disappears partially into the sand, Roman numeral depth markings at the stern just in front of the rudder, and various pieces of china, some of it Royal Doulton, etc. etc. This ship is beautifully loaded. Please help keep it that way for the benefit of all future scuba visitors.

Hazards: Be constantly aware of the depth and bottom time, since this is considered a deep dive. There are some modern fishing nets snagged along portions of the wreck, particularly at the bow; do not get entangled in that. Take at least one sharp dive knife with you in case you need to cut your way out of some netting. The silt, especially below deck, stirs up easily and reduces visibility dramatically.

The unidentified Port Stanley coal schooner very likely resembled this vessel, the Fayette Brown, *whose measurements were similar.* (Photo: Institute for Great Lakes Research, Bowling Green State University, Ohio.) *Below, a diver studies the midship bilge pump with its broken handle.* (Photo by Cris Kohl.)

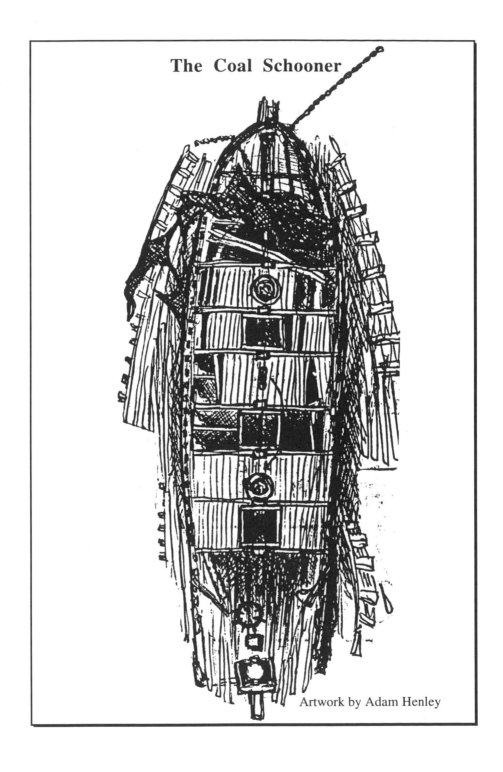

The Coal Schooner

Artwork by Adam Henley

Site 66: The Wreck of the *Nimrod*

Location:	Lake Erie, off Port Stanley, Ontario.
Loran Co-ordinates:	58053.2/44279.7
Access:	Boat.
Skill Level:	Intermediate - advanced.
Depth:	70 feet (21 metres).
Visibility:	6 - 25 feet (1.8 - 7.5 metres).

Background: The schooner *Nimrod* was 184' (55.2 metres) long; with the addition of her 28.5' (8.5-metre) bowsprit, she had an impressive length of over 200' (60 metres). The *Nimrod* sank in November, 1874, with a load of corn.

Description: The vessel is sitting upright in 70' (21 metres) of Lake Erie water several miles out of Port Stanley/Port Burwell, Ontario. She is the victim of shifting sand and soft lake bottom. The keel and the bottom half of the wreck have sunk into the sand and silt; the rudder is also buried, and the hull is impenetrable due to the accumulation of sediment. The superstructure is well worth diving. Only 18' (5.4 metres) of her bowsprit remain, but there is the spectacle of a large anchor off her bow. There are three large, dark, round holes on the deck; these were for the masts, which are missing except for part of one. There are numerous belaying pins and plenty of chain to conjure up a diver's fantasy about the sailing life on a Great Lakes schooner a century ago.

Hazards: Since this is considered a deep dive, be constantly aware of the depth and bottom time. There may be some modern fishing nets snagged along portions of the wreck, so take at least one sharp dive knife with you in case you need to cut your way out of some netting. The silt stirs up easily and reduces visibility dramatically.

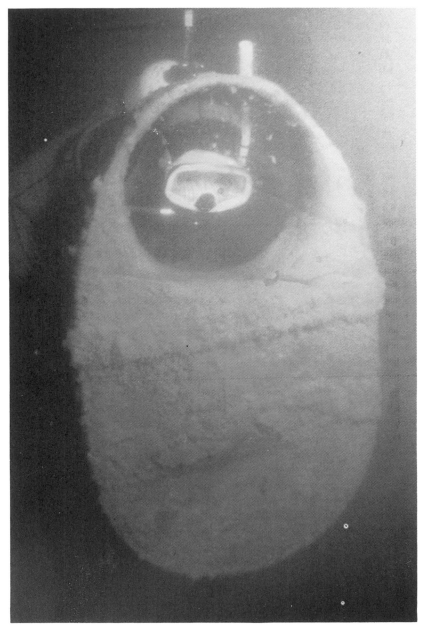

The bowsprit cap of the schooner Nimrod *frames diver Frank Troxell. The wreck is upright, but it sits deep in the sand and mud in about 70' (21 metres) of Lake Erie water many miles offshore.* (Photo by Cris Kohl.)

The Schooner, *Nimrod*

Artwork by Adam Henley

Site 67: The Wreck of the *Merida*

Location:	Lake Erie, off Pt. Stanley/Erieau, Ontario.
Loran Co-ordinates:	57843.9/44159.2
Access:	Boat.
Skill Level:	Intermediate - advanced.
Depth:	80 feet (24 metres).
Visibility:	8 - 30 feet (2.4 - 9 metres).

Background: The *Merida,* with an overall length of 380' (114 metres), a beam of 45' (13.5 metres), a draft of 26' (7.8 metres), and a gross tonnage of 3,329, was the largest ship of her kind on the Great Lakes when she was launched at Bay City, Michigan, in 1892. A steel freighter with wooden deckhouses, she could make 14 miles (22.4 kilometres) an hour, but her solid hull construction and good speed could not save her from the Black Friday Storm of October 20, 1916, which claimed a total of four ships and 51 lives on Lake Erie. The *Merida* was lost with all 23 hands. Local fishermen discovered the wreck site in 1975.

Description: The wreck of the *Merida* is sitting upright and intact in about 80' (24 metres) of water. The visibility can vary, and is usually best at the *Merida's* bow. There you will find an unusual anchor with hinged flukes mounted flat on the deck. Many brass portholes and a large capstan also adorn the bow. Stanchions and railings are also intact. While exploring the length of the ship, the visibility is usually better if you follow the port rail to the stern rather than the starboard rail, which sinks into the mud completely out of sight at midship. The vessel's spine seems to have snapped, probably from the weight of her iron ore cargo, and most of the hull at midship is buried in Lake Erie, with the bow and stern sticking up at tortured angles. Usually, many burbot can be found on this wreck, including a couple of enormous ones below deck at the stern.

Hazards: This site is considered a deep dive site, so utilize the proper precautions. Silt is easily stirred up, especially below deck, so don't dive with a mud-shoveller if you wish to get good underwater photographs. Stirring up the silt can also lead to diver disorientation. Do not enter this shipwreck unless you have been specially trained in penetration diving and are taking all the precautions. It is surprisingly easy to lose this huge shipwreck completely while attempting to swim from the bow to the stern or vice-versa.

The Merida *was lost with all hands in Lake Erie during the severe Black Friday Storm of October 20, 1916. She was discovered in 1975 in 80' (24 metres) of water by Port Stanley fishermen.* (Photo: Great Lakes Historical Society, Vermilion, Ohio.) *Below, a pair of burbots "guard" what remains of a porthole on the* Merida. *The brass rings are still there, but the glass is missing, probably knocked out when the ship hit the bottom of the lake.* (Photo by Cris Kohl.)

Diver Roy Pickering studies the bow capstan on the steel freighter, Merida, *lying in 80' (24 metres) of Lake Erie water.* (Photo by Cris Kohl.)

Diver Gary Kennedy examines the lantern from the Merida *on board the late Mike Verbrugge's* Check Mate *in the summer of 1985. Located in the lake bottom about 15' (4.5 metres) off the shipwreck, this electric lantern was still attached to the* Merida *by its wiring. The lantern was removed from this site "under an archaeological licence," according to the overseer of the salvage.* (Photo by Ken Long.)

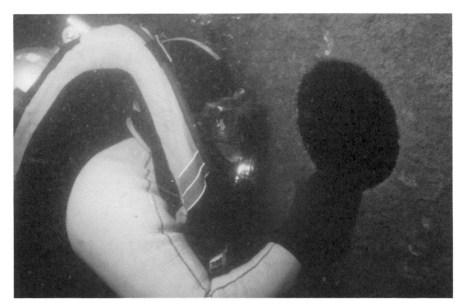

The upper level of the Merida *shows obvious signs of wreckstripping. Being readily accessible to divers both internally and externally, most of the portholes here have been stolen. The gaping black hole that remains is a black eye on the face of the* Merida *(above.) Below, diver Joe Corsaro examines a brass porthole, complete with glass still intact, on the lower level of the wreck. (Photos by Cris Kohl.)*

Site 68: The *Majestic* Shipwreck

Location:	Lake Erie, out of Port Burwell, Ontario.
Access:	Boat.
Skill Level:	Intermediate - advanced.
Depth:	55 feet (16.5 metres).
Visibility:	8 - 30 feet (2.4 - 9 metres).

Background: The wooden freighter, *Majestic,* measured 291' (87.3 metres) in length, 40' (12 metres) in beam, and 21' 1" (6.3 meters) in draft, with a gross tonnage of 1,985.82. Built in 1889 at West Bay City, Michigan, by James Davidson, she was launched as hull #25. The Majestic burned to the water's edge on September 10, 1907, 12 miles (19.2 kms.) west of Long Point. The entire crew was rescued by the propeller *Charlemagne Tower Jr.*

Description: Little remains of the wooden portion of this wreck, since she burned to the waterline. However, her enormous double boiler and propeller are interesting and worthy of inspection.

Hazards: Be aware of possible modern fishnetting snagged on the wreck.

The large, wooden propeller, Majestic, *underway.* (Photo: Institute for Great Lakes Research, Bowling Green State University, Ohio.)

Site 69: The *H. A. Barr* Shipwreck

Location:	Lake Erie, out of Erieau, Ontario.
Loran Co-ordinates:	57803.2/44118.3
Access:	Boat.
Skill Level:	Intermediate - advanced.
Depth:	80 feet (24 metres).
Visibility:	8 - 30 feet (2.4 - 9 metres).

Background: The bow half of a large, unidentified schooner lies in the middle of Lake Erie, just within the Canadian side of the shipping channel. This wreck seems to be the remains of the schooner-barge, *H. A. Barr,* which sank in a storm on August 24, 1902, while in tow of the steamer *Theano.* The *H. A. Barr,* launched at West Bay City, Michigan, in 1893, measured 225' (67.5 metres) in length, 35' (10.5 metres) in beam, and 17' (5.1 metres) in draft. She was owned by the Algoma Central Steamship Company at the time of her demise. Positive identification of this shipwreck has not yet been made.

Description: Resting at a depth of 80' (24 metres), this bow portion shipwreck is upright and intact. Its most striking feature is the long line of deadeyes of various sizes along its port rail. Belaying pins can still be seen in their original holders. A capstan and a windlass, the latter unfortunately recently collapsed into the hull due to natural elements, also adorn this shipwreck. The stern half of this ship may be the large pile of rubble nearby that has been detected by scuba divers, but they did not approach too closely because of the incredible profusion of dangerous fishing nets on those timbers.

Hazards: Be very wary and cautious about modern fishing nets snagged on portions of this shipwreck. The bottom time and depth also present special consideration, since this is considered a deep dive.

Diver Joe Corsaro exchanges stares with a deadeye along the port rail of a schooner in Lake Erie believed to be the H. A. Barr. *Deadeyes, so-named due to their resemblance to human skulls, were part of a sailing ship's standing rigging.* (Photo by Cris Kohl.)

Site 70: The Erieau Dock

Location: Erieau, Ontario.
Access: Shore.
Skill Level: Novice - intermediate.
Depth: To 22 feet (6.6 metres).
Visibility: 4 - 20 feet (1.2 - 6 metres). Extremely variable!
Description: The harbour of Erieau, Ontario, has a long, concrete dock that is a good shore dive site. Levels of cement close to the waterline make entries and exits relatively easy. We have found everything from fishing equipment to lighters and golf balls off this dock.
Hazards: Since there are usually people fishing from this dock, beware of fishing lines and take a dive flag with you on this dive. On the channel side, beware of boaters that sometimes come very close to the pier. You may experience the "washing machine" effect (churning wave action) if you round the end of the pier underwater.

Site 71: The Wreck of the *Robert*

Location: About five miles (8 kms.) off Erieau, Ontario.
Loran Co-ordinates: 57510.6/44044.0
Access: Boat.
Skill Level: Novice - intermediate.
Depth: 47 feet (14.2 metres).
Visibility: 6 - 20 feet (1.8 - 6 metres).
Description: The 50' tug *Robert* sank in a collision with another tugboat in Sept., 1982, with no loss of life. This wreck, sitting on a sand and silt bottom, is interesting in that the dangerous fishing nets have, for the most part, been removed, and much of the original ship is still there: radar, engine, fire extinguisher, autopilot, the key still in the ignition.
Hazards: Visibility is easily eradicated due to silt at this site; make sure you know how to keep your buoyancy neutral. Some fishing nets may snag divers; take two knives along.

Site 72: The Erieau Wreck, *Lycoming*

Location:	Lake Erie, just off Erieau, Ontario.
Loran Co-ordinates:	57566.4/44073.0.
Access:	Boat.
Skill Level:	Novice - intermediate.
Depth:	28 feet (8.4 metres).
Visibility:	4 - 25 feet (1.2 - 7.5 metres).

Background: Long popular with local divers, the "Erieau wreck," was discovered in 1977 by gas divers from Toronto. An intense survey undertaken by Kent Divers Association of Chatham in 1990, under the organization of then-President, Roy Pickering, indicated that the wreck is the *Lycoming*. This wooden bulk freight steamer caught fire while at berth at Erieau on Oct. 21, 1910 and was towed away to save the dock. Built by Frederick N. Jones at the F. W. Wheeler & Company yard in West Bay City, Michigan, in 1880, the *Lycoming,* which was the sister ship to the *Conemaugh* (which coincidentally lies further up the lake off Point Pelee!) measured 251' (75.3 metres) by 36' (10.8 metres) by 15' 3" (4.5 metres).

Description: The badly broken-up wreck rests on a silt, sand, and stone bottom. Well-worth viewing, however, are her steeple compound engine, enormous boiler, capstan, anchor chain, and four-bladed propeller.

Hazards: Brown water occasionally emerging from Rondeau Bay, especially after a rainfall, heavily obscures visibility. Don't lose your dive buddy!

The steamer Lycoming *proved to be the "unidentified Erieau wreck."* (Photo: Institute for Great Lakes Research, Perrysburg, Ohio.)

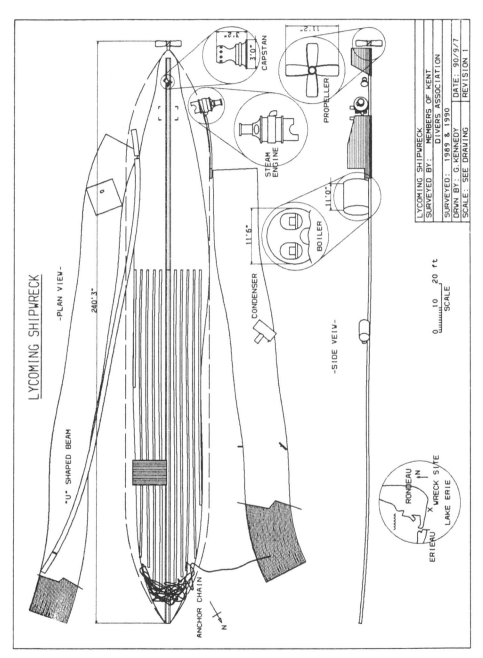

(Computer drawing of the Lycoming *shipwreck layout courtesy of Gary Kennedy and Kent Divers Association, Chatham, Ontario. Used with permission.)*

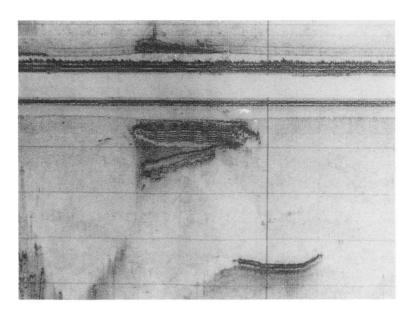

Sidescan sonar is a modern, electronic device which maps out the bottom of a body of water. This is how the broken-up wreck of the Lycoming *appears printed out on sidescan. Note that one of the hogging arches of the vessel is a fair distance away (lower right) from the main wreckage, a fact that was hitherto unknown* (above; photo courtesy of Roy Pickering). *Below, diver Roy Pickering examines a zebra-mussel-encrusted propeller blade from the* Lycoming. (Photo by Cris Kohl.)

Site 73: The Steamer *Frank E. Vigor*

Location:	Middle of Lake Erie, off Erieau, Ontario.
Loran Co-ordinates:	57464.5/43941.9
Access:	Boat.
Skill Level:	Advanced.
Depth:	90 feet (27 metres).
Visibility:	6 - 30 feet (1.8 - 9 metres).

Background: This steel freighter, originally named the *Sir William Siemans* when she was launched in Cleveland in 1896, measured 418' 3" (125.5 metres) by 48' 2" (14.4 metres) by 23' 9" (7.1 metres), with a gross tonnage of 4,067, at the time of her sinking. She became the *William B. Pilkey* in 1929 and was further renamed the *Frank E. Vigor* in 1942 when she was converted to a crane ship. In a collision with the steam propeller *Philip Minch* in the foggy, morning hours of April 27, 1944., the *Vigor* capsized and went to the bottom with her sulphur load. The *Minch* rescued her crew.

Description: This is a big wreck in deep water in the middle of Lake Erie. Like the *Charles S. Price* in lower Lake Huron, the *Frank E. Vigor* lies upside-down, with her rudder and propeller the most interesting features. Cargo sulphur rocks, a crane, and air vents lie scattered to the east side.

Hazards: Due to depth, low visibility, and silt, penetration of this wreck is extremely dangerous. Fishing nets also exist. Beware of passing freighters.

The steel freighter *Frank E. Vigor* underway. (Photo: author's collection.)

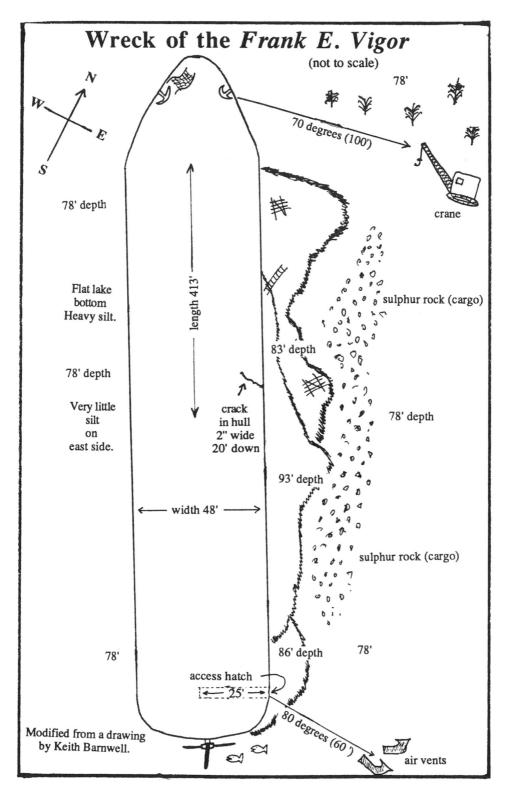

Wreck of the *Frank E. Vigor*

(not to scale)

N
W   E
S

78'

70 degrees (100')

crane

78' depth

sulphur rock (cargo)

Flat lake
bottom
Heavy silt.

length 413'

83' depth

78' depth

78' depth

Very little
silt
on
east side.

crack
in hull
2" wide
20' down

93' depth

width 48'

sulphur rock (cargo)

78'

86' depth

78'

access hatch
25'

80 degrees (60')

air vents

Modified from a drawing
by Keith Barnwell.

Scuba instructor Joe Corsaro hovers above one of the four huge propeller blades on the Frank E. Vigor. *At a depth of about 80' (24 metres), it can be quite dark in Lake Erie on an overcast day, as this photo indicates. As in the case of the* Charles S. Price *in lower Lake Huron, the stern area of this shipwreck, where the propeller and the rudder are located, is of greatest interest to the scuba diver. The rest of the ship, for several hundred feet, is the seemingly endless steel plating of an overturned hull.* (Photo by Cris Kohl.)

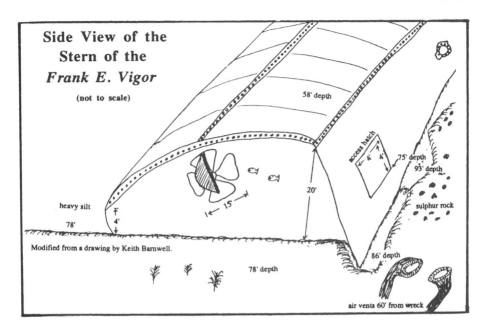

Side View of the
Stern of the
Frank E. Vigor

(not to scale)

58' depth

access hatch
4' 4'

75' depth
93' depth

20'

1← 15 →

heavy silt

78'
4'

sulphur rock

Modified from a drawing by Keith Barnwell.

86' depth

78' depth

air vents 60' from wreck

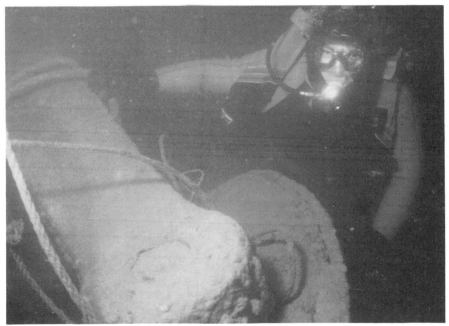

The Frank E. Vigor *lies upside-down in 85' - 90' (25.5 - 27 metres) of water. Exploring the stern area, diver Joe Corsaro inspects the lower gudgeon of the large, wooden, steel-encased rudder.* (Photo by Cris Kohl.)

Site 74: The *Little Wissahickon*

Location:	Middle of Lake Erie, off Erieau, Ontario.
Loran Co-ordinates:	57454.9/43919.4
Access:	Boat.
Skill Level:	Intermediate - advanced.
Depth:	80 feet (24 metres).
Visibility:	8 - 25 feet (2.4 - 7.5 metres).

Background: The wooden schooner-barge, *Little Wissahickon,* measuring 146' (43.8 metres) in length, was towed by the steamer *Donaldson* when she sank on July 10, 1896, with the loss of three lives.

Description: This site boasts a relatively complete shipwreck sitting upright on a sand and silt bottom. At the bow, the diver can appreciate two wooden stock anchors, the ship's bell (which was returned to this wreck site in Canadian waters by Ohio divers who had removed it in the late 1980's and is now bolted to a cement block at the bow) a windlass, and a Save Ontario Shipwreck's plaque on the bow post. There are also three deadeyes on each rail, port and starboard, plus a large rudder post, the ship's wheel, part of a water pump, and miscellaneous hardware.

Hazards: Depth, an occasional slight current, fishing nets, and easily-disturbed silt which impairs visibility are the main potential hazards at this site.

The ship's wheel on the wreck of the schooner-barge Little Wissahickon *is one of several sight highlights.* (Photo by Cris Kohl.)

Site 75: The "Light" Wreck

Location: Middle of Lake Erie, off Erieau/Wheatley, Ontario.
Loran Co-ordinates: 57414.4/43942.0
Access: Boat.
Skill Level: Intermediate - advanced.
Depth: 76 feet (22.8 metres).
Visibility: 5 - 18 feet (1.5 - 5.4 metres).
Description: This unidentified wooden vessel, nicknamed the "light
wreck" because the first divers on her lost their underwater
lights, burned. The highlights of this site are the planking of
the hull, a huge rudder post and a steering quadrant.
Hazards: The depth makes this a deep dive, so special
precautions must be taken. This site is, like most Lake Erie
sites, silt-covered, so maintain neutral buoyancy in order to
maintain good visibility. Beware of snagged, modern fishing
nets. There is also a slight current at this site.

Site 76: The *Valentine* Wreck

Location: Middle of Lake Erie, off Erieau/Wheatley, Ontario.
Loran Co-ordinates: 57475.9/43931.2
Access: Boat.
Skill Level: Intermediate - advanced.
Depth: 78 feet (23.4 metres).
Visibility: 5 - 18 feet (1.5 - 5.4 metres).
Description: This schooner-barge, which sank in 1877 and lies
about 23.6 miles (38 kms.) off Erieau, will impress the diver
with the windlass and chain at the bow (although the anchors
are missing, as is the ship's wheel). The wreck also features
two pumps and a capstan which has an interesting design on
its top. The stern and parts of the hull have collapsed (as
usual) outwards. Portions of the coal cargo are visible.
Hazards: There is a slight current at this site, and the fine layer
of silt on the wreck is easily disturbed, which reduces
visibility for divers who cannot control their buoyancy or who
are mud-shovellers for other reasons.

Site 77: The Wreck of the *F.A.Meyer*

Location:	Middle of Lake Erie, off Erieau, Ontario.
Loran Co-ordinates:	57406.1/43911.8
Access:	Boat.
Skill Level:	Intermediate - advanced.
Depth:	78 feet. (23.4 metres).
Visibility:	6 - 30 feet (1.8 - 9 metres).

Background: This wooden freighter, launched as the *J. Emory Owen* at Detroit, Michigan, on May 14, 1888, received her new name, the *F.A. Meyer,* in 1905, four years before she sank. Measuring 256' 4" (76.9 metres) by 38' 5" (11.5 metres) by 19' 8" (5.9 metres), she was bound from Boyne City, Michigan, for Buffalo, New York, with a load of lumber, when early-winter ice punctured her hull on Dec. 18, 1909. The passing propeller, *Mapleton,* rescued her entire crew.

Description: The huge triple expansion engine and the two enormous boilers, as well as a capstan and a beautiful, wooden, rounded railing, still grace the stern of this wreck. The vessel is upright and intact, and can, to a degree, be penetrated. The bow section is in collapsed disarray.

Hazards: Freighter traffic is heavy and the depth and the snagged fishing nets pose potential problems for divers. Visibility can be bad at times.

The F.A. Meyer *at Duluth, on Lake Superior. She was still named the* J. Emory Owen *at the time of this picture.* (Photo: Seaway Port Authority of Duluth.)

A diver studies a pair of bollards at the stern of the steamer, F. A. Meyer, which lies in about 78' (23.4 metres) of Lake Erie water. (Photo by Cris Kohl.) Below, diver Roy Pickering cautiously approaches one of the several snagged fishing nets which pose a potential hazard to divers at this site. (Photo by Cris Kohl.)

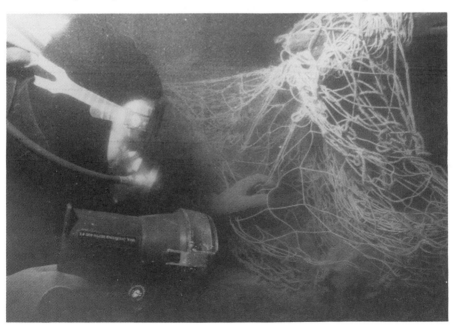

Site 78: The Wreck of the *Willis*

Location:	Lake Erie, off Erieau/Wheatley, Ontario.
Loran Co-ordinates:	57349.8/43897.4
Access:	Boat.
Skill Level:	Intermediate - advanced.
Depth:	70 feet (21 metres).
Visibility:	8 - 30 feet (2.4 - 9 metres).

Background: The three-masted schooner, *Willis,* sank within ten minutes after a collision with the bark, *Elizabeth Jones,* an hour before daylight on Nov. 11, 1872. Measuring 131' 7" (39.5 metres) by 27' 9" (8.3 metres) by 9' (2.7 metres) draft, and built at Manitowoc, Wisconsin by Peter Larson in 1872, the short-lived *Willis* was downbound with grain from Escanaba, Michigan, at the time of loss. A long courtcase ensued.

Description: This shipwreck was originally located by Michael Schoger, a retired hardhat diver who spent much of his life working on the submerged gas wells in western Lake Erie. Definite identification resulted when Cleveland diver, James Paskert, found the tonnage numbers on the rear hatch combing.

　　The steering gear at the stern of this vessel is impressive to behold, even though the ship's wheel has been removed. Several deadeyes and blocks remain, even though a diver went on a wreck-stripping rampage in the summer of 1989. Two teardrop-shaped brass portholes are missing from the ship's transom. A capstan, bilge pump, and long portion of the bowsprit make this an exciting dive. The smallest of the spars straddling the starboard rail could possibly be the bowsprit of the bark, *Elizabeth Jones,* left there after the collision (even though the collision occurred on the port side of the *Willis,* the *Elizabeth Jones'* bowsprit could conceivably have come to rest on the other side.)

Hazards: Modern, snagged fishing nets, especially on the starboard side, can be hazardous to divers as well as fish; take along at least one good diveknife.

This artist's rendition of the Willis *shows how she rests in Lake Erie.* (Artwork by Peter Rindlisbacher, courtesy of the owner, Roy Pickering). Below: *These blocks, deadeyes, and other items of standing rigging lying on the deck of the schooner* Willis *were keenly appreciated by visiting divers. Unfortunately, most of these items were stolen in the summer of 1989.* (Photo by Cris Kohl.)

Site 79: The *Jay Gould* Shipwreck

Location:	Lake Erie, southeast of Point Pelee.
Loran Co-ordinates:	57202.6/43829.2
Access:	Boat.
Skill Level:	Novice - intermediate.
Depth:	40 feet (12 metres).
Visibility:	8 - 30 feet (2.4 - 9 metres).

Background: This wooden propeller, *Jay Gould,* built in Buffalo, New York, in 1869, measured, at the time of her demise, 213' 8" (64 metres) in length, 33' 9" (10.1 metres) in beam, and 11' 5" (3.4 metres) in draft, with a gross tonnage of 840. Towing the barge, *Commodore,* the *Jay Gould* was bound from Cleveland, Ohio, for Sandwich (Windsor), Ont., with a cargo of coal when she foundered southeast of the Southeast Shoal Light Ship off Point Pelee on June 17, 1918. The propeller *Midvale* rescued the captain and crew.

Description: Dynamited as a threat to navigation, this wreck still displays her propeller, stern capstan, and rare lay steeple compound steam engine which was built by the Shepard Iron Works in Buffalo, New York, in 1869.

Hazards: Occasionally poor visibility, slight currents, and a couple of snagged fishing nets are the only hazards to be aware of at this divesite.

The steamer, Jay Gould, *served the Great Lakes for nearly 50 years.* (Photo: Institute for Great Lakes Research, Bowling Green State University, Ohio.)

The Jay Gould's *huge, four-bladed propeller, here encrusted with layers of zebra mussels, appeals to visiting diver Mike Nalepa.* (Photo by Cris Kohl).

Site 80: The Wreck of the *Tasmania*

Location:	Lake Erie, southwest of Point Pelee.
Loran Co-ordinates:	57140.1/43786.8
Access:	Boat.
Skill Level:	Novice - intermediate.
Depth:	40 feet (12 metres).
Visibility:	6 - 18 feet (1.8 - 5.4 metres).

Background: The large, wooden schooner, *Tasmania,* originally named the *James Couch* when she was launched on April 22, 1871, at Port Huron, Michigan, foundered about three miles (4.8 kilometres) southwest by south from Southeast Shoal Light off Point Pelee on October 20, 1905, with the loss of all eight people on board. She and another schooner-barge, *Ashland,* were towed by the propeller, *Bulgaria,* with a load of iron ore from Escanaba, Michigan, bound for Cleveland, Ohio, at the time of the foundering during a violent storm. The other vessels survived. Considered a menace to navigation, the wreck of the *Tasmania* was dynamited on July 13, 1906. She was a huge vessel, 221 feet (66.5 metres) in length, 35 feet (10.5 metres) in beam, and 16 feet (4.8 metres) in draft.

Description: Today, the *Tasmania's* large timber remains and iron ore cargo are scattered on a sand and rock bottom. The site offers many mounds of iron ore, part of the original cargo, as well as a small donkey boiler used for cargo handling. Probably the most impressive sights are the ship's two, enormous, wooden-stock bow anchors. In the late summer of 1987, one of these gigantic anchors was stolen by Ohio divers utilizing two boats, a hacksaw to cut through the chain, and airlift bags. Undaunted by having crossed an international border with stolen goods from an historic site in Ontario, the divers, upon request from the Windsor chapter of Save Ontario Shipwrecks, refused to return the anchor to the site. U. S. Customs officials and other law enforcement agents swooped down on the storage site and confiscated the anchor, as well as the boats used to acquire it, thereby beginning, for the culprits, legal headaches that continue to this day. S.O.S. Windsor, with assistance from the Canadian Coast Guard and other agencies and individuals, returned the anchor to its shipwreck on June 3, 1989. The bow of the wreck displays two Save Ontario Shipwrecks plaques.

Hazards: There is a fair amount of boating traffic through the Pelee Passage between Pelee Island and Point Pelee, so fly a divers down flag when divers are in the water. In poor visibility, diver disorientation can occur. A very few snagged fishing nets exist at this site. Zebra mussels are also plentiful.

The four-masted Tasmania, *launched as the* James Couch *at Port Huron, Michigan, in 1871, was one of the largest schooners that ever plied Great Lakes waters.* (Photo: Institute for Great Lakes Research, Bowling Green State University, Ohio.)

One of the enormous bow anchors from the Tasmania *was studied by local historian, James Gilbert, when it was on display in the town of Kingsville, Ontario. The author's son, Geoffrey Kohl, played on the flukes. U. S. authorities had confiscated the anchor from the Ohio divers who had stolen it from this shipwreck in Canadian waters. On June 3, 1989, the anchor was returned to the original shipwreck site by members of Save Ontario Shipwrecks, Windsor chapter, and the Canadian Coast Guard vessel,* Kenoki. *(Photo by Cris Kohl.)*

Minutes after the Canadian Coast Guard vessel, Kenoki, *lowered the* Tasmania's *anchor to the shipwreck site, diver Art Vermette was there to videotape it (safety requirements prevented divers from being in the water at the time of lowering). The Coast Guard, with uncanny precision, placed the anchor right at the wreck's bow. The Save Ontario Shipwrecks plaques, one telling the story of the ship's sinking in 1905, the other recounting the theft and eventual return of the anchor in 1987-1989, were placed with equal accuracy.* (Photos by Cris Kohl.)

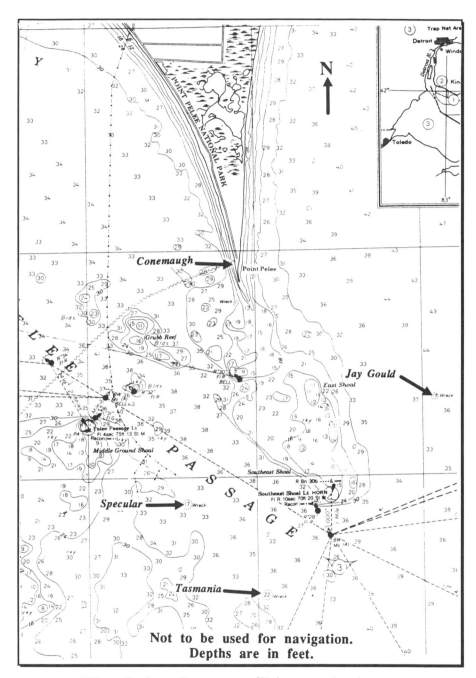

Not to be used for navigation.
Depths are in feet.

The Pelee Passage Shipwreck Area, western Lake Erie.

Site 81: The Wreck of the *America*

Location:	Off northeast Pelee Island, Lake Erie.
Access:	Shore or boat.
Skill Level:	Novice - intermediate.
Depth:	15 feet (4.5 metres).
Visibility:	4 - 10 feet (1.2 - 3 metres).

Directions: One needs to get over to Pelee Island. If you take the ferry to the island, take a vehicle, as you will need transportation around the island for you and your gear. Better yet, take a private diveboat directly to this site.

Background: The *America,* a wooden sidewheel passenger steamer built in 1847 in Port Huron, Michigan, measured 240' (72 metres) in length, 34' (10.2 metres) in beam, almost 14' (4.2 metres) in draft, and had a gross tonnage of 1,083. Her paddlewheels were 32' (9.6 metres) in diametre. On April 5, 1854, *America* ran aground just off Pelee Island; all on board were evacuated by April 8, when the increasing winds sounded *America's* death knell.

Description: The wreck lies about a half mile (0.8 km.) below the lighthouse at Lighthouse Point. Locate the first house south of the lighthouse; 75' (22.5 metres) north of this house and 175' (52,5 metres) offshore, *America* lies in shallow water with her boiler rising to within a few feet of the surface. Although badly broken up, planking, spikes and other remains can be located and explored by divers.

Hazards: There is occasional boating traffic this close inshore, so fly a divers down flag. Low visibility is frequent due to wave and weather conditions.

The *America, based on a drawing by Heyl.*

Site 82: The Wreck of the *Specular*

Location:	Lake Erie, southwest off Point Pelee.
Loran Co-ordinates:	57128.5/43795.5
Access:	Boat.
Skill Level:	Novice - intermediate.
Depth:	37 feet (11.1 metres).
Visibility:	7 - 30 feet (2.1 - 9 metres).

Background: This wooden vessel measured 263' 4" (79 metres) by 38' 4" (11.5 metres) by 20' (6 metres), with a gross tonnage of 1,687, when she was launched on Sept. 7, 1882 at Cleveland, Ohio. Originally constructed as a schooner, her rig was changed to a propeller at Marquette, Michigan, in 1888. Her function as a transport vessel for iron ore remained unchanged. "Specular," in fact, is the name of a high-grade type of iron ore. The *Specular* sank in a collision with the steamer *Denver* on August 22, 1900, about five miles (8 kms.) off Point Pelee. The wreck was dynamited as a menace to navigation on Oct. 23, 1900.

Description: Divers from both Ontario and Ohio have been visiting this interesting site since the early 1960's, and most of the vessel's brass and other fittings have been stolen. The boiler, engine, portions of the hull, and bow anchors, however, are still well worth seeing.

Hazards: Fly a diveflag, since boating traffic exists, especially during the summer months. Low visibility on occasion can disorient a diver. Zebra mussels have covered this site; keep your skin away from their sharp shells.

The Zebra Mussel Problem

Our Great Lakes shipwrecks are being threatened by multi-layered zebra mussel encrustation. Ocean-going vessels, discharging ballast water from coastal Europe into our Great Lakes, have introduced several foreign invaders that have acclimatized to our freshwater conditions; the zebra mussel seems destined to be the most destructive. Besides disfiguring our shipwrecks, these millions of rapidly-reproducing, diminutive (the size of a dime) aliens have cost us millions of dollars in clogged water intake pipes; native fish spawning grounds, our freshwater clams, and the safety of public beaches are also at risk. To date, zebra mussels are entrenched in Lakes St. Clair and Erie, the Detroit R., parts of L. Ontario and the St. Lawrence R., and have colonized the harbours of Goderich, Kincardine, Southampton, Port Elgin (Ontario), Alpena and Saginaw Bay (Michigan), Green Bay (Wisconsin) on L. Michigan, and Duluth (Minnesota) and Thunder Bay (Ontario) in L. Superior. Although there are no known predators to keep zebra mussels in check, the hope exists that water characteristics will retard or halt their encroachment onto many shipwreck sites.

Above, *the steamer,* Specular. (Photo: Institute for Great Lakes Research, Bowling Green State University, Ohio.) Below, *diver Jennifer Elcomb studies the zebra mussel encrustation on a* Specular *anchor fluke.* (Photo by Cris Kohl.)

Site 83: The Wreck of the *Conemaugh*

Location:	Off the tip of Point Pelee National Park.
Loran Co-ordinates:	57163.1/43835.7
Access:	Shore or boat.
Skill Level:	Novice - intermediate.
Depth:	18 feet (5.4 metres).
Visibility:	6 - 20 feet (1.8 - 6 metres).

Directions: This can be done as a boat dive (ideally) or as a shore dive (for those willing to lug their scuba gear a fair distance.) For the latter, park your car at the Interpretive Centre in Point Pelee National Park and get yourself and your dive gear on board one of the park "trains" that take visitors regularly out to the actual Point. From the end of the "train" ride, haul your equipment about a quarter of a mile (400 metres) to the west side of the Point just north of where the trees end. The wreck lies parallel to the shore, with the bow facing north, about 300' (90 metres) offshore.

Background: Built in Bay City, Michigan, in 1880, the 251' (75.1-metre) wooden package freighter, *Conemaugh,* had a beam of 36' (10.8 metres), a draft of 15' (4.5 metres), and a gross tonnage of 1,609. On Nov. 24, 1906, a violent storm beached the *Conemaugh* just off Point Pelee with such smashing force that three of her four propeller blades broke on the sandbar. The entire crew was fortunately rescued by the men at the nearby Point Pelee Lifesaving Station. Over a period of six days, salvage teams were able to work only 22 hours, recovering 799 cases of dry goods (each case weighing 700 pounds!), 1,000 packages of canned goods, and 130 bags of oyster shells. Winter set in quickly, and by spring, any hopes of salvaging the vessel were pounded to pieces just like the ship.

Description: Lying on a shallow sand and silt bottom, the *Conemaugh* is broken up, but items of interest include the huge boiler, what is left of the propeller and the shaft, steam engine pieces, chain, a spare propeller blade near the boiler, bollards, and much planking and twisted pipes, bolts, and spikes. Remnants of the canned goods cargo can be located. Save Ontario Shipwrecks (Windsor chapter), under the direction of John Karry, has done a survey of this wreck site. As recently as 1986, a small brass porthole was discovered in the remains. A local scuba diver salvaged the capstan and donated it to Point Pelee National Park, which put it on outdoor display. Unfortunately, it was not properly preserved and it soon became a broken pile of rust, especially after vandals rolled it around the concession stand.

Hazards: Occasional boating traffic, low visibility, and rough water conditions are likely hazards. Little current exists, a surprise considering the site's close proximity to the Point, where currents clash and are severe undertow threats.

Above, *the* Conemaugh, *a package freight steamer of the design which featured distinctive support arches in midship, ran aground and was wrecked at Point Pelee in late 1906.* (Photo: Institute for Great Lakes Research, Bowling Green State University, Ohio.) Below, *diver Joyce Hayward explores the remains of the* Conemaugh's *propulsion system at the vessel's stern.* (Photo by Cris Kohl.)

Site 84: The *George Worthington*

Location:	Off Colchester Reef, Western Lake Erie.
Loran Co-ordinates:	56994.4/43800.0
Access:	Boat.
Skill Level:	Novice - intermediate.
Depth:	40 feet (12 metres).
Visibility:	5 - 20 feet (1.5 - 6 metres).

Background: This wooden, two-masted schooner, built in 1852 at Euclid, Ohio by William Treat, measured 119' 9" (36 metres) in length, 25' 2" (7.5 metres) in beam, and 10' 1" (3 metres) in draft, with a gross tonnage of 231. The *George Worthington* sank on July 12, 1887, in a collision with the schooner *George W. Davis* off Colchester Reef. This site was located by E.R. Fabok and Art Vermette on July 28, 1987.

Description: The wreck sits upright in relatively shallow water, and is an excellent dive when the visibility is good (10', or 3 metres, or better). Items to appreciate are the two large, wooden stock anchors at the bow, still connected to the windlass by their anchor chain, the centreboard and its winch, portions of the coal cargo. numerous deadeyes, the mast locations, and tools at the stern. Of interest is one pipe which has absolutely no zebra mussel attachment at all -- that pipe is made of copper, one of the elements, along with brass and bronze, that zebra mussels seem to shun.

Hazards: When the silt stirs up (and that happens often in this silt-laden area), this becomes something of a Braille dive. However, when the visibility is good, this is an excellent, easy shipwreck to explore and appreciate. This shipwreck was one of the first to be totally encrusted by zebra mussels, and they are several layers thick. Do not try to scrape them off the wreck, as this will only do damage to the site, and possibly to yourself. The zebra mussel shells have been known to produce small, painful slices in divers' hands, similar to paper cuts, even through dive gloves.

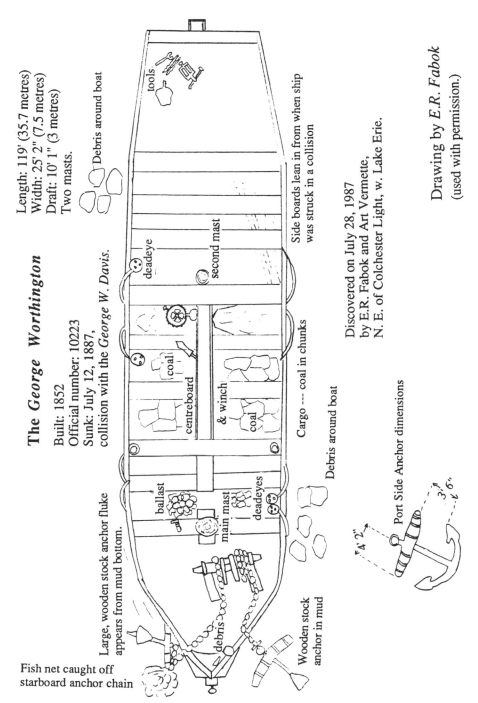

Length: 119' (35.7 metres)
Width: 25' 2" (7.5 metres)
Draft: 10' 1" (3 metres)
Two masts.

Debris around boat

Side boards lean in from when ship
was struck in a collision

Drawing by *E.R. Fabok*
(used with permission.)

The George Worthington

Built: 1852
Official number: 10223
Sunk: July 12, 1887,
collision with the *George W. Davis.*

deadeye

second mast

Discovered on July 28, 1987
by E.R. Fabok and Art Vermette,
N. E. of Colchester Light, w. Lake Erie.

coal

centreboard

& winch

coal

Cargo --- coal in chunks

Debris around boat

Port Side Anchor dimensions

3'

6"

4' 2"

Large, wooden stock anchor fluke
appears from mud bottom.

ballast

main mast

deadeyes

debris

Wooden stock
anchor in mud

Fish net caught off
starboard anchor chain

tools

(Drawing of the George Worthington *site by Ed Fabok, of the South Shore
Scuba Club, Leamington, Ontario. Used with permission.)*

Site 85: The Wreck of the *Armenia*

Location:	Off Colchester Reef, western Lake Erie.
Loran Co-ordinates:	56975.1/43795.9
Access:	Boat.
Skill Level:	Intermediate - advanced.
Depth:	38 feet (11.4 metres).
Visibility:	6 - 20 feet (1.8 - 6 metres).

Background: A large wooden bulk freight schooner named the *Armenia,* while in tow of the propeller, *Fred Pabst,* swamped and foundered in a severe storm off Colchester Light on May 9, 1906, with no loss of life. Built in 1896 by James Davidson of West Bay City, Michigan, she measured 288' 6" (86.5 metres) in length, 44' 6" (13.4 metres) in beam, and 19' 1" (5.7 metres) in draft, with a gross tonnage of 2,040.

Description: The *Armenia* was dynamited to eliminate her as a hazard to navigation. Her wooden hull and decking lie scattered "all over the place." This is one of the wrecks marked on the chart.

Hazards: This is an area with bad silt conditions. One good fin-kick an arm's length above the shipwreck will destroy the visibility in that area for the rest of the day. It is easy to lose your dive buddy in conditions like this, and that's all the more dangerous because of the presence of modern fishing nets!

The bulk freight schooner-barge, Armenia, *at dock.* (Photo: Institute for Great Lakes Research, Bowling Green State University, Ohio.)

Site 86: The *Charles B. Packard*

Location: Off Colchester Reef, western Lake Erie.
Loran Co-ordinates: 57053.8/43808.3
Access: Boat.
Skill Level: Intermediate - advanced.
Depth: 40 feet (12 metres).
Visibility: 6 - 20 feet (1.8 - 6 metres).

Description: About four months after the *Armenia* sank, the wooden propeller, *Charles B. Packard,* struck the schooner's remains and sank 45 minutes later, a total loss, but also with no loss of life. This occurred on Sept. 16, 1906. Originally launched as the *Elfin-Mere* at West Bay City, Michigan, on Aug. 18, 1887, the *Charles B. Packard,* at the time of her sinking, measured 180' 5" (54.1 metres) by 35' 7" (10.7 metres) by 13' 3" (4 metres), with a gross tonnage of 676. This wreck, too, was dynamited because she was a threat to navigation, but she is in better shape than the *Armenia.* Her prop and engine were salvaged, but there is a huge boiler at this site.

Hazards: The silt is easily disturbed and destroys visibility. Many modern fish nets have found their permanent homes snagged on this wreck, so dive cautiously; take one, if not two, good knives with you.

The large, wooden steamer, Charles B. Packard, *sank on a stormy night after striking the wreckage of the* Armenia *in Pelee Passage.* (Photo: The Great Lakes Marine Collection of the Milwaukee Public Library.)

Site 87: The *Grand Traverse* Wreck

Location: Off Colchester Reef, western Lake Erie.
Loran Co-ordinates: 57073.67/43817.22
Access: Boat.
Skill Level: Intermediate - advanced.
Depth: 38 feet (11.4 metres).
Visibility: 6 - 20 feet (1.8 - 6 metres).

Description: On Oct. 19, 1896, the 181' (54.3-metre) wooden propeller *Grand Traverse* (launched in 1879 as the *Morley* at Marine City, Michigan) sank in a collision with the propeller *Livingstone* 1.5 miles (2.4 kilometres) north of Colchester Light. The *Grand Traverse,* upbound from Buffalo, New York, to Green Bay, Wisconsin, with a load of 800 tons of hard coal, 900 bbls. of apples, 240 kegs of fish, and 140 half-barrels of cider, was a total loss, but fortunately no lives were lost. Her beam was 33' (9.9 metres), draft, 14' 1" (4.23 metres), and gross tonnage, 870.

Hazards: Low visibility due to silt disturbance is common. Any scuba divers finding the kegs of fish are advised to leave them down there!

The Grand Traverse *sank in a collision in 1896.* (Photo: Institute for Great Lakes Research, Bowling Green State University, Ohio.)

The Detroit River

Site 88: Crystal Bay/Hidden Lake

Location:	Detroit River, Amherstburg, Ontario.
Access:	Boat to island; shore dive from there.
Skill Level:	Novice - intermediate.
Depth:	30 feet (9 metres).
Visibility:	10 - 25 feet (3 - 7.5 metres).

Background: Windsor, Ontario, product, the late Jack McKenney, in his book, "Dive to Adventure," wrote, "The polluted Detroit River...played little part in my fantasies of pristine coral reefs." (page 13). Well, Jack might be interested to know that there are still no coral reefs out there!

The Detroit River is full of modern debris as well as historical artifacts. One Windsor diver retrieves scores of anchors, mostly the modern five to fifteen pounders, every year. In the summer of 1984, an 18th-century cannon was recovered off Cobo Hall; three more were retrieved three years later.

The waters off Fort Malden have also yielded historically-valuable artifacts recently. However, the visibility is almost always nil, there is a strong, three-to-four knot current, and the boating traffic is usually heavy.

The one really bright spot in this river is Crystal Bay on a manmade island. Jack McKenney wrote, "Visibility in the Detroit River never got above one foot, but in Crystal Bay, we could see 40 to 50 feet...." (page 4).

Directions: Divers will need a boat to get to Crystal Bay, and they will have lots of company on a hot, summer weekend. Boat over to Crystal Bay itself and dive there, or go to green buoy number "77D" which marks a small landing place and short trail over to the cut known as Hidden Lake.

Description: There are plenty of rocks along the walls of Hidden Lake and much fish life, especially at the upstream end of the cut where the rocks and sand filter the Detroit River water that feeds the cut. There is a negligible current in this protected area. An old rowboat poses as an interesting shipwreck near the mouth of Hidden Lake. Closer to the upstream end, there is an underwater habitat (a large, steel barrel on legs; one can enter and look out through a small rectangular window. It's much like playing "fort.") A wrecked barge lies at the north end of Crystal Bay, some of it on shore. A boiler with its top usually exposed lies in the shallows there. The diving is reportedly good also at the south end of Bois Blanc (Bob-Lo) Island.

Hazards: Boating traffic is heavy, especially on weekends, so use a dive flag. If you find the old submerged habitat and enter, don't get stuck in it!

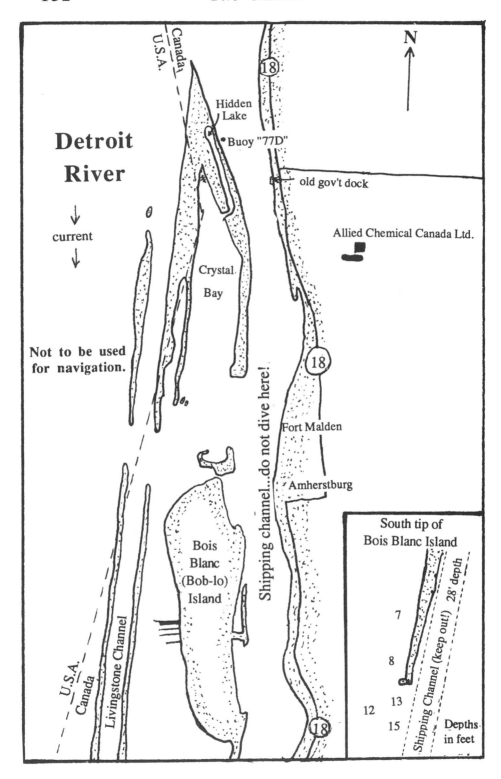

N

**Detroit
River**

↓
current
↓

**Not to be used
for navigation.**

Canada
U.S.A.

Hidden
Lake

• Buoy "77D"

old gov't dock

Allied Chemical Canada Ltd.

Crystal
Bay

Fort Malden

Amherstburg

Shipping channel..do not dive here!

Bois
Blanc
(Bob-lo)
Island

Livingstone Channel

U.S.A.
Canada

South tip of
Bois Blanc Island

7

8

12

13

15

28' depth

Shipping Channel (keep out!)

Depths
in feet

Above, *Winston Smith prepares to do a long dive in the shallow cut known as Hidden Lake, a man-made site on an island in the Detroit River. Although in existence only since the 1950's when it was excavated as a potential marina site in connection with the development of the St. Lawrence Seaway-Great Lakes Waterway system, Hidden Lake has a vast assortment of trash, such as this steel barrel and a discarded fir tree* (below). (Photos by Cris Kohl.)

Above, *scuba divers in Hidden Lake can easily locate the "bar" in the cut's bottom, where several of the empty bottles have found a permanent home in the mud.* Below, *inside the steel habitat standing at a depth of about 26' (7.8 metres) in Hidden Lake, Winston Smith peers out of the small, square opening. There has been enough air trapped in the small space above this window that divers have removed their regulators and talked with one another. The habitat, however, is corroding and is no longer completely air-tight.* (Photos by Cris Kohl.)

The St. Clair River

Site 89: The Snye Channel

Location:	A branch of the lower St. Clair River.
Access:	Shore or boat.
Skill Level:	Novice - intermediate.
Depth:	To 35 feet (10.5 metres).
Visibility:	6 - 20 feet (1.8 - 6 metres).

Background: The Snye River, or Channel (or the Chenal Ecarte, as the navigation charts label it) has, for many years, been an easy, readily accessible site for local divers.

Directions: The Snye Channel is about 30 miles (48 kms.) south of Sarnia, Ontario, or about four miles (6.5 kms.) west of Wallaceburg, Ontario, along the old Highway #40, today's St. Clair River Parkway.

Description: The current is two to three knots average, and the scuba diver can remain stationary on the bottom of the river, or even move upstream slowly, without much difficulty. There are many private residences and cottages along the Snye River; please respect the rights of these owners by not trespassing on their properties, including their docks. Some owners have been liberal about permission to dive from their property as long as they are asked in advance. Share your old bottles or other finds with them after.

A sunken hull lies at the mouth of the Snye River near Baby Point, resting in about 15' (4.5 metres) off the high banks. This, at one time, was believed to be the burned-out hull of the steamer/sandsucker *Sachem,* which was destroyed by fire on Oct. 8, 1928, near Port Lambton. However, information located in Ottawa recently proved otherwise: the *Sachem* was scuttled in lower Lake Huron instead of being abandoned at this location. These shipwreck remains still remain a mystery.

Hazards: Boating traffic is heavy, especially on weekends, so use of a dive flag is wise. Diver disorientation in low visibility will not likely occur, since the direction of the current helps keep a diver oriented. There is no confusing backwash in the Snye. Entanglement in old, snagged fishing line is a possibility, so bring along a good, accessible dive knife. Present-day fisherpeople might also find divers to be a nuisance, so try to steer clear of them and their fishing lines.

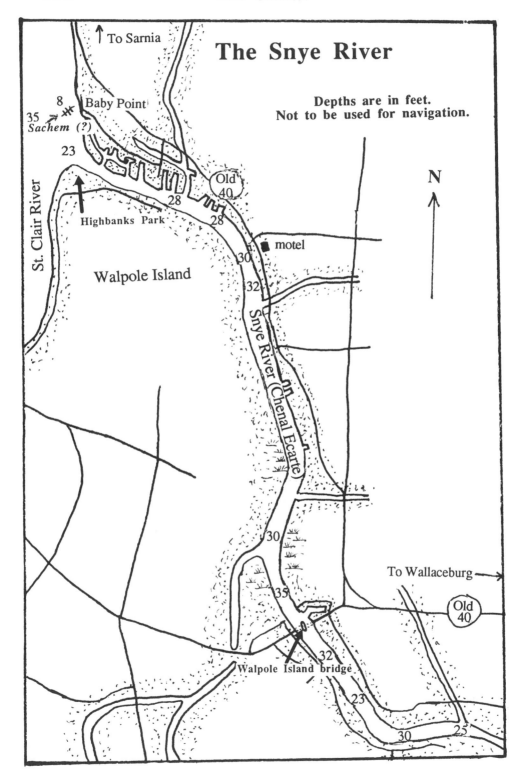

The Snye River

To Sarnia

8
Baby Point
35
Sachem (?)
23

Depths are in feet.
Not to be used for navigation.

Old
40

28
28

Highbanks Park

N

motel

30

St. Clair River

32

Walpole Island

Snye River Chenal Ecarte

30

35

To Wallaceburg

Old
40

32

Walpole Island bridge

23

30   23

Site 90: Walpole Island Bridge

Location: About four miles (6.5 kms.) west of Wallaceburg.
Access: Shore or boat.
Skill Level: Novice - intermediate.
Depth: To 35 feet (10.5 metres).
Visibility: 6 - 20 feet (1.8 - 6 metres).
Description: The bridge to Walpole Island, which is First Nation land, is an easy access site for locating bottles or other items cast from the bridge or along this old, historic shore. To find the truly old bottles, one should concentrate on a relatively small area on the river's bottom while probing or digging.
Hazards: The current can pose a problem for the totally inexperienced (although this is a good place to gradually adjust to swiftwater diving conditions.) Speeding boaters are also a threat to diver safety, so use a divers down flag. Take a knife in case of entanglement in snagged fishing line.

Site 91: Highbanks Park, Walpole I.

Location: At the north end of Walpole Island, where the Snye River branches off from the St. Clair River.
Access: Shore or boat.
Skill Level: Novice - intermediate.
Depth: To 30 feet (9 metres).
Visibility: 6 - 20 feet (1.8 - 6 metres).
Description: Walpole Island is set aside as First Nation land. Please respect the rights of private property owners in the area of Highbanks Park, for both scuba entries and exits. This area has been used by picnickers for many, many years, and the natural split of the Snye and the St. Clair Rivers has also made this point a sort of catch-basin for old bottles washed down from upstream.
Hazards: There is a two-to-three knot current here, with much boating traffic, so make your presence known by flying a divers down flag. Take along a good diveknife in case of entanglement in snagged fishing line.

Site 92: The St. Clair Parkway

Location:	Along the St. Clair River, south of Sarnia.
Access:	Shore or boat.
Skill Level:	Intermediate - advanced.
Depth:	To 60 feet (18 metres).
Visibility:	6 - 30 feet (1.8 - 9 metres).

Directions: There are approximately a dozen parks in the St. Clair Parkway system picturesquely dotting the drive on old highway #40 along the St. Clair River from Port Lambton to Sarnia.

Description: Most of these parks make excellent entry and exit points for drift dives in the river. Four of them offer boat launching (Sarnia Centennial, Willow, Cathcart, and Lambton-Cundick). Two have camping facilities (Cathcart and Lambton-Cundick). Two offer boat morring (Courtright Waterfront and Cathcart). All of them offer fishing, so scuba divers should either do their drift dives on slow days when no or few people are fishing, or dive out further from shore along the drop-off where it is deeper, the current is faster, and the drift dive pickings are better. Most of these riverfront parks have washroom (toilet) facilities, although MacKenzie, Seaway Centre, Courtright Waterfront, Sombra, and Port Lambton have only basic, portable outhouses. Playgrounds are found at Sarnia Centennial, Cathcart, Lambton-Cundick, and Marshy Creek (for divers' post-dive activities?). There are change shelters at Willow, Lambton-Cundick, and Brander. Only Cathcart has picnic shelters, although all of these parks certainly allow picnicking and offer opportunities for seaway shipping traffic observation. When using any of these parks for scuba diving activities, please respect the rights of picnickers and other visitors.

We have found drift dives in the St. Clair River exhilarating because of the strong current, and exciting because of the artifacts one might find: old plates, cups, and other china cast overboard from one of the numerous early-twentieth-century passenger steamers, pop bottles, beer bottles (sometimes full!), milk bottles, jugs, inkwells, anchors, chains, planking, indeed anything that could fall from a boat probably has done just that here in the St. Clair River. All these items await the adventurous scuba diver.

Hazards: Problems that divers may encounter, besides a profusion of active fishing lines from shore and offshore boats, are the strong current, low visibility (especially after a storm or during a northern wind), and boating traffic. With large ships entering the St. Clair River about every 12 minutes during the shipping season, their occasional close encounter with a scuba diver is a dangerous possibility.

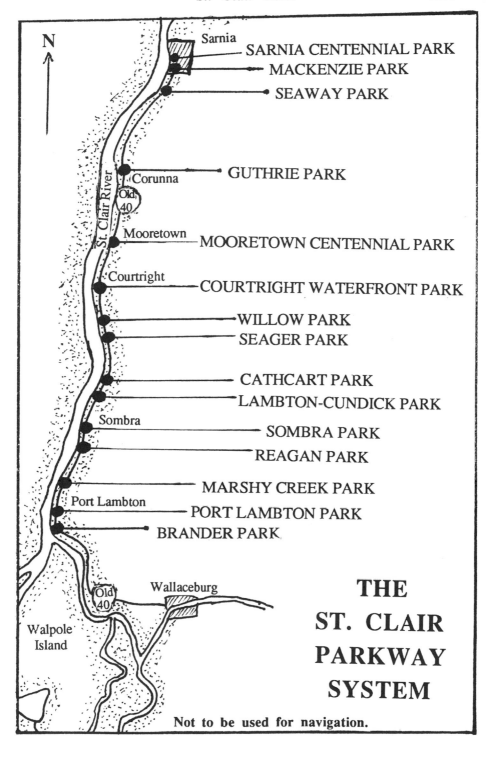

N

Sarnia
SARNIA CENTENNIAL PARK
MACKENZIE PARK
SEAWAY PARK

GUTHRIE PARK

Corunna
Old 40

St. Clair River

Mooretown
MOORETOWN CENTENNIAL PARK

Courtright
COURTRIGHT WATERFRONT PARK

WILLOW PARK
SEAGER PARK

CATHCART PARK
LAMBTON-CUNDICK PARK

Sombra
SOMBRA PARK
REAGAN PARK

MARSHY CREEK PARK

Port Lambton
PORT LAMBTON PARK
BRANDER PARK

Wallaceburg

Old 40

Walpole
Island

THE
ST. CLAIR
PARKWAY
SYSTEM

Not to be used for navigation.

The St. Clair Parkway system offers over a dozen parks, like the two pictured here, that make excellent entrance and exit points for drift dives. All have washroom and parking facilities, some have boat launch ramps, and one even offers camping and hot showers. (Photos by Cris Kohl.)

Divers in the shallow water near the bank of the St. Clair River (above) *prepare to go "over the edge" into deeper water. Many old bottles have been located near former docks* (below). (Photos by Cris Kohl.)

Scuba divers drifting along the bottom of the St. Clair River have located many old plates, bottles, anchors, chains, propellers, and other items from, and implements of, boats. Above, a diver carefully extricates an intact plate from the bottom of the river. (Photo by Cris Kohl.)

"Tokens of accomplishment" found at random in the St. Clair River and its tributaries include "torpedo" bottles, "blob-top" bottles, inkwells, various "bowling pin" bottles (one, below, is embossed with the words "O'Keefe's Toronto"), small medicine bottles, and various milk and cream bottles. (Photos by Cris Kohl.)

The author examines closely some of the old bottles found in the St. Clair River after a good afternoon's worth of diving, including "bowling pin" style bottles and rounded bottom "blob-tops." (Photo by Ken Shaw.)

Above, bottles and porcelain shards, ranging in age from about 30 years to about 100 years, were randomly located at the bottom of the St. Clair River. Two of the old bottles are still capped. Below, diver Ron DeBoer poses with an embossed cream bottle which was found in the Snye River (Chenal Ecarte). The bottle is probably about 40 years old. (Photos by Cris Kohl.)

Site 93: The *William H. Wolf* Wreck

Location:	St. Clair River, south of Sarnia, Ontario.
Loran Co-ordinates:	Not necessary to locate this site.
Access:	Shore or boat.
Skill Level:	Intermediate - advanced.
Depth:	5 - 60 feet (1.5 - 18 metres).
Visibility:	6 - 20 feet (1.8 - 6 metres).

Background: The wooden freighter, *William H. Wolf,* built at Milwaukee, Wisconsin, in 1887, was 285 feet (85 metres) long with a beam of 42 feet (12.6 metres) and a gross tonnage of 2,265. The vessel caught fire and sank just south of Fawn Island on October 20, 1921 with the loss of two lives.

Directions: Take the St. Clair River Parkway (which is the old highway 40) to Marshy Creek Park just south of the town of Sombra, Ontario. Suit up at the park, enter the water, and wade upstream in the shallows until you are opposite the brown A-frame house (this is the home of Bob Renaud, who is the avid St. Clair River diver who usually puts a buoy marker at the bow of the wreck in the shallows). Wreckage can be seen and felt right at the river's drop-off, which suddenly slopes like a very steep hill from about 3 feet (1 metre) of water to a final depth of about 60 feet (18 metres). Since this shipwreck lies about 250 feet (75 metres) off the Canadian shore, and this shore is mostly privately owned, using a boat may be a better way to reach this site. The public launch ramp is opposite Fawn Island between Sombra and Marshy Creek Park upstream from the wreck and huge gravel mounds.

Description: The superstructure of the *William H. Wolf* has burned off and/or caved in, so there is no penetration diving on this wreck. She lies east-to-west in about 5 to 60 feet (1.5 to 18 metres), perpendicular to the current and the shore. The bow is in the shallows and the stern points westward from deeper water. Inside the broken, open hull, the explorable machinery includes the triple expansion steam engine and boiler. The stern, which is in very good shape, still displays the huge four-bladed propeller. The rudder lies flat, with other debris, about 100 feet (30 metres) off the stern. The bottom is a combination of sand, clay, and stones.

Hazards: Boating traffic is heavy, especially on weekends, so use of a dive flag is wise. The three-knot current is not usually a problem for a diver with some river experience, and once inside or on the downstream side of the wreck, the diver is protected. In poor visibility, diver disorientation can occur. Entanglement in old, snagged fishing line is also a possibility.

Above, the huge, wooden steamer, William H. Wolf, *underway.* (Photo: Institute for Great Lakes Research, Bowling Green State University, Ohio.) *Below, a sense of humour overcomes any difficulties at a depth of 55' (16.5 metres) in fast-moving St. Clair River water at the propeller of the* William H. Wolf. (Photo by Cris Kohl.)

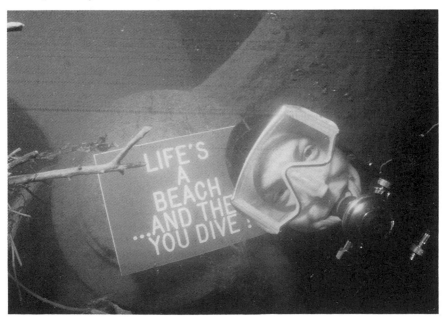

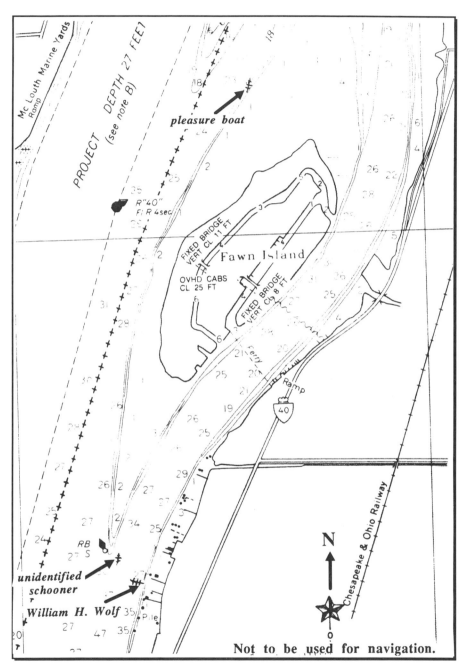

Not to be used for navigation.

Fawn Island, St. Clair River

This chart portion is not to be used for navigation.

Site 94: Wreck near Fawn Island

Location:	Near the *William H. Wolf* wreck, but a bit upstream, and still over the drop-off point in deep water closer to Fawn Island.
Access:	Boat.
Skill Level:	Intermediate - advanced.
Depth:	35 feet (10.5 metres).
Visibility:	6 - 20 feet (1.8 - 6 metres).
Description:	These are the remains of an unidentified, larger, older, wooden, sailing vessel with a centreboard box.
Hazards:	The usual river current and heavy boating traffic, especially in the spring and summer, plus the fact that this site is not readily accessible from a close shore, may pose hazards for the diver.

Site 95: Fawn Island Pleasure Boat

Location:	North of Fawn Island where the shallows drop off into deep water towards the international boundary and the shipping channel.
Access:	Boat.
Skill Level:	Intermediate - advanced.
Depth:	20 feet. (6 metres).
Visibility:	6 - 20 feet (1.8 - 6 metres).
Description:	This small pleasure boat is about 20 feet (6 metres) long. Little is known about this mishap.
Hazards:	A speedy river current and boating traffic will be your main problems. Propwash from passing freighters can confuse the diver with the temporary dropping of the water level and a chaos of currents underwater.

Site 96: The Stag Island Wrecks

Location:	St. Clair River, opposite Corunna, Ontario
Access:	Boat.
Skill Level:	Intermediate.
Depth:	25 feet (7.5 metres).
Visibility:	6 - 20 feet (1.8 - 6 metres).

Background: The remains of at least three shipwrecks lie in relatively shallow water around Stag Island.

Description: The wrecks of two old, wooden vessels, one a schooner, lie off the south end of the island. One wreck has, besides planking, an old toilet, pipes, and machinery on it. The wreck on the west side was dynamited years ago because it was a navigational hazard to boats that moved close to the island. This site is opposite the former location of a coal depot. The remains of an old, unidentified vessel lie in the shallows off the north end of the island as well. A complete tour of these wrecks can easily be done in one day by launching a boat from Corunna.

Hazards: Potential problems are the current (three to four knots, more if you go out too far from the island) and the recreational boaters, some of whom do not know what a divers down flag means. It is recommended that you dive from a boat with a lookout keeping constant watch on board. Also, if there was a recent storm, the current will be faster, the visibility will be lower, and the water will be higher. These factors must all be considered to ensure a safe dive.

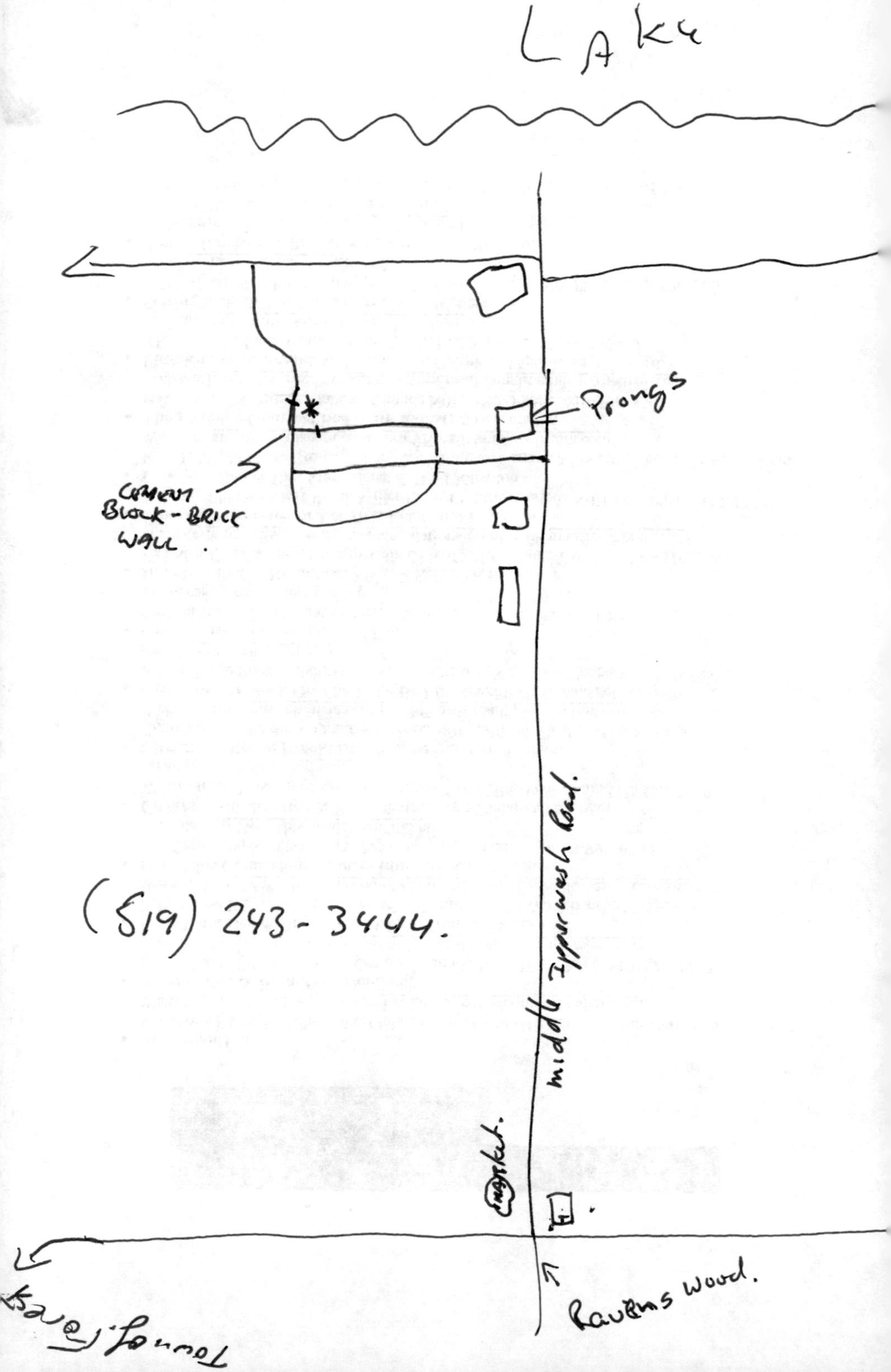

Town of Forest

Rowans Wood

middle Ipswich Road

market.

(519) 243-3444.

Prongs

Cement
Block - Brick
Wall

Lake

- **Applewood Inn**
  878 Dyers Bay Rd., Miller Lake, Ontario, Canada N0H 1Z0. Phone and Fax: 519-795-7552
  Website: http://www.applewoodinn.net Email:applewoodinn@yahoo.com
- **Bayside Bed & Breakfast:** Don Smith
  R.R. 1, Eagle Rd., Tobermory, Ontario, Canada N0H 2R0. Phone: 519-596-2712.
  Website: http://www.bbcanada.com/4220.html Email:donsmith@log.on.ca
- **Bear Walk Bed & Breakfast:** Diane & Duncan MacDonald
  R.R. 4, East Rd., Lion's Head, Ontario, Canada N0H 1W0. Phone: 519-592-4506.
  Website: http://www.bbcanada.com/2923.html Email: dianemac@amtelecom.net
- **Cape Chin Connection Country Inn:** Ann & Don Bard
  418 Cape Chin N.: Phone 519-795-7525. Reservations 1-888-999-6254.
  Website: http://www.bbcanada.com/765.html
- **Cedars & Birches Bed & Breakfast:** Louise Clohosey - Morgan
  Water Street, Tobermory, Ontario, Canada N0H 2R0. Phone/Fax: 519-596-2100.
  Email:cedar@littletubharbour.com
- **Christine's Bed & Breakfast:** Christine and Bob Chisholm
  Elgin Street, Tobermory, Ontario, Canada N0H 2R0. Phone: 519-596-8014.
  Website: http://www.bbcanada.com/3274.html Email: pisces@bmts.com
- **Crack In The Rock On The Lake Bed & Breakfast:** Ronald Pollock
  R.R. 1, Eagle Road, Tobermory, Ontario, Canada N0H 2R0. Phone/Fax: 519-596-2230.
  Email:ropollo@hotmail.com
- **Guesthouse, The:** Jo Ann McMillan
  Carlton Street, Tobermory, Ontario, Canada N0H 2R0. Phone: 519-596-2350.
  Email:captainm@amtelecom.net
- **Innisfree Bed & Breakfast:** Mark & Kellie McDade
  Bay Street, Tobermory, Ontario, Canada N0H 2R0. Phone/Fax: 519-596-8190.
  Website: http://www.tobermoryaccomodations.com Email: innisfree@bmts.com
- **Moeke's Ankerstee Bed & Breakfast:** Ina Toxopeus
  R.R. #1, 479 Dyers Bay Road, Miller Lake, Ontario, Canada N0H 1Z0. Phone:519-795-7769
- **Our Nest Bed & Breakfast:** Janet & Brad Johnston
  R.R. 1, Maple Grove Cresc., Tobermory, Ontario, Canada N0H 2R0. Phone: 519-596-2936.
  Website: http://www.niagara.com/~bradj Email: bradj@niagara.com
- **The Paddling Gourmet Bed & Breakfast:** Jane Hamilton
  Bay Street, Tobermory, Ontario, Canada N0H 2R0. Phone: 519-596-8343.
  Website: http://www.paddlinggourmet.com Email: junglehamilton@hotmail.com
- **Plumica Bed & Breakfast** (Dyers Bay): Celine and Jean-Denis Girouard,
  RR #1, Miller Lake, Ontario, Canada N0H 1Z0. Phone: 519-795-7499.
  Website: http://www.bbcanada.com/1493.html
- **Setting Sails Bed & Breakfast:** Louise Weber
  R.R. 1, Eagle Road, Tobermory, Ontario, Canada N0H 2R0. Phone: 519-596-2038.
  Email:warnerb@amtelecom.net
- **Sunset Bay Bed & Breakfast:** Phone 519-596-2286.
  Website: http://www.bbcanada.com/4223.html
- **Taylors Bed & Breakfast:** Lynette & Jim Taylor
  Box 379, Lion's Head, Ontario, Canada N0H 1W0. Phone: 519-793-4853. Fax 519-793-

4682
Website: http://www.bbcanada.com/1311.html
- **Tobermory Shores Bed & Breakfast:** Dan and Alice Crocco
35 Grant Watson Drive, Tobermory, Ontario, Canada N0H 2R0. Phone: 519-596-2010.
Website: http://www.oe-pages.com/AUTO/Travel/tobermoryshoresbedandbreakfast

See maps to cross-reference numbers in red to specific locations.

Divers Den.
519 596 2363
divers@Amtelecom.net

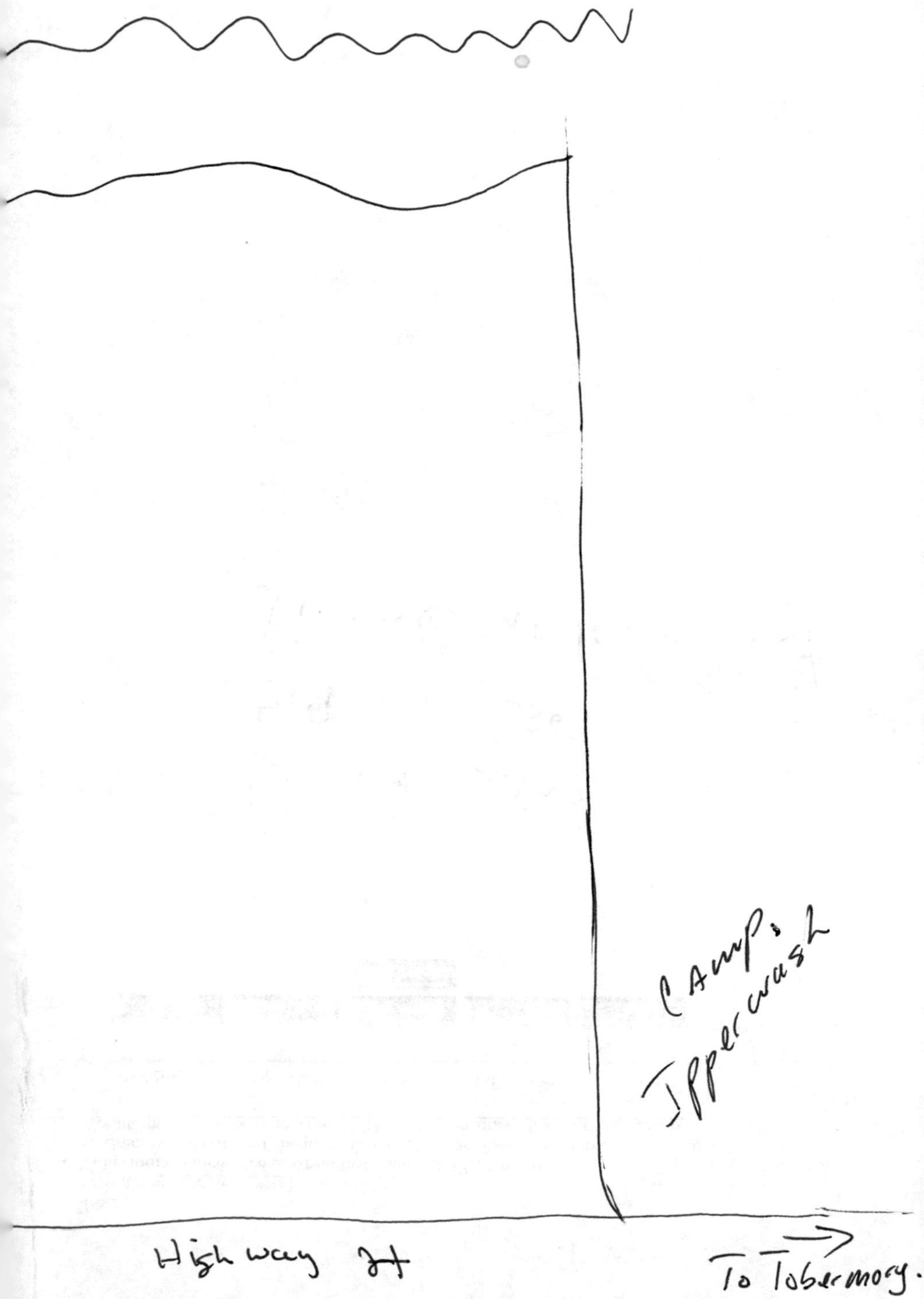
Camp Ipperwash
Highway 21
To Tobermory.

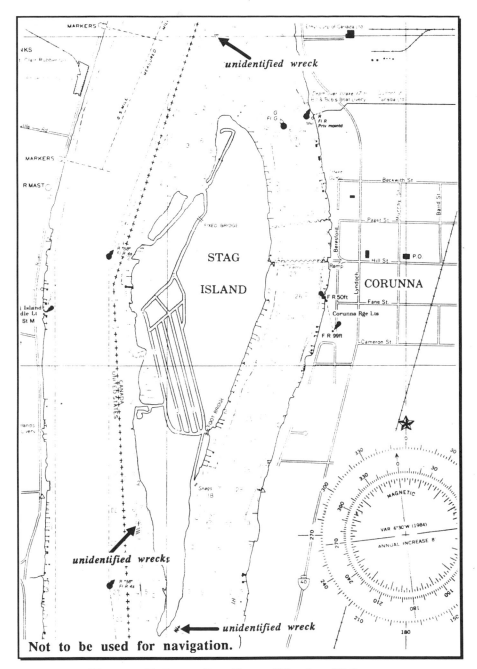

unidentified wreck

unidentified wrecks

unidentified wreck

STAG

ISLAND

CORUNNA

Not to be used for navigation.

Stag Island, St. Clair River

This chart portion is not to be used for navigation.

Site 97: The *Chembarge 2* Dock

Location:	Sarnia, Ontario.
Access:	Shore.
Skill Level:	Novice - intermediate.
Depth:	To 30 feet (9 metres).
Visibility:	5 - 20 feet (1.5 - 6 metres).

Directions: The *Chembarge 2* dock is at the end of Exmouth Street, Sarnia.

Background: This dock was once a steel steamer originally launched at Hull, England, as the *Casco* in 1927. Measuring 261' (78.3 metres) in length, 43' 3" (13 metres) in beam, and 20' (6 metres) in draft, she was renamed *Thordoc* in 1955. She was converted to a barge in 1961, renamed *Chembarge 2,* and, in the mid-1960's, used as a dock support.

Description: Since fishing is popular at this site, respect the rights of those people participating in that pastime. After all, they are the ones who are losing their fishing tackle that you will someday retrieve. This location is considered a rooting dive, where anything and everything might be found.

Hazards: Boating traffic can be heavy in this area, so use a divers down flag. Take at least one good diveknife with you in case you become entangled in snagged fishing line.

The steamer Thordoc, *later renamed the* Chembarge 2, *underway in a canal. She ended her days as a dock in Sarnia.* (Photo: author's collection.)

Site 98: The *Sydney E. Smith Jr.*

Location:	Sarnia, Ontario.
Access:	Shore.
Skill Level:	Novice - intermediate.
Depth:	To 30 feet (9 metres).
Visibility:	6 - 20 feet (1.8 - 6 metres).

Directions: In Sarnia, take Exmouth Street towards the St. Clair River, turn left (south) at Harbour Road, and swing west on that road to the government dock. The *Sydney E. Smith Jr.* is part of that dock.

Background: On June 5, 1972, the 356' (106.8-metre) steel freighter, *Sydney E. Smith Jr.,* sank in 20 minutes following a collision with the downbound freighter, *Parker Evans.* There was no loss of life. The ship broke in two, and part of the wreck became this retaining wall.

Description: This ship-turned-dock may be hard to imagine as once having been a vessel, but the bow thrusters located near the rocks help identify it. Going south, at midship, the part where the hull is broken is covered with sheets of steel; fish usually congregate in the hollows under the wreck here.

Hazards: Boating traffic, disorientation due to poor visibility, and getting caught in snagged fishing lines are the major concerns for the diver.

The salvage of the Sydney E. Smith Jr. *in the St. Clair River.* (Photo: Institute for Great Lakes Research, Bowling Green State University, Ohio.)

Site 99: The C.S.L. Docks

Location: North of the Canada Steamship Line sheds and dock, a
                     short distance south of the Bluewater Bridge and the wreck of
                     the *Monarch*. In fact, divers could explore the *Monarch* first
                     and then follow the shoreline downstream to this site.

Access: Shore.

Skill Level: Novice - intermediate.

Depth: 20 feet (6 metres).

Visibility: 6 - 20 feet (1.8 - 6 metres).

Description: This dive features all sorts of treasures, from bottles
                     and cans to fishing rods and lures and bicycles. Tour the
                     submerged posts and root for rare, remunerative reimbursement
                     (and look at the fish, too.) Exit at the same point where you
                     entered.

Hazards: Beware of submerged posts in the water as you enter.
                     Keep off the bottom so you can maintain your visibility.

*The relatively-protected waters at the old Canada Steamship Lines docks on the
St. Clair River at Point Edward are frequently used by scuba instructors to train
students.* (Photo by Cris Kohl).

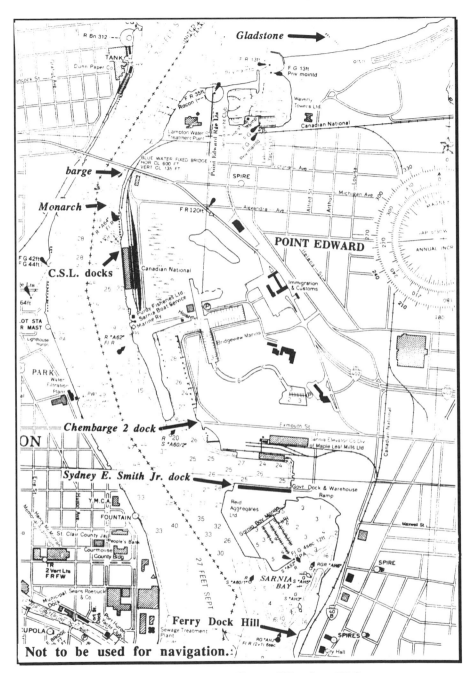

Sarnia Area, St. Clair River

This chart portion is not to be used for navigation.

Site 100: The Wreck of the *Monarch*

Location:	South of the Bluewater Bridge, Sarnia, Ont.
Access:	Shore.
Skill Level:	Advanced.
Depth:	60 feet (18 metres).
Visibility:	5 - 30 feet. (1.5 - 9 metres).

Background: On July 6, 1934, the 49-ton, 63' (18.9-metre) tugboat, the *Monarch,* launched as the *W.H. Simpson* at Sheboygan, Wisconsin, in 1889, towed an old hulk named the *C.F. Bielman* upriver. The *Bielman's* bow was caught at an off-angle by the swift current and swung awkwardly towards the U.S. shore, and the *Monarch,* attempting to compensate, ran into problems. The unusually-short tow-line forced the tug, which was heavily laden with fuel coal, onto her beam ends. Her stern suddenly disappeared underwater, which was enough to flood her open holds. The ship sank in less than two minutes, taking with her four of the eight men on board, including the captain. The blame was placed on a missing deckhand who, had he been at his post, could have prevented the disaster by cutting the towline. The deckhand also died in this mishap.

Directions: Entry point is a convenient set of steel stairs, left over from the early days of the Canada Steamship Lines, leading down to the water about 500' (150 metres) south of the Bluewater Bridge.

Description: The *Monarch* lies relatively intact in about 60' (18 metres) of fast-moving water, about 200' (60 metres) offshore. Enter the water and swim cautiously over some submerged posts to deeper water. At the top of the submerged retaining wall is the beginning of the oily, braided steel cable (wear old gloves!) that leads to the wreck site. This new cable was placed in the spring of 1990 as a project of Save Ontario Shipwrecks (Sarnia). The wreck lies on its starboard side, hatch covers removed, bow pointing into the current. The deck side offers protection from the strong current. Explore the bow, the wheelhouse with head (toilet), the engine area with much machinery, the steering mechanism and a huge coil of cable at the stern. More experienced divers may follow the upper rail or ride with the current from the bow to the stern along the smooth hull side. To exit, take the cable back to shore. Near shore, don't let the backwash current disorient you.

Hazards: Since the current can vary from four to eight knots, this dive is not recommended for the inexperienced. There have been two diving fatalities at this site, one in 1965, the other, 1990. If you get washed off the wreck, stay calm and swim along the sandy bottom towards shore (the **Canadian** shore) as quickly as possible to avoid being swept downstream too far. Do not surface immediately after you have been washed off; the dangerous boating traffic could include freighters, and surface swimming in a current is very tiring. On the wreck, don't let the strong current remove your mask; hang onto it when turning your head. There are numerous fishing lines on this wreck, so take a good knife along.

This rare photo of the tug, Monarch, *was taken when she was still named the* W.H. Simpson. *Her name change occurred in 1933, a year before she sank in the fast-moving St. Clair River.* (Photo: author's collection.) Below, *diver Tim Philp studies the mechanism of the* Monarch's *exposed steering quadrant.* (Photo by Cris Kohl.)

Diver Alan Armbruster takes a wild ride by pulling himself upstream along the Monarch's *port railing, which puts him in the strongest current. Below, a diver examines items that look as though they might have come from the* Monarch, *since they lie near the wreck in shallower water. In reality, these objects are the anchor mechanism for a Coast Guard river buoy!* (Photos by Cris Kohl.)

The author with five modern anchors, mostly 10 and 15 pounders, that he retrieved from the St. Clair River during two dives one day. No, none of them had a ship or a shipwreck attached to it! (Photo by Cris Kohl.)

Site 101: Ferry Dock Hill

Location:	Just off Front Street, along the southern portion of Sarnia Bay, Sarnia, Ontario.
Access:	Shore.
Skill Level:	Novice - intermediate.
Depth:	To 20 feet (6 metres).
Visibility:	4 - 12 feet. (1.2 - 3.6 metres).
Description:	This site is the location of the Canadian side of the Sarnia-Port Huron ferry service, which ran until shortly after the Bluewater Bridge eliminated their need in the late 1930's. This is a rooting dive.
Hazards:	Beware of boating traffic, people fishing from the dock, and snagged fishing lines which could cause entanglement. Carry a good diveknife with you.

Site 102: The Barge

Location:	Just south of the Bluewater Bridge, Sarnia.
Access:	Shore.
Skill Level:	Advanced.
Depth:	40 feet (12 metres).
Visibility:	5 - 25 feet (1.5 - 7.5 metres).

Background: This unnamed barge is the dump scow that sank on May 7, 1948, about 250' (75 metres) south of the Bluewater Bridge. Loaded with mud, she was being towed into Lake Huron by the tug, *Patricia McQueen,* when suddenly she nosed under and sank quickly at 5::00 A.M., about 100' (30 metres) offshore. One unidentified man was aboard the scow, and he quickly swam ashore.

Directions: Once again, just like at the site of the *Monarch,* a cable is attached, connecting the wreck to one of the posts near this north corner of the cement retaining wall.

Description: The trap door, chains, and the three holds can be studied, one by one, air permitting. For the truly experienced diver who has lots of air left afterwards, a drift dive can be made from the barge to the wreck of the *Monarch* further downstream at somewhat greater depth.

Hazards: This site is for very experienced and strong divers only, due to the extreme current. Boating traffic can be heavy and the current can play tricks some days because of its variable nature. On the wreck, don't let the strong current remove your mask; hang onto it when turning your head. There are numerous fishing lines on this wreck, so take a good knife along.

Lower Lake Huron
Site 103: The *Gladstone*

Location:	Off Canatara Park, north of Sarnia, Ont.
Access:	Shore or boat.
Skill Level:	Novice - intermediate.
Depth:	10 - 15 feet (3 - 4.5 metres).
Visibility:	8 - 20 feet (2.4 - 6 metres).

Directions: Canatara Park is situated on L. Huron to the north of Sarnia. The wreck of the *Gladstone* lies about 200' (60 metres) offshore from the western end of the park. Leave your car in the sandy, unpaved lot just north of the traffic circle at the park's western entrance. Enter Lake Huron about 200' (60 metres) east of the old boat ramp at the end of the parking lot.

Background: The wooden freighter, *Gladstone,* built in 1888 in Cleveland, Ohio, measured 282' (84.6 metres) by 40' 3' (12 metres) by 23' (6.9 metres). In 1923, the aged vessel was sunk, along with two old schooners, as a foundation for a dock at its present site; in 1936, this dock burned.

Description: Follow the underwater wooden wall to the end; the *Gladstone* is a bit further out. Scattered planking, the engine, a mass of pipes, and part of the propeller can be found at the western end. This is a good novice site.

Hazards: Boating traffic is heavy in summer, so use a divers down flag, and divers must compensate for the mild current which takes them southwest.

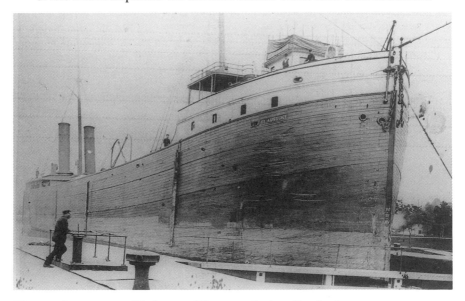

The wooden steamer, Gladstone. (Photo: author's collection.)

Worth Checking Out? The *Charles S. Price*

Location:	About 11 miles (18 kms.) north of Sarnia, just inside U.S. waters.
Loran Co-ordinates:	49622.7/30799.3
Access:	Boat.
Skill Level:	Intermediate - advanced.
Depth:	65 feet (19.5 metres).
Visibility:	8 - 25 feet (2.4 - 7.5 metres).

Background: The Great Storm of Nov. 9, 1913, the most severe ever recorded on the lakes, lasted for 16 howling hours and resulted in the loss of 19 ships, the stranding of 19 others, and the deaths of 244 people. The *Charles S. Price* is one of the more famous of these lost vessels. The *Charles S. Price* was a 504' (151.2-metre) steel steamer, with a huge beam of 54' (16.2 metres), a draft of 30' (9 metres), and a gross tonnage of 6,322. Built in 1910 at Lorain, Ohio, she carried heavy loads of iron ore during her short, three-year life.

On the first day after the Great Storm, an enormous, overturned ship was seem floating in the lake above Port Huron. For days, this unidentified "mystery" ship made the headlines until a Detroit hardhat diver discovered the name: the *Charles S. Price*. Two days later, the hull sank. No one from the *Price* survived to tell the tale of what happened. The story about the mysterious situation of *Charles S. Price* crewmembers wearing *Regina* (another vessel lost with all hands in the same storm) lifejackets has become ingrained in Lake Huron folklore; recent attempts at historical analysis conjecture that the reversed lifejacket situation may have been caused by scavenging shore opportunists who stripped the bodies of anything valuable but, upon learning that the law was nearby, hastily returned the loot indiscriminately to the cadavers. Not all the lifejackets ended up on their original bearers.

Description: The *Charles S. Price* wreck lies upside down on a sand-and-rock bottom. Several scrap-metal salvage attempts, plus the ravages of time and weather, have left the wreck in a broken, caved-in condition. Although most heavily deteriorating in midship, the rest of the vessel is also getting weaker every year. The huge, impressive, four-bladed propeller is worth seeing, but penetration dives are not recommended on this wreck.

Hazards: Boat diving procedures must be followed carefully, since this site is several miles offshore. Because of the *Price's* depth, bottom time must be carefully heeded. A slight current exists at this site. Once again, penetration of this deteriorating shipwreck is not recommended.

The steel steamer, Charles S. Price, (above; photo: Great Lakes Historical Society, Vermilion, Ohio) *lies upside-down in about 65' (19.5 metres) of Lake Huron water, several miles north of Sarnia.* Below: *The pilothouse of the* Price *contained all the modern conveniences for precision navigation.* (Photo: Institute for Great Lakes Research, Bowling Green State University, Ohio.)

Above: *For several days after the Great Storm of November 9, 1913, the floating shipwreck of the* Charles S. Price *made headlines as an unidentified mystery ship.* (Photo: Moore Museum, Mooretown, Ontario). Below: *Diver Winston Smith explores the wreck of the* Charles S. Price *at a depth of about 45' (13.5 metres).* (Photo by Cris Kohl.)

Winston Smith gazes at the steel bow of the Charles S. Price, *which rises to about 40' (12 metres) from the surface. Three years after the* Price *sank, her bow was raised to the surface and examined; deckhouses, superstructure, and machinery were all missing, broken clean off, possibly while the hull floated upside-down for eight days after the Nov., 1913, storm.* (Photo by Cris Kohl.)

Above: *The funeral procession, complete with marching band, for five unidentified sailors who perished in the Great Storm of November, 1913, occurred at Goderich.* (Photo: Ontario Public Archives). Below: *The Maitland Cemetery, just outside Goderich, is the resting place of these five sailors.* (Photo by Cris Kohl.)

Site 104: The Sad, Little *Sweetheart*

Location:	About 3 miles north of Sarnia, Ontario.
Loran Co-ordinates:	30834.0/49671.6
Access:	Boat.
Skill Level:	Novice - intermediate.
Depth:	30 feet (9 metres) maximum.
Visibility:	8 - 20 feet (2.4 - 6 metres).

Background: This two-masted schooner was 176' (52.8 metres) in length.

Description: This is a relatively easy dive in shallow water. The wreck, however, is badly broken up and scattered by wind, waves, and ice. The remains, resting on the sand-and-rock bottom, attract many fish. The keelson, some ribbing, and portions of planking , as well as part of the rudder, remain.

Hazards: Silt disturbance may cause diver disorientation. Fishing nets may be snagged on portions of the wreck, so dive with caution.

The two-masted schooner-barge, Sweetheart. (Photo: author's collection.)

Worth Checking Out? The *City of Genoa* Wreck

Location:	About 11 miles north of Sarnia, Ontario, just inside U.S. waters, near the *Price.*
Loran Co-ordinates:	30805.1/49624.9
Access:	Boat.
Skill Level:	Intermediate - advanced.
Depth:	60 feet. (18 metres).
Visibility:	8 - 25 feet (2.4 - 7.5 metres).

Background: This wreck was the unidentified "wheelbarrow wreck" until Michigan marine historian and scuba diver, Paul J. Schmitt, took measurements, did some research, and concluded that this was the *City of Genoa.* This wooden steamer sank in a collision with the *W.H. Gilbert* in the St. Clair River on Aug. 26, 1911. Raised, she was towed to a Sarnia dock, where she sank again. Reraised and stripped of her machinery, the hull was abandoned at the dock. In 1915, vandals set fire to her; later, her hull was towed into Lake Huron and scuttled. The *City of Genoa,* built in 1892 by James Davidson of West Bay City, Michigan, measured 301' (90 metres) long by 42' 5" (12.7 metres) beam, with a gross tonnage of 2,446.

Description: Lying near the *Charles S. Price,* the *City of Genoa's* massive hull size and large propeller impress visiting scuba divers.

Hazards: Depth demands caution and watching bottom time, while silt disturbance can cause diver disorientation. Dive cautiously and thoughtfully!

The wooden-hulled steamer, City of Genoa, *underway.* (Photo: Institute for Great Lakes Research, Bowling Green State University, Ohio.)

Former navy and commercial diver, Frank Troxell, explores the port side of the "wheelbarrow wreck," the City of Genoa, *in about 65' (19.5 metres) of Lake Huron water. Only the steel wheel and part of the frame of the wheelbarrow itself remain in the middle of the hull near the stern of the vessel. The vessel's large propeller is still in place and is of interest to divers. (Photo by Cris Kohl.)*

Worth Checking Out?: Kettle Point Shipwrecks

Kettle Point has not been on a major shipping route since the last century, but its geographical situation made it perfect then for turning unwary ships into shipwrecks. The wreck of the *Northerner,* which sank in 1856 after a collision with the *Forest Queen* and took a reported $25,000 in silver to the bottom, lies somewhere just off Kettle Point. The steel freighter, *Wexford,* a victim of the Great Storm of Nov., 1913, lies somewhere to the north. There are shipwrecks just off the point; S.O.S. London did a survey of a schooner in the shallows, and local fishermen know of the existence of a "big, steel wreck" just off the point in deeper water. Exciting possibilities exist for the adventurous diver. The rock formations are also of interest: the "stone kettles" just offshore are thought to be over a billion years old. There are also fish fossils to be found --- one common type are fish vertebrae, round, small and nicknamed "Cheerios" by local divers.

Site 105:Southampton's "Long Dock"

Location:	Just off the northeast point of Chantry Island, arching to the mainland at the town of Southampton (see chart).
Access:	Shore or boat (see chart on next page).
Skill Level:	Intermediate - advanced.
Depth:	To 25 feet (7.5 metres).
Visibility:	4 - 10 feet (1.2 - 3 metres).
Description:	Begun in 1871, this submerged breakwall consists of massive timber cribs, rock-filled and 30' (9 metres) square, on a gravel bottom. The upper works have been destroyed by ice.
Hazards:	Boating traffic can get heavy; use a dive flag.

Site 106: The *W. E. Gladstone* Wreck

Location:	Off the "Long Dock" ruins, Southampton, Ontario.
Access:	Shore or boat (see chart, next page).
Skill Level:	Intermediate - advanced.
Depth:	15 feet (4.5 metres).
Visibility:	4 - 10 feet (1.2 - 3 metres).
Description:	The small schooner, *W.E. Gladstone,* built at Goderich in 1886, broke up along the north wall of the mainland portion of the Long Dock on Nov. 23, 1908. Deadeyes and other fittings have been removed from this site by local divers over the years.
Hazards:	Boating traffic requires a divers down flag.

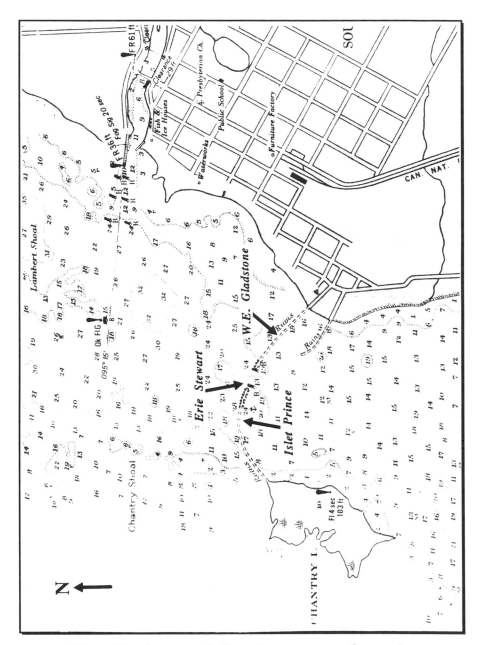

The Harbour of Southampton, Ontario

The Charts and Publications Regulations of the Canada Shipping Act require vessels operating in Canadian waters to carry the latest, best scale, corrected Canadian Hydrographic Service (CHS) charts. This document does not meet the requirements of the Act. (Portion of CHS chart 2292.)

Site 107: The *Erie Stewart* Wreck

Location:	In the gap of the "Long Dock," Southampton, Ontario.
Access:	Boat.
Skill Level:	Intermediate - advanced.
Depth:	18 feet (5.4 metres).
Visibility:	4 - 12 feet. (1.2 - 3.6 metres).

Background: Built by G. S. Waterbury at Port Dover, Ontario, on Lake Erie, launched on May 13, 1874, and owned by John Piggot & Sons of Chatham, Ontario, at the time of her demise, the oak-hulled schooner, *Erie Stewart,* was heading to Parry Sound from Chatham on October 7, 1907, to take on a load of lumber. The vessel was already north of Chantry Island when the weather quickly worsened, and the ship retreated towards Southampton harbour. Attempting to clear the gap in the "Long Dock," the captain missed the entrance by about 300' (90 metres) because of the faintness of the single light and the low visibility due to the weather. The vessel rammed into the breakwater. Amidst breaking seas and shattering masts, the crew clung to the lifeline which had been stretched along the breakwall as a safety measure, and they eventually reached the boathouse on the lee side of the breakwall, where they launched two small boats which conveyed them to the safety of the harbour at the Chantry Island light station. The *Erie Stewart* was a total loss. She had measured 117' (35.1 metres) in length by 23' (6.9 metres) in beam, and 10' (3 metres) in draft, with 230 gross tons.

Directions: About halfway between the mainland at the town of Southampton, Ontario, and the northeast corner of Chantry Island, is the "gap," or cut, which allowed vessels in the late 1800's to pass between the two "Long Dock" sections. The wreck of the schooner, *Erie Stewart,* lies in this gap.

Description: The battered bow of the *Erie Stewart* lies wedged against the island portion of the submerged, historic "Long Dock."

Hazards: Boating traffic can be heavy on some days, so take a dive flag with you and make great effort to keep track of where you are in relation to the wreck, the "Long Dock," and your dive boat.

The oak-hulled schooner, Erie Stewart, *broke into pieces in an October, 1907, storm at Southampton, Ontario. Fortunately, the crew reached safety.* (Photo: Institute for Great Lakes Research, Bowling Green State University, Ohio.)

Site 108: The *Islet Prince* Wreck

Location:	Near the "Long Dock," Southampton, Ont.
Access:	Boat.
Skill Level:	Intermediate - advanced.
Depth:	15 feet (4.5 metres).
Visibility:	4 - 10 feet (1.2 - 3 metres).

Background: On July 19, 1938, the wooden passenger and freight steamer, *Islet Prince,* while enroute from Amherstburg to Owen Sound, Ontario, encountered a thunderstorm, caught fire, and sank at the "Long Dock" near Southampton. Her boiler and engine were salvaged a year later. Built at Saugatuck, Michigan, in 1894 as the *Mariposa,* her dimensions were 118' (35.4 metres) by 24' 6" (7.4 metres) by 8' (2.4 metres).

Description: Since this vessel burned, there is very little left. The least inviting of the shipwrecks at Southampton, the *Islet Prince* hull is largely buried in the bottom of the lake just off the Chantry Island portion of the "Long Dock" (south side; see chart on page 155).

Hazards: Boating traffic is occasionally heavy, so use a divers down flag.

The steamer, Islet Prince, *burned at Southampton.* (Photo: author's collection.)

Worth Checking Out?: The Wreck of the *Azov*

The wreck of the Canadian schooner, *Azov,* lies in 6' - 10' (1.8 - 3 metres) of water close to shore inside the boundaries of McGregor Point Provincial Park, one concession south of Port Elgin, Ontario. These remains can be seen from the surface on a calm day. Take a boat, as car access to the shore is non-existent. The visibility is usually poor, so this is not a very popular dive site.

The *Azov,* built by John Simpson at Wellington Square (Hamilton), Ontario, in 1866, measured 108' 4" (32.6 metres) in length, 23' 7" (7.1 metres) in beam, and 10' (3 metres) in draft, with a gross tonnage of 195.

Loaded with piling logs taken on board at Gore Bay, Manitoulin Island, bound for Chatham, Ontario, the old schooner, *Azov,* capsized and foundered on Lake Huron during a gale on Oct. 25, 1911, about twenty miles (32 kilometres) east by north of Point aux Barques, Michigan. The hull drifted about 60 miles (96 kilometres) clear across the lake before settling near Port Elgin. The ship's captain, his wife and son, plus the crew, jury-rigged the schooner's yawl boat and sailed to safety in Goderich, Ontario.

The wreck was located by the captain's grandson in the 1950's, and an *Azov* anchor, recovered by scuba divers in August, 1956, is on display at the Marine Museum at the harbour in Goderich.

Site 109: Early Kincardine Wrecks

Location:	Just north of the harbour channel at Kincardine, Ont.
Access:	Shore or boat.
Skill Level:	Intermediate.
Depth:	To 15 feet (4.5 metres).
Visibility:	4 - 8 feet (1.2 - 2.4 metres) average.
Description:	The 374-ton schooner, *A. J. Rich,* loaded with 17,000 bushels of wheat from Chicago bound for Goderich, was blown into the shallows on Nov. 10, 1864, and broke up. Lying a bit further out from shore are the remains of the sidewheeler, *Bonnie Maggie,* which was driven ashore by the wind on Oct. 14, 1869. Both vessels went to pieces within a day, and most of the remains lie beneath the sand, gravel, and clay. Tools, brass and iron fittings, and chain, among other items, have been located with metal detectors.
Hazards:	Boating traffic and low visibility at this silt-prone site must be considered before doing a dive here.

Site 110: Wreck of the *John S. Miner*

Location:	North side of the demolished boat launching ramp at the foot of Harbour Street, Kincardine, Ontario (see chart, page 198).
Access:	Shore.
Skill Level:	Novice - intermediate.
Depth:	To 8 feet (2.4 metres).
Visibility:	3 - 6 feet (0.9 - 1.8 metres) average.
Description:	On Oct. 15, 1871, a fierce gale grounded the 97-ton schooner, *John S. Miner,* and she quickly disintegrated. Built at Port Huron in 1857 by J. H. Randall, her cargo of 1,200 bushels of oats was salvaged. Only the bottom timbers of this wreck remain at the site.
Hazards:	Low visibility and the occasional boating traffic are the main concerns of divers at this site.

Site 111: The *Adelaide Horton* Wreck

Location:	Along the south side of the south pier, about halfway out along its length, Kincardine, Ontario (see chart on page 198).
Access:	Shore.
Skill Level:	Novice - intermediate.
Depth:	6 feet. (1.8 metres).
Visibility:	3 - 5 feet (0.9 - 1.5 metres) average.
Description:	On Oct. 19, 1871, the newly-launched-at-Goderich propeller, *Adelaide Horton,* struck the South Pier while departing Kincardine for Sarnia. Heavy seas broke up this vessel, which had measured 107' (32.1 metres) in length, 18' (5.4 metres) in beam, and 8' (2.4 metres) of draft, with a gross tonnage of 91.
Hazards:	Low visibility along the pier, plus random fishing lines and boaters, make this an occasionally challenging site.

Site 112: The Wreck of the *Singapore*

Location:	About 300' (90 metres) southwest of the wreck of the *Ann Maria,* Kincardine harbour, Ontario (see chart on page 198.)
Access:	Shore or boat.
Skill Level:	Novice - intermediate.
Depth:	8 feet (2.4 metres).
Visibility:	4 - 6 feet (1.2 - 1.8 metres) average.

Background: On September 15, 1904, a storm grounded the Canadian schooner, *Singapore,* in the shallows south of Kincardine harbour. Built at Kingston by William Powers and Company, and launched there on July 31, 1878, she was bound from Tobermory for Kincardine with a cargo of lumber at the time of loss. Owned by her skipper, James C. Sutherland of Goderich, the 186-gross-ton *Singapore* measured 110' 9" (33.3 metres) in length, 25' 4" (7.6 metres) in beam, and 9' 9" (2.9 metres) in draft.

Description: The timbers of the hull of this wreck are largely buried in the shifting sands at a depth of about 8' (2.4 metres).

Hazards: Boating traffic is heavy in the summertime, and spring and autumn weekends. Take a dive flag with you and make great effort to keep track of where you are in relation to the shore and/or your dive boat.

The gaff-rigged schooner, Singapore, *underway.* (Photo: Institute for Great Lakes Research, Bowling Green State University, Ohio.)

Site 113: The Wreck of the *Ann Maria*

Location:	Just off the beach, south of the South Pier, Kincardine harbour, Ontario.
Access:	Shore.
Skill Level:	Novice - intermediate.
Depth:	To 6 feet (1.8 metres).
Visibility:	3 - 5 feet. (0.9 - 1.5 metres).

Background: Bound from Cleveland, Ohio, for Kincardine with a cargo of coal, the *Ann Maria* stranded in heavy weather on Oct.7, 1902, with the loss of four of her six crew members. Built by Marshall Capron in Conneaut, Ohio, in 1864, and named after the captain's daughter, the 256-gross-ton *Ann Maria* measured 131' 2" (39.3 metres) in length, 26' 3" (7.9 metres) in beam, and 11' 3" (3.4 metres) in draft.

Directions: The hulk of the schooner, *Ann Maria,* is visible at the water's edge, opposite the railway station.

Description: Most of the wreck is wedged deep in the sand, with the centreboard showing above water during low-water stages. Some wreckage, a bit further out, gets covered and uncovered by the shifting sands.

Hazards: Boating traffic can get heavy, so take a dive flag with you. The major difficulty will be locating sizable, recognizable shipwreck portions.

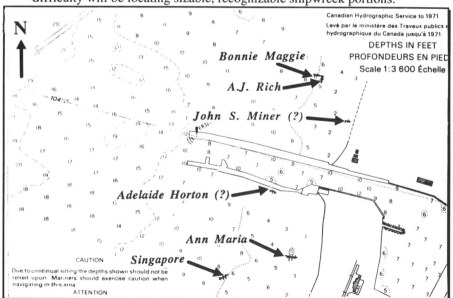

Kincardine, Ontario, Harbour Wrecks

The Charts and Publications Regulations of the Canada Shipping Act require vessels operating in Canadian waters to carry the latest, best scale, corrected Canadian Hydrographic Service (CHS) charts. This document does not meet the requirements of the Act. (Portion of CHS chart 2291.)

The oak-hulled schooner, Ann Maria, *grounded and sank at Kincardine, Ontario, in 1902 with the loss of four lives. The wreck is mostly buried in sand.* (Photo: Institute for Great Lakes Research, Bowling Green State University, Ohio.)

Site 114: The Fishing Islands Wrecks

Location:	The Fishing Islands consist of a series of islands and shoals stretching from Chiefs Point about 5 miles (8 kilometres) north of Sauble Beach, Ontario, to Pike Bay just south of Stokes Bay and Lyal Island. The largest of the Fishing Islands is Cranberry Island, just off the mainland community of Oliphant. The incredible number of shoals makes this area a navigator's nightmare.
Access:	Boat. Since this is an area of high inaccessibility, comparatively little shipwreck search and exploration has been done. This area is ripe for diving.
Skill Level:	Novice - intermediate.
Depth:	Variable; all are shallow.
Visibility:	Usually 6 - 15 feet (1.8 - 4.5 metres).

Some Fishing Islands Shipwrecks

Blanche Shelby: This wooden tug hit a submerged rock on Oct. 15, 1885 and sank almost immediately at the entrance to the channel between Main Station and Burke Island. All hands escaped in the yawl boat.

Phoenix: This 25-ton tug is mostly buried in the sand of the shallow channel between Indian Island and the east shore of Main Station Island. She stranded during a storm and was lost on Nov. 30, 1901. Boiler and machinery were salvaged and only the ship's bottom remains now in 4' (1.2 metres) of water. Her length measured 53' 5" (16 metres); her beam, 13' 7" (4 metres).

Gold Hunter: Built in 1862 at Milford, Ontario, by John Tait, this schooner struck a shoal off Ghegheto (Round) Island in October, 1890, while attempting to pass the narrow channel to the open lake. She and her cedar logs cargo went to pieces within days. The vessel's value in 1866 was $8,000, but her 1872 rebuild raised that to $12,000. By the time of her loss in 1890, the *Gold Hunter* was valued at $2,000. The wreck lies about 600' (180 metres) off the west shore of Ghegheto (Round) Island, near Howdenvale, in 6' - 18' (1.8 - 5.4 metres) of water. She is on the north side of the reef extending west of the island. The anchors and other items of interest are scattered over a wide area.

Site 115: The Schooner, *Sarah*

Location:	On the east shore of Burke Island, Ont.
Access:	Boat.
Skill Level:	Novice - intermediate.
Depth:	10 feet (3 metres).
Visibility:	6 - 10 feet (1.8 - 3 metres).

Background: This two-masted, 64.86-ton schooner, measuring 73' 3" (22 metres) by 19' 4" (5.9 metres) by 6' 6" (2 metres), became trapped in an ice floe and was abandoned on Nov. 28, 1906. The captain, his wife, and two crewmen struggled for hours to get their yawl boat through the floe. Originally launched as the *Emma Laura* (or *Lurea Emma,* depending upon your source of information), she was rebuilt at Port Burwell in 1864 and again at Port Dover in 1871. She was remeasured and renamed the *Sarah* at Port Burwell in 1881. Her register was finally closed on Feb. 14, 1923, at Port Burwell, and endorsed "broken up."

Description: This wreck lies broken up in 10' (3 metres) about 900' (270 metres) off the east shore of Burke Island.

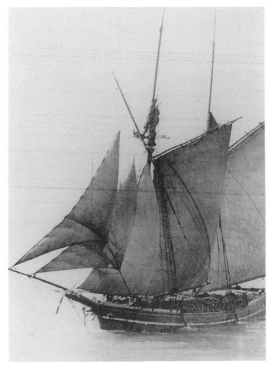

Underway, the graceful lines of the small schooner, Sarah, *rocked gently.* (Photo: The Great Lakes Marine Collection of the Milwaukee Public Library).

Site 116: Stokes Bay, The *Goudreau*

Location:	S. of Lyal Island, near Stokes Bay, Ont.
Lat./Long.:	N 46 03' 45, W 82 12' 55
Access:	Boat.
Skill Level:	Novice - intermediate.
Depth:	18 - 28 feet (5.4 - 8.4 metres).
Visibility:	10 - 20 feet (3 - 6 metres).

Background: This 2,298-ton steel freighter, built by the Cleveland Ship Building Company and launched as the *Pontiac* on July 3, 1889, measured 300' (90 metres) by 40' (12 metres) by 24' 8" (7.4 metres). As the *Pontiac,* she set a record in her first year by hauling a payload of 2,849 tonnes of ore in a single trip. She sank in a collision with the *Athabasca* in the St. Mary's River on July 14, 1891, in 30 feet (9 metres) of water, but was salvaged and returned to service.

Renamed the *Goudreau* in 1916, she stranded on Nov. 23, 1917, after losing her rudder and trying to make the shelter of Stokes Bay, on a shoal about 5 miles (8 kilometres) southwest of Lyal Island. There were 24 people on board at the time, and fortunately no lives were lost. The *Goudreau* was loaded with pyrites at the time of loss. Abandoned to the underwriters, the loss of the *Goudreau* was set at $117,198.

Much of the wreck's steel was salvaged for the war effort in 1942.

Description: This wreck rests on a rocky shoal, and the visibility is good. The boilers and engine were salvaged, but two acres of steel hull plates, iron ore cargo, numerous large gears and winches with coiled cable, hatchways, and steel portholes make this ideal for photography and exploration.

The sturdy ore carrier, Goudreau, *foundered near Lyal Island in 1917.* (Photo: Institute for Great Lakes Research, Bowling Green State University, Ohio.) Below: *A winch with braided steel cable offers one of many photographic opportunities at this site.* (Photo by Cris Kohl.)

Site 117: The Steamer, *Africa*

Location:	W. of Lyal Island, near Stokes Bay, Ont.
Access:	Boat.
Skill Level:	Novice - intermediate.
Depth:	18 - 28 feet (5.4 - 8.4 metres).
Visibility:	10 - 20 feet (3 - 6 metres).

Background: On October 5, 1895, this 482-ton steamer, towing the schooner-barge, *Severn,* headed towards Owen Sound from Ashtabula, Ohio, loaded with 1,270 tons of coal. Two days later, a storm caught the vessels southwest of the Tobermory straits. The steamer released the *Severn* in order to save itself. The *Severn* stranded on a shoal off Bradley Harbour and went to pieces, although her crew was saved by local fishermen. The *Africa,* however, was never seen again. A few days later, an *Africa* crewmember's body was found on the beach at the Lyal Island lighthouse. A smashed lifeboat and life-preservers were also located, but there was no trace of the ship or her other ten crewmembers. Two washed-up bodies were ultimately found the following summer, one near Stokes Bay, the other at Sauble Beach. The *Africa* measured 148' (44.4 metres) in length by 26' (7.8 metres) in beam, by 13' (3.9 metres) of draft.

Description: The wreck lies scattered along a wide swath of hazardous shoal just south of the wreck of the *Explorer.*

The white steamer, Africa, *at dock amidst a forest of masts from sailing vessels sharing the harbour.* (Photo: The Great Lakes Marine Collection of the Milwaukee Public Library.)

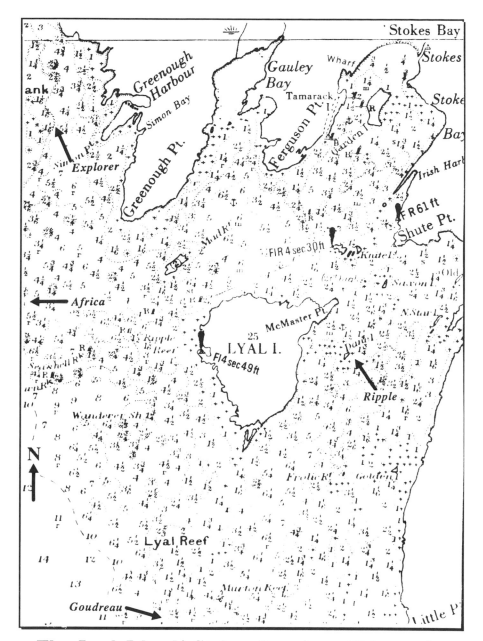

The Lyal Island/ Stokes Bay Area Shipwrecks

The Charts and Publications Regulations of the Canada Shipping Act require vessels operating in Canadian waters to carry the latest, best scale, corrected Canadian Hydrographic Service (CHS) charts. This document does not meet the requirements of the Act. (Portion of CHS chart 2292.)

Site 118: More Stokes Bay Wrecks

Ripple: This tug, built at Chatham, Ontario, in 1884 and owned by W. McRae of Wallaceburg, hit a reef on September 9, 1905 and quickly broke up. The hull lies upside-down and the rest of the wreck is scattered in less than 10' (3 metres) of water close alongside the east shore of the diminutive Dane Island, a mere patch of scrubby rock located off the east side of Lyal Island. Ice and weather have damaged these remains over the years, and today there is little more than one side of the ship's ribs left.

Explorer: On Tuesday, September 4, 1883, this small (32.6 tons, measuring 48', or 14.4 metres, in length, 16', 4.8 metres, in beam, and 5' 6", or 1.7 metres, in draft) two-masted schooner ran aground on the rocks at Greenough Bank, northwest of Lyal Island. With her crew of four clinging to the rigging, and while sailors from within the safety of Greenough Harbour observed them through a telescope, the storm buffeted the helpless vessel across the shoal into deeper water, where she sank, drowning the sailors.

This vessel, built in Chatham, Ontario, in 1866, had a tumultuous history. The little vessel disappeared mysteriously near Tobermory a year after her construction, with the loss of the two crew (captain/owner John Waddell somehow survived and emerged from the wilderness several days later at Wiarton to tell his sad tale of how he lost his ship and crew).

Time passed. Captain John Waddell made a series of clandestine trips in a small boat up to the western Bruce Peninsula area. It was on his return from such a trip that he and his teenage son were accidentally drowned off Goderich in July, 1870.

In Tobermory in 1876, a fisherman accidentally found the resting place of the sunken, but intact-looking, *Explorer.* The schooner was finally raised in 1881 and examined. Shocking discoveries were made. Before she sank in 1867, the ship had been stripped of everything, including cargo, and loaded with rocks; the bodies of the two crew members were found locked below deck, and auger holes were located in the hull.

The general conclusion was that Waddell had his crew unload the cargo and hide it along the shore before he got them incapacitatingly inebriated; then Waddell bored holes in the hull, locked his hapless crew below deck, and headed for shore in the small yawlboat as the schooner sank beneath the waves. Waddell, formerly the Sheriff of the Western District of Upper Canada, even collected the vessel's insurance money! Those secret trips to the wilderness shoreline in the years immediately following the loss of the *Explorer* were likely to pick up portions of the hidden cargo.

The *Explorer* was rebuilt, with final and disastrous results in 1883, as described earlier. This time, the *Explorer* was not raised from the dead.

The *Explorer* is hard to locate in her 35' (10.5-metre) depth, but diligence and possible assistance from experienced sailors in Stokes Bay will make it all worthwhile for the diver. Much remains of the ship's wooden hull and deck, including deadeyes, rigging, winches, and anchor chain.

The Tobermory Area

Ranked by most diving authorities as the prime scuba diving area in Ontario, this mecca offers a variety of superb shipwrecks, excellent underwater visibility, geological formation dives, several dive shops, the greatest concentration of scuba charter boats in the province, beautiful scenery, a huge range of accommodations (from rudimentary camping to first-class resorts), restaurants, and interesting land sites for diver and non-diver alike.

The Canadian Parks Service, in cooperation with the sport diving associations and training agencies, supports and encourages all divers to adhere to the following safe diving practices:

1. CERTIFICATION: All divers should be trained and certified by a recognized organization. Trainees must be under the supervision of a certified diving instructor.
2. NEVER DIVE ALONE: The buddy system is your protection in the event of unexpected problems.
3. USE THE DIVE FLAG: Always display a fully visibile and recognized dive flag when in the water. Restrict all diving to within 100' (30 metres) of the flag and do not confuse boaters by flying the flag when no activity is underway. In turn, boat operators must use extreme caution when operating near a displayed dive flag.
4. COLD WATER: Low water temperatures in this area can create special hazards. Only experienced divers should exceed 60' (18 metres) in depth. Regulator freeze-up can occur, so divers should take appropriate precautions.
5. DRUGS AND ALCOHOL: The use of alcohol or drugs when diving can have disastrous effects.
6. PROHIBITED AREAS: Avoid diving in prohibited areas such as vessel channels and docking areas. Details regarding these restricted areas are available at the park Diver Registration
7. UNATTENDED BOATS: Never leave a boat unattended, especially when it is used for diving. At least one person must be left on board when the boat is anchored or moored.
8. NIGHT DIVING: Only experienced divers should engage in night diving. Each diver should be equipped with an adequate underwater light and should never exceed 30' (9 metres) in depth.

EACH DIVER is required to REGISTER at the Registration Centre PRIOR to diving in the park.

Tobermory, the scuba diving mecca of Ontario. (Photo by Cris Kohl.)

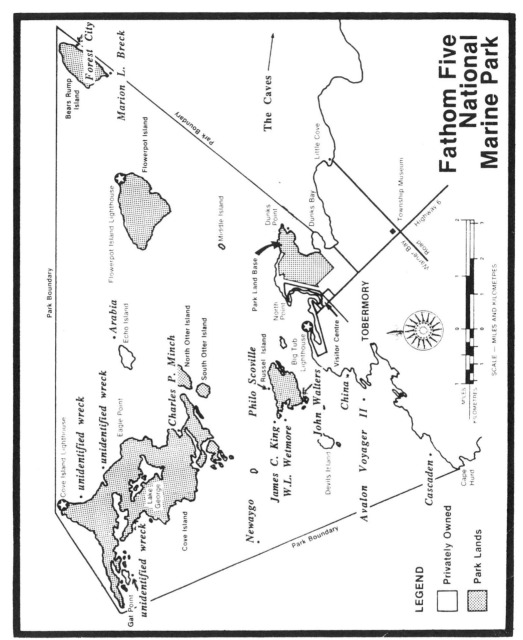

Fathom Five National Marine Park
Tobermory, Ontario

(The author thanks Fathom Five National Marine Park for permission to slightly alter and use their map of the shipwreck sites and park boundaries.)

Site 119: The Wreck of the *Cascaden*

Location:	Just northeast of Cape Hurd.
Access:	Boat.
Skill Level:	Novice.
Depth:	20 feet (6 metres).
Visibility:	6 - 20 feet (1.8 - 6 metres).

Background: The 138-ton, wooden schooner, *Cascaden,* built in Southampton, Ontario in 1866, was wrecked just to the northeast of Cape Hurd on October 15, 1871.

Directions: This site, although still within the park boundaries, is a fair distance southwest of Tobermory, and a boat is required.

Description: This schooner broke up in an autumn gale when she went onto the rocks. Her wreckage lies scattered over a large, shallow area, and because of those facts, this is not a popular dive site.

Hazards: The greatest hazard would be disappointment due to the inability to make head or tail of any of the strewn wreckage at this site. Since this site lies in waters that become dangerously shallow, damage to the dive boat is also a concern.

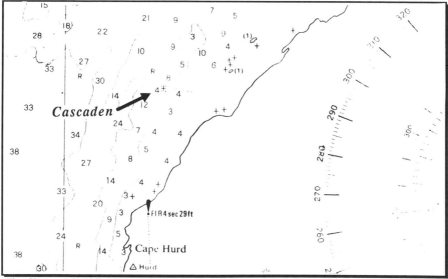

The Charts and Publications Regulations of the Canada Shipping Act require vessels operating in Canadian waters to carry the latest, best scale, corrected Canadian Hydrographic Service (CHS) charts. This document does not meet the requirements of the Act. (Portion from CHS chart 2274.)

Site 120: The Wreck of the *China*

Location:	On China Reef, just southwest of Tobermory.
Access:	Boat.
Skill Level:	Novice.
Depth:	10 feet (3 metres).
Visibility:	6 - 20 feet (1.8 - 6 metres).
Description:	The 314-ton schooner, *China,* built at Port Robinson, Ontario, in 1863 and having a length of 137' (41.8 metres), was wrecked on Nov. 20, 1883, at the reef which was subsequently named after her. The wreckage is badly broken up, lying between China Cove and Wreck Point; the largest and most interesting portion lies close to shore.
Hazards:	Diving this shallow site when the swells are up could prove dangerous. Numerous rocks and ledges form boating hazards.

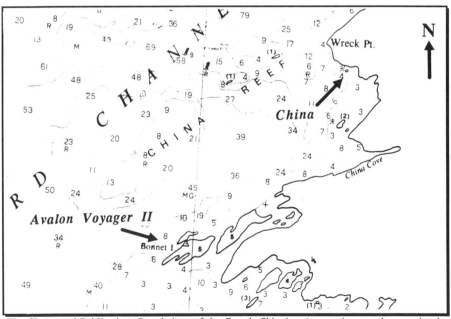

The Charts and Publications Regulations of the Canada Shipping Act require vessels operating in Canadian waters to carry the latest, best scale, corrected Canadian Hydrographic Service (CHS) charts. This document does not meet the requirements of the Act. (Portion ofCHS chart 2274.)

The schooner, China, *lies in shallow water, with her features, such as wooden ribbing, easily viewed from the surface. Below: The bow end of the keelson is one of the several interesting sights of this wreck.* (Photos by Cris Kohl.)

Site 121: *Avalon Voyager II* Wreck

Location:	Just off the west end of Bonnet Island near Hay Bay, southwest of Tobermory.
Access:	Boat.
Skill Level:	Novice.
Depth:	To 25 feet (7.5 metres).
Visibility:	10-25 feet (3 - 7.5 metres).

Description: This 325-ton, 135' (41-metre) long wooden propeller, built at Clarenville, Newfoundland in 1946 and launched as the *Twillingate,* with various other name changes (*Thomas V. Hollett* from 1951 to 1967, *Avalon Voyager* from 1967 to 1976, *Avalon Voyager II* from 1976 to 1981) struck ground off Cape Hurd on Oct. 31, 1980, while enroute from Kincardine to Owen Sound for use there as the floating restaurant she had become. Her anchor failed to hold, and she dragged into Hay Bay. Her registration was closed on March 5, 1981. Weather and firebug vandals have taken their toll on this vessel, but she is still photogenic.

Hazards: On occasion, a current exists at this site.

The extensive debris and artifact field around the main hull sections of the Avalon Voyager II *make exciting exploration.* (Photo by Cris Kohl.)

The Wreck of the *Avalon Voyager II*

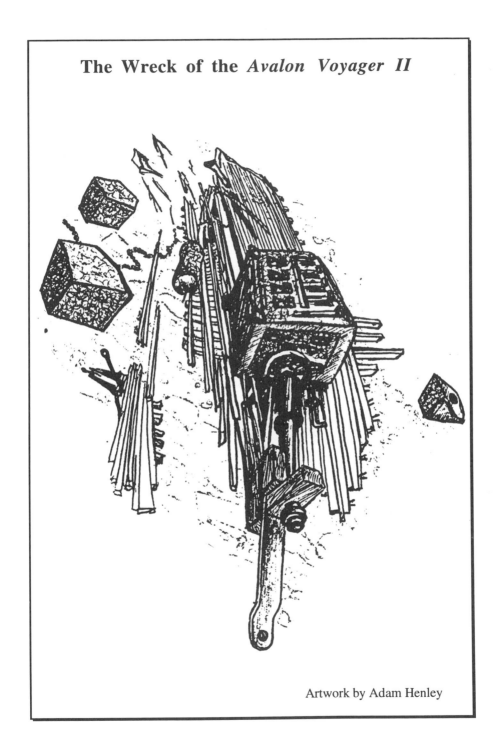

Artwork by Adam Henley

Site 122: The *Sweepstakes*

Location:	Near the head of Big Tub Harbour.
Access:	Boat.
Skill Level:	Novice.
Depth:	20 feet (6 metres).
Visibility:	8 - 20 feet (2.4 - 6 metres).

Background: The 218-ton, two-masted schooner, *Sweepstakes,* built at Burlington, Ontario, by Melancthon Simpson in 1867, measured 120' by 23' by 10' (36 by 6.9 by 3 metres). She was driven ashore and seriously damaged at Cove Island in August, 1885, but was pulled off and towed by the tug, *Jessie,* to Big Tub Harbour, where she sank before repairs could be made. Her coal cargo was salvaged.

Directions: The *Sweepstakes* lies about 150' (45 metres) from the head of Big Tub Harbour. Below-deck access is limited due to the wood corrosion caused by divers' bubbles staying below deck. This wreck is buoyed every year.

Description: The *Sweepstakes* is one of the best preserved 1800's Great Lakes schooners to be found, in spite of nature taking her toll every year. Of interest are the bow's starboard railing, the windlass, the Roman numeral draught markings, the mast holes, and the centreboard box below deck.

Hazards: Boating traffic can be heavy, especially the glassbottom tourist boats. Diver/tourboat access hours are limited during summer; check the office for times. Please respect the rights of the private landowners around the site.

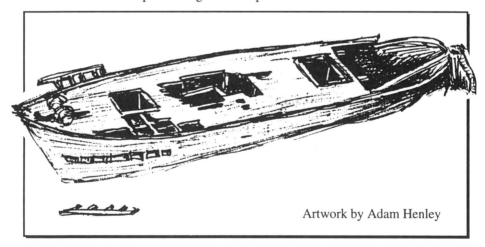

Artwork by Adam Henley

REMEMBER

All divers are required to register and obtain an annual diver registration at the park Dive Registration Centre for diving at Fathom Five National Marine Park.

The schooner, Sweepstakes, *is probably the most dived shipwreck in the entire Great Lakes.* Above: *Diver Kathy Everson glides up to the windlass at the bow.* Below: *Kathy views the Roman numeral bow markings.* (Photos by Cris Kohl.)

Site 123: The *City of Grand Rapids*

Location:	Near the head of Big Tub Harbour.
Access:	Boat.
Skill Level:	Novice.
Depth:	15 feet (4.5 metres) maximum.
Visibility:	7 - 16 feet (2.1 - 4.8 metres).

Background: This 327-ton wooden propeller measured 123' (36.9 metres) in length, 25' (7.5 metres) in beam, and 9' 3" (2.8 metres) in draft. Built at Grand Haven, Michigan, by Duncan Robertson in 1879, she was sold to Canadian interests in 1907, with whom she saw very brief service. On Oct. 29, 1907, while at dock in Big Tub Harbour, the *City of Grand Rapids* mysteriously caught fire and burned to a total loss.

Directions: The wreck is located about 100' (30 metres) off the starboard bow of the schooner, *Sweepstakes.*

Description: The port side of this wreck rises close to the surface, and protrudes in years of low water. The charred, mostly-buried hull lies filled with burned deck and superstructure debris. Portions of the engine and boiler remain in place, while the propeller and rudder are on display at the Tobermory and St. Edmunds Township Museum just south of Tobermory.

Hazards: Boating traffic is frequently heavy at this site. Fly a divers down flag.

Big Tub Harbour Shipwrecks

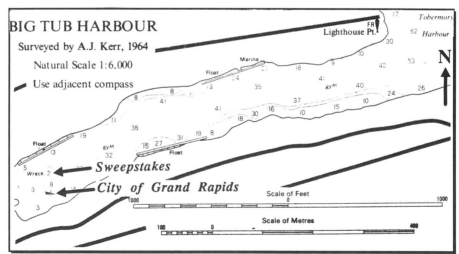

The Charts and Publications Regulations of the Canada Shipping Act require vessels operating in Canadian waters to carry the latest, best scale, corrected Canadian Hydrographic Service (CHS) charts. This document does not meet the requirements of the Act. (portion of CHS chart 2274.)

Flames consumed the steamer, City of Grand Rapids, *when the vessel was 28 years old.* (Photo: Institute for Great Lakes Research, Bowling Green State University, Ohio). Below: *The boiler box is one of the large metal items remaining of this shipwreck.* (Photo by Cris Kohl.)

Site 124: The Anchor at Big Tub

Location: Just off the shoreline almost halfway between Big
                Tub Harbour and Little Tub Harbour, Tobermory, Ontario.
Access: Shore or boat.
Skill Level: Intermediate - advanced.
Depth: 70 feet (21 metres).
Visibility: 5 - 15 feet (1.5 - 4.5 metres).
Description: This huge wooden-stocked iron anchor from an
                unknown vessel provides a unique viewing opportunity. The
                length of large-links chain is also of interest to divers. The
                suit-up and entry area is at the "gap" just to the east of the
                church at the end of Highway 6. Parking is limited. Please
                respect the rights of all landowners adjacent to the parking and
                suit-up area, and the site itself.
Hazards: Be aware of depth, windy wave-producing weather,
                and boating hazards. Other than those, the greatest hazard is
                not being able to locate this site! Once you get to the huge
                underwater boulder from the "gap,", the anchor lies just beyond
                it. Stay at about the 65' level and keep a sharp eye.

Artwork by Adam Henley

*Most of a diver's air supply will be used reaching, and returning from, the Big
Tub Harbour anchor site. Studying the enormous wooden-stocked anchor (above)
and its chain will not take much time, so divers can casually appreciate the
geological wonders of huge boulders and "Tobermory coral" (pitted, limestone
rocks) while en route to and from this site. (Photo by Cris Kohl.)*

Site 125: Little Tub Tugs

Location:	At Little Tub Harbour, Tobermory Ontario.
Access:	Shore.
Skill Level:	Novice - intermediate.
Depth:	40 feet (12 metres) maximum.
Visibility:	7 - 20 feet (2.1 - 6 metres).

Background: These four tugs have different stories: the *John & Alex,* a 59' (17.7-metre) fishing tug built at Port Dover, Ont., in 1924, burned here on Dec. 6, 1947. The *Bob Foote* sank in 1905. The 68' (20.4-metre) *Robert K.,* built at Port Dover, Ont. in 1917, burned June 23, 1935. The 67' (20.1-metre) *Alice G.* went aground in gale force winds and sank in Nov., 1927.

Directions: The area enclosing these four tugs is marked by restricted boating buoys. Diver access is from the diver's platform just off the road.

Description: For the most part, the first three of these wrecks, all of which burned, are badly broken and scattered in the harbour. The *Alice G.,* however, is nearly intact; her steam engine, boiler, driveshaft, and propeller are interesting and photogenic. The stern railing gracefully curving with the lines of the fantail attests to the beauty and workmanship of that era.

Reaching the remains of the four small steam tugs in Little Tub Harbour at Tobermory is facilitated by this specially-constructed divers' suit-up/access platform, reached by means of a short trail from the road. (Photo by Cris Kohl.)

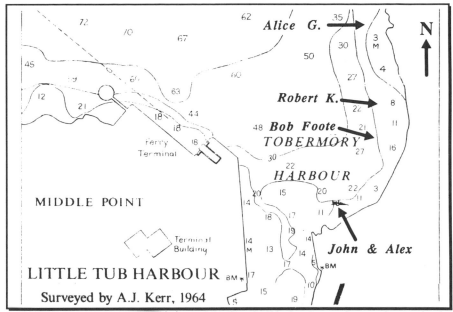

The Charts and Publications Regulations of the Canada Shipping Act require vessels operating in Canadian waters to carry the latest, best scale, corrected Canadian Hydrographic Service (CHS) charts. This document does not meet the requirements of the Act. (Portion of CHS chart 2274.)

The tugboat, John & Alex, *one of four shipwrecks frequently explored at Little Tub Harbour, burned in late 1947.* (Photo: author's collection.)

Thirteen-year-old Christoff Kohl, the author's second cousin, explores the tugboat that is in the most intact shape, the Alice G., *which ran aground here during a storm in late 1927.The beautiful curved stern railing is one of the highlights of this shipwreck.* (Photos by Cris Kohl.)

The Wreck of the tug, *Alice G.*

Artwork by Adam Henley

Site 126: Big Tub Lighthouse

Location: Lighthouse Point, Big Tub Harbour, near Tobermory.
Access: Shore.
Skill Level: Novice - intermediate.
Depth: To 75 feet (22.5 metres).
Visibility: 8 - 20 feet (2.4 - 6 metres).
Description: Interesting geological features can be oserved just
                   below the historic (1885) lighthouse. This area, marked off
                   with restricted boating buoys, is frequently used for check-out
                   dives in the shallower depths. There is limited parking near
                   this access point.
Hazards: Beware of your depth limitations.

*The Fathom Five National Marine Park Visitor Centre is worth a visit for
anyone. Please keep in mind that scuba divers planning to dive in the park must
register at a nearby office before diving.* (Photo by Cris Kohl.)

Site 127: Wreck of the *John Walters*

Location:	Southeast tip of Russel Island, near Tobermory.
Access:	Boat. (Shore dive from Russel Island).
Skill Level:	Novice.
Depth:	15 feet (4.5 metres) maximum.
Visibility:	6 - 20 feet (1.8 - 6 metres).

Description: This 176-ton schooner, built in 1852 at Kingston, Ontario, by George Thurston (the same man who constructed the *Arabia),* and launched as the *Sarah Bond,* was owned by Henry Patterson of Chatham, Ontario, when she was driven ashore at this site in 1899. The bow lies broken near the shore, while the stern and rudder are in deeper water. The thick keelson and centreboard box are also of interest. The *Walters* measured 108 feet (32.4 metres) in length, with a beam of 23' (6.9 metres).

Hazards: This sheltered site is easy for snorkelers and novice divers.

Exploring the centreboard box of the schooner, John Walters, *diver Tim Philp is made aware of the powerful forces of nature (rocks, ice, wave action) that bent the huge bolts extending towards the surface.* (Photo by Cris Kohl.)

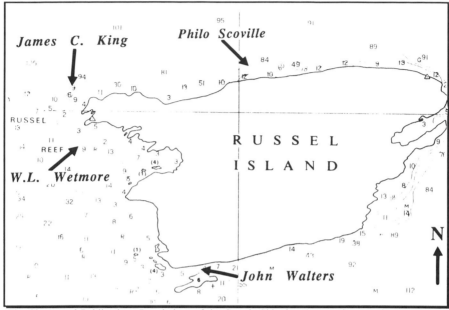

James C. King

Philo Scoville

RUSSEL

REEF

W.L. Wetmore

R U S S E L

I S L A N D

John Walters

N

The Charts and Publications Regulations of the Canada Shipping Act require vessels operating in Canadian waters to carry the latest, best scale, corrected Canadian Hydrographic Service (CHS) charts. This document does not meet the requirements of the Act. (portion of CHS chart 2274.)

Site 128: The *W.L.Wetmore* Wreck

Location: Just below the west end of Russel Island.
Access: Boat.
Skill Level: Novice - intermediate.
Depth: 28 feet (8.4 metres) maximum.
Visibility: 7 - 20 feet (2.1 - 6 metres).
Description: Considered one of the best wrecks in the Tobermory area, the 819.74-ton steamer, *W.L. Wetmore,* while towing her usual barges, *Brunette* and *James C. King,* was driven ashore on Russel Island in a storm on Nov. 29, 1901. No lives were lost, but only the *Brunette* was salvaged. Built by Quayle & Martin in Cleveland, Ohio, and launched on May 17, 1871, the *Wetmore* measured 213' 7" (64 metres) in length, 33' 4" (10 metres) in beam, and 12' 6" (3.7 metres) in draft. Highlights of the site include the massive rudder, the sheared-off propeller, the striking boilers, bow anchor chain, hawse pipes, an anchor, and much planking with hanging knees and other features.
Hazards: A west wind will whip up the waves.

The steamer, W.L. Wetmore, *fell victim to the gales of November, 1901, at Russel Island near Tobermory.* (Photo: Institute for Great Lakes Research, Bowling Green State University, Ohio.) Below, *an enormous mound of anchor chain lies just off the bow of the* W.L. Wetmore *wreck.* (Photo by Cris Kohl.)

The Wetmore's *boilers* (above) *are an easily- recognizable characteristic. Rising to within a few feet of the surface, they can usually be spotted from a boat approaching the site. Brass portions of the boiler piping are also recognizable (below). (Photos by Cris Kohl.)*

The Wreck of the steamer, *Wetmore*

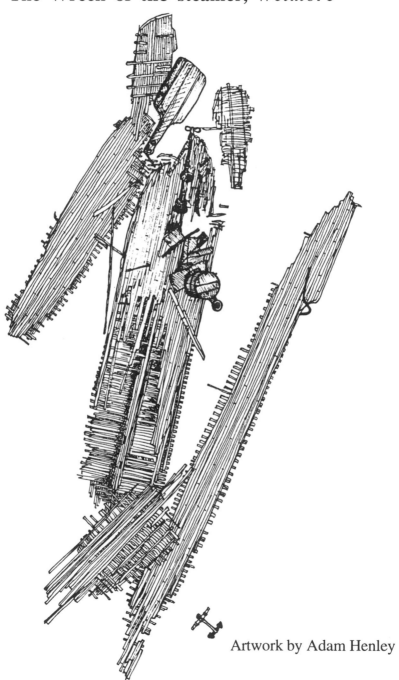

Artwork by Adam Henley

Site 129: Wreck of the *James C. King*

Location:	Off the western tip of Russel Island.
Access:	Boat.
Skill Level:	Intermediate - advanced.
Depth:	22 - 93 feet (6.6 - 27.9 metres).
Visibility:	7 - 20 feet (2.1 - 6 metres).

Background: This schooner-barge (one of thousands of sailing vessels that was denigrated to this position when steam replaced sail) was in tow of the steamer, *W.L. Wetmore,* when both vessels were driven ashore at Russel Island near Tobermory by a fierce gale on Nov. 29, 1901. Unlike the *Wetmore,* the *James C. King* slide into deep water. Built by Bruce Tripp at East Saginaw, Michigan in 1867 as a 512-ton, three-masted schooner, this large wooden vessel measured 181' 6" (54.5 metres) in length, 33' (9.9 metres) in beam, and 13' (3.9 metres) in draft.

Description: The wreck lies on a steep incline, with the rudder resting in about 22' (6.6 metres) of water close to the broken, split hull, while at depth, a capstan and the Roman numeral draught markings can be viewed.

Hazards: The depth and cold water must be considered when diving this site.

The stern of the schooner, James C. King, *is seen at the right in this dock scene.* (Photo: The Great Lakes Marine Collection of the Milwaukee Public Library.)

The rudder of the schooner, James C. King, *explored by diver Roy Pickering, lies on the hard limestone bottom in the shallows.* (Photo by Cris Kohl.)

Site 130: The *Philo Scoville* Wreck

Location: North shore of Russel Island, near Tobermory.

Access: Boat.

Skill Level: Intermediate - advanced.

Depth: 35 - 95 feet (10.5 - 28.5 metres).

Visibility: 7 - 20 feet (2.1 - 6 metres).

Description: The 325-ton schooner, *Philo Scoville,* built by Quayle & Martin at Cleveland, Ohio, in 1863, drifted off course during a storm on Oct. 6, 1889 while enroute light (that is, carrying no cargo) from Collingwood, Ont. to Escanaba, Mich. Dragging her anchors, she struck Russel Island, where her captain died when he fell between the ship and some rocks. A Tobermory tug rescued the other four crewmen. Lying on a steep incline, the *Scoville's* bowsprit lies in about 93' (27.9 metres) near the mooring buoy anchor. An anchor about 150' (45 metres) to the east lies at the same depth, with chain running uphill to about 30' (9 metres). Part of the stern lies in 35' (10.5 metres) about 100' (30 metres) west of the main wreckage.

Hazards: The depth and cold water must be considered when diving this site.

The twin set of anchor chains from the Philo Scoville *tumble down the limestone drop-off some distance to the east of the wreck; at the bottom, as diver Joe Drummond discovered, they disappear under vast silt. (Photo by Cris Kohl.)*

Site 131: The Wreck of the *Newaygo*

Location: Northwest Bank, Devil Island Channel.
Access: Boat.
Skill Level: Novice - intermediate.
Depth: To 25 feet (7.5 metres).
Visibility: 8 - 18 feet (2.4 - 5.4 metres).
Description: Launched at Marine City, Michigan, on July 18, 1890, by builder Alexander Anderson, the 906.26-ton wooden steamer, *Newaygo,* stranded at this site on Nov. 17, 1903, and broke up. No lives were lost. The ship was underway light from Cleveland for French River, Ontario, towing the schooner-barge, *Checotah,* at the time of loss (the *Checotah* survived this storm.) The *Newaygo* measured 196' (58.8 metres) by 37' 2" (11.1 metres) by 13' 4" (4 metres). The scattered wreckage highlights are a boiler and the huge, heavily-built bottom of the hull, 160' (48 metres) long.
Hazards: This open site is susceptible to bad weather.

The steamer, Newaygo, *loaded with coal when she grounded at McGregor Channel, was owned by Port Huron businessman, Henry McMorran.* (Photo: Institute for Great Lakes Research, Bowling Green State University, Ohio.)

Site 132: *Charles P. Minch* Wreck

Location:	South shore, Tecumseh Cove, Cove Island.
Access:	Boat. (Shore dive from Cove Island).
Skill Level:	Novice - intermediate.
Depth:	20 - 60 feet (6 - 18 metres).
Visibility:	10 - 25 feet (3 - 7.5 metres).

Background: The *Charles P. Minch,* a 408.21-ton, three-masted schooner built
  by Isaac W. Nicholas at Vermilion, Ohio, in 1867, was enroute to Chicago
  with a lumber cargo on Oct. 26, 1898, when adverse weather forced her into
  the protected harbour of Tecumseh Cove. When the wind suddenly shifted,
  and the safe harbour lost its "safe" status, the captain and crew just barely
  reached the island, and the *Minch* was destroyed within three hours. The
  Minch measured 154' 7" x 28' 2" x 11' 8" (46.3 x 8.4 x 3.5 metres).

Directions: North-northwest of Tobermory, the *Minch* wreckage is marked by
  two mooring buoys in beautiful Tecumseh Cove.

Description: The centreboard box, sides, bow and bottom of the hull lie on
  the incline east the submerged cribs near the head of the cove, a good place
  to make an entry. (The rudder situated west of this mooring buoy is likely
  from the schooner, *Tecumseh,* wrecked here in 1882.) Between the second
  mooring buoy, about 600' (180 metres) south of the cove, and the shore lie
  a keel and rudder portion, plus part of the deck, from the *Charles P. Minch.*
  Numerous artifacts, including a .38 revolver, were recovered here years ago.

Hazards: Occasional adverse weather and boating traffic are potential hazards.

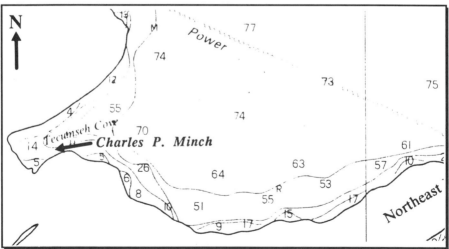

Broken wreckage from the schooner, Charles P. Minch, *in Tecumseh Cove offers interesting views of 19th-century sailing ship construction. Planking and hardware can be appreciated by visiting divers.* (Photos by Cris Kohl.)

Site 133: Three Cove Island Wrecks

Background: Nothing is known of the backgrounds of these three unidentified shipwrecks off various parts of Cove Island north of Tobermory.

Directions and Descriptions: The remains of one wreck lie in the shallows just east of Gat Point (maximum 8', or 2.4 metres, of water), protected by an islet, on the western shore of Cove Island. A section 62' (18.6 metres) in length, thought to be a forward hull portion, exists, with framing, planking, and miscellaneous debris covering a large area. A shallow-draft boat is necessary, as these are dangerously shallow waters.

The second is the "Cassle's Cove Wreck," a centreboard schooner, below Cove Island lighthouse off Boat Harbour. An 88' (26.4-metre) section lies in the sand at a depth of 70' (21 metres), while the vessel's sides rest at about 60' (18 metres), with the rudder, complete with a decorative, scalloped design carved in the top of its blade, sits in pebbles at 50' (15 metres).

The third wreck is also on the east side of Cove Island, near Boat Harbour, but a bit southeast of "Cassle's Cove Wreck." There is a Parks Canada Service sign naming "Cove Island." Dive at this sign. The wreckage, mainly three chunks of boards, lies in 20' - 80' (6 - 24 metres). One reliable source has indicated that this site is the wreckage described in one recent T.V. film as being a previously-undiscovered wreck close to the *Arabia*. However, this is a great distance from the *Arabia*. Do not search for another shipwreck within swimming distance of the deep *Arabia*. There is none.

The blue waters of Cove Island sparkle an enthusiastic welcome for divers. At least three unidentified shipwrecks lie in this area. (Photo by Cris Kohl.)

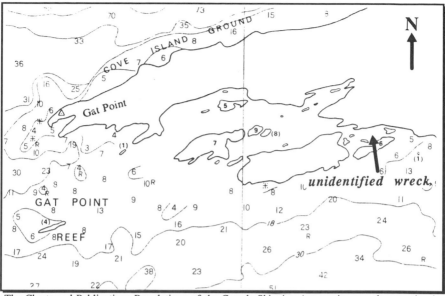

The Charts and Publications Regulations of the Canada Shipping Act require vessels operating in Canadian waters to carry the latest, best scale, corrected Canadian Hydrographic Service (CHS) charts. This document does not meet the requirements of the Act. (Portion of CHS chart 2274.)

As shallow as it is, the unidentified wreck at Gat Point makes for interesting discoveries and underwater photography. Great cove, too! (Photo by Cris Kohl.)

Site 134: The Wreck of the *Arabia*

Location:	Off Echo Island, near Tobermory, Ontario.
Loran Co-ordinates:	30202.9/48669.8
Access:	Boat.
Skill Level:	Advanced.
Depth:	117 feet (35.1 metres).
Visibility:	8 - 15 feet (2.4 - 4.5 metres).

Background: The 309-ton barque, *Arabia,* bound from Chicago to Midland, Ontario, with 20,000 bushels of corn, began taking on water during heavy seas on Oct. 4, 1884. After hours of pumping, the weary crew, realizing the hopelessness of the situation, abandoned ship in their yawlboat; the vessel sank in deep water off Echo Island. This three-masted ship, built by George Thurston at Kingston, Ontario, in 1853, measured 131' (39.3 metres) in length, 26' (7.8 metres) in beam, and 12' (3.6 metres) in draft.

Description: This wreck is in pristine condition. The mostly-intact hull, lying north-to-south, has two mooring buoys positioned about 30' (9 metres) to the east. The bow is impressive with its bowsprit, windlass, anchors, catheads, and bilgepump. Deadeyes and pulleys decorate the railings. The afterdeck, separated form the hull, rests against the starboard quarter. The ship's wheel and steering mechanism are located alongside the afterdeck. The three masts have all collapsed and lie alongside the wreck.

Hazards: This is a deep, cold, low-visibility site for very experienced divers only. Give this site all the preparation and experience it demands; at least 12 scuba divers have died here over the past 25 years.

Roy Pickering explores the Arabia's *port rail.* (Photo by Cris Kohl.)

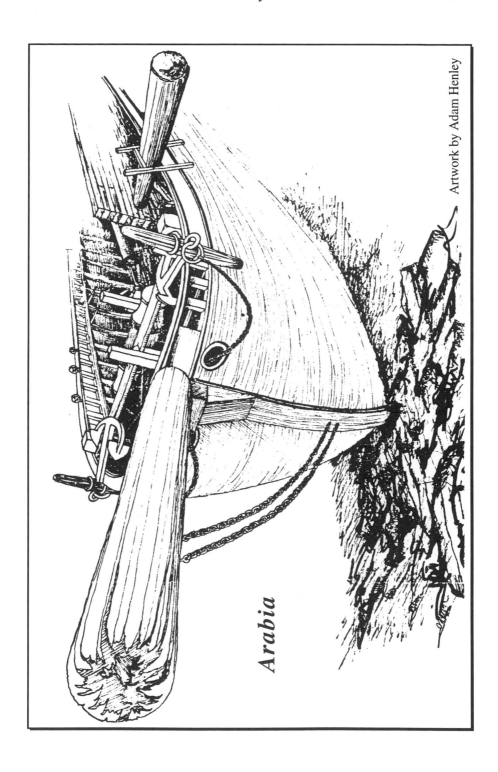

Arabia

Artwork by Adam Henley

Site 135: Dave's Bay (Little Cove)

Location:	East of Tobermory, Ontario.
Access:	Shore or boat.
Skill Level:	All levels of experience.
Depth:	To 40 feet (12 metres).
Visibility:	8 - 18 feet (2.4 - 5.4 metres).
Description:	Take Warner Bay Road near the Township Museum east to Little Cove. Besides being a picturesque cove, this site offers interesting geological formations such as glacial erratics, pitting, and layered dolomite along the bay's south shore. Used sometimes for diver checkouts, this site offers limited parking at the access point. Please respect the rights of private property owners in this area, which is outside the Fathom Five National Marine Park boundaries.

Site 136: Dunk's Point

Location:	About one mile (1.6 kilometres) east of Tobermory.
Access:	Boat.
Skill Level:	Variable, depending upon depth.
Depth:	To 60 feet (18 metres).
Visibility:	8 - 20 feet (2.4 - 6 metres).
Description:	Dunk's Point is accessible only by boat (an inflatable is ideal.) Interesting underwater geological formations, such as prime examples of gracial pitting, abound at this site. There is a wooden-stock anchor off Dunk's Point. In the water just to the left of a small island in the bay are three visible rocks. Dive off the first and second rocks for the anchor; the anchor chain rests in 45' - 55' (13.5 - 16.5 metres), with the anchor at the 60' (18-metre) level.

Site 137: Flowerpot I. Shore Dive

Location: North-northeast of Tobermory, Ontario

Access: Boat to Flowerpot Island, shore dive from there.

Skill Level: All levels of experience, depending upon depth.

Depth: 30 - 130 feet (9 - 39 metres).

Visibility: 10 - 20 feet (3 - 6 metres).

Description: This site abounds with underwater cliffs, rock formations, and submerged ledges. The area just off the "flowerpots" themselves is the most popular site, and is just to the east of the small dock at the southeast side of Flowerpot Island. Simply follow the trail a short distance.

Hazards: Cold water and depth limitations must be taken seriously at this site, since you're a fair distance from help in case of an accident. Be aware of occasional boating traffic as well; fly a divers down flag.

Limestone cliffs form walls and other interesting geological features underwater just off Flowerpot Island near the famous flowerpots. (Photo by Cris Kohl.)

Site 138: The *Marion L. Breck* Wreck

Location:	Off the south end of Bear's Rump Island.
Access:	Boat.
Skill Level:	Variable, depending upon depth.
Depth:	10 - 100 feet (3 - 30 metres).
Visibility:	8 - 18 feet (2.4 - 5.4 metres).

Background: With much of her canvas lost to the fury of November gales, the schooner, *Marion L. Breck,* stranded on the southeast side of Bear's Rump Shoal on Nov. 15, 1900. The crew abandoned ship and reached the safety of Flowerpot Island, where the lighthouse keeper rescued them. The wind and waves quickly pounded the 396-ton *Breck* into pieces, scattered with her cargo of brick fragments. Authorities consider the *Breck* to be an 1863 rebuild of the 1840 vessel, *William Penn,* constructed at Garden Island, near Kingston, Ontario. The *Breck* measured 127' (38.1 metres) by 23' 6" (7 metres) by 12' (3.6 metres).

Description: Scattered over a vast area, the *Breck's* remains include: a 40' (12-metre) hull section in 75' (22.5 metres) of water, a section of keel at 50' (15 metres), a capstan and anchor in 25' (7.5 metres) further southwest along the shoal's edge, and the major portion of the wreck at about 90' (27 metres).

Hazards: Be cautious of depth and the potential for hypothermia at this site.

The schooner, Marion L. Breck, *at dock.* (Photo: author's collection.)

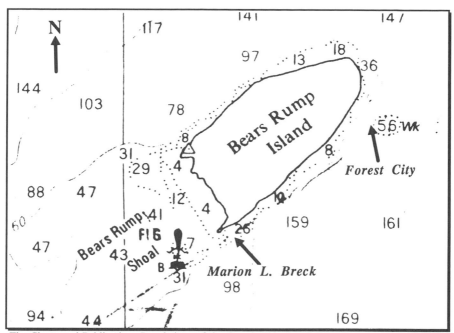

The Charts and Publications Regulations of the Canada Shipping Act require vessels operating in Canadian waters to carry the latest, best scale, corrected Canadian Hydrographic Service (CHS) charts. This document does not meet the requirements of the Act. (Portion of CHS chart 2235.)

Diver Joe Drummond explores expansive timbers from the Marion L. Breck *scattered over a wide area along the island's drop-off.* (Photo by Cris Kohl.)

Site 139: Wreck of the *Forest City*

Location:	Off northeast Bear's Rump Island.
Loran Co-ordinates:	30158.0/48675.1
Access:	Boat.
Skill Level:	Advanced.
Depth:	60 -150 feet (18 - 45 metres).
Visibility:	10 - 20 feet (3 - 6 metres).

Background: Built by Elihu M. Peck at Cleveland, Ohio, and launched on May 7, 1870, as a 740.13-ton, three-masted schooner, the *Forest City* was converted to a 1,236-ton propeller in 1872. Her measurements were 213' 7" (64 metres) in length, 33' 5" (10 metres) in beam, and 21' 3" (6.3 metres) in draft. On June 5, 1904, heavy fog, a slight wavering off course, and a rocky island combined to put a sudden, solid end to the career of the *Forest City*. Several weeks' worth of salvage efforts succeeded only in stripping this vessel; then, suddenly, the hull filled and slid into deep water.

Description: On shore, a chunk of rusty, iron bow-plating marks the impact point. In the water, the broken-up bow is situated in 60' (18 metres), while the relatively intact stern drops off on a steep, rocky incline to depths beyond sport-diving range. This site is for experienced divers only.

Hazards: Deep, coldwater diving is demanding. Plan your dive well, and don't waver off course. Careless and/or inexperienced divers have died at this site.

Since the wreck of the Forest City *is in deep water, caution is vital.* (Photo: Institute for Great Lakes Research, Bowling Green State University, Ohio.)

The *Forest City* Shipwreck

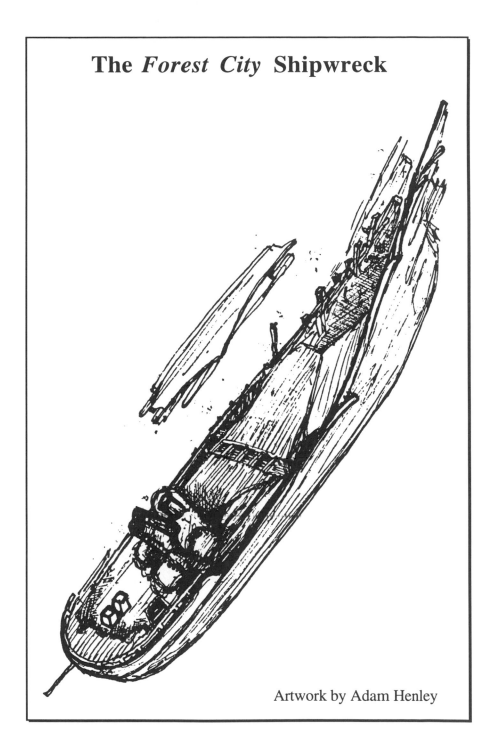

Artwork by Adam Henley

Site 140: The *Lady Dufferin* Wreck

Location:	About 1.5 miles (2.4 kilometres) east of Little Cove, just west of Driftwood Cove, near Tobermory, Ont.
Access:	Boat.
Skill Level:	Advanced.
Depth:	40 - 100 feet (12 - 30 metres).
Visibility:	8 - 18 feet (2.4 - 5.4 metres).

Description: In Oct., 1886, the schooner-barge, *Lady Dufferin,* was towed by the steamer, *W.B. Hall,* to Cabot Head to recover the cargo of lumber from the stranded schooner, *John Bentley.* Heavy seas arose, and the strained towline to the *Lady Dufferin* parted. The schooner was swept onto the rocks and sank, but fortunately, the crew escaped with their lives. The *Lady Dufferin,* built at Port Burwell, Ontario, was 135' (40.5 metres) long. To locate the *Lady Dufferin* site, take a boat to Dufferin Point and look for two orange, fluorescent circles on the rock wall in a niche. Dive there. The wreck is broken up on a steep incline, with a steam engine, probably for use in the lumber salvage, located in the deepest part of the wreckage.

Hazards: This remote site is considered a deep dive, and diveplans must be made accordingly. This site is for experienced divers only.

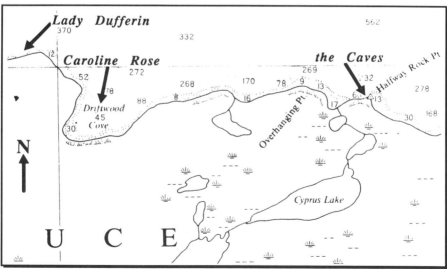

The Charts and Publications Regulations of the Canada Shipping Act require vessels operating in Canadian waters to carry the latest, best scale, corrected Canadian Hydrographic Service (CHS) charts. This document does not meet the requirements of the Act. (Portion of CHS chart 2235.)

Large slabs of timbers which comprised the hull and decking of the schooner, Lady Dufferin, *cascade down the steep, rocky slope.* (Photo by Cris Kohl.)

Site 141: The Caves

Location: About 10 miles (16 kms.) east of Tobermory.

Access: Shore or boat (boat preferred). A long trail from a parking lot past Cyprus Lake leads to this site, but it can be quite strenuous carrying scuba gear that distance.

Skill Level: Novice - intermediate.

Depth: 30 feet (9 metres) maximum at the base of the submerged cave entrance, but the rock face just beyond that point drops off to much greater depths.

Visibility: 10 - 25 feet (3 - 7.5 metres).

Description: Two small, submerged caves lead from the open bay waters to *the grotto,* a secluded, hushed pool protected by a massive limestone vault, where scuba divers and skinnydippers have been known to unexpectedly encounter each other. Interesting sights, in the shape of underwater rock formations, exist outside *the grotto* as well.

Hazards: Watch your depth at the rock face drop-off. Dive lights are useful for crevice investigations, but not necessary to dive the caves.

Site 142: Wreck of the *Caroline Rose*

Location: In Driftwood Cove, about 6.5 kilometres southeast of Tobermory and about one kilometre outside the park boundary.

Access: Boat. This wreck site is buoyed.

Skill Level: Intermediate.

Depth: Maximum 55 feet (16.5 metres).

Visibility: 8 - 20 feet (2.4 - 6 metres).

Description: The 250-ton, 132' (39.6-metre) schooner, *Caroline Rose,* built in 1940 by Smith and Rhuland of Lunenburg, Nova Scotia (the same company which had earlier built the famous *Bluenose,* depicted on the Canadian dime), was one of the last Grand Bank schooners to be used for fishing. She is one of the three ships shown on our $100 bill. Abandoned after being used as a cruise ship and sinking at her dock at Owen Sound, the *Caroline Rose* was raised amidst controversy, towed north, and purposely sunk in late August, 1990, as a dive site, by Peter Dean and Rod Anderson, both of Tobermory, and Toronto diver Don MacIntyre. On board were left most of the original tools, fittings, and usual ship's items. The vessel sits upright on a 30-degree list.

Hazards: In September, 1990, a severe storm moved the wreck 150' (45 metres) closer towards shore, causing extensive damage. It is now considered dangerous to penetrate the weakened hull of the *Caroline Rose.*

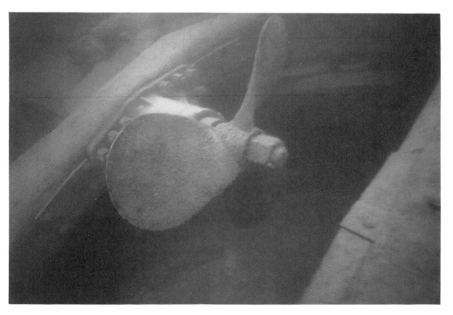

The propeller of the purposely-scuttled Caroline Rose. (Photo by Cris Kohl.)

Site 143: The *Vita* Shipwreck

Location:	West of Yeo Island, north of Tobermory.
Loran Co-ordinates:	Not necessary to locate this site.
Access:	Boat.
Skill Level:	Novice - intermediate.
Depth:	2 - 18 feet (0.6 - 5.4 metres).
Visibility:	8 - 16 feet (2.4 - 4.8 metres).

Background: The opulent steam yacht, *Vita,* built by John Craig at Trenton, Michigan in 1888 and owned by Frank S. Upton of Charlotte, New York, measured 86' 4" (25.9 metres) in length, 18' 4" (5.5 metres) in beam, and 6' 8" (2 metres) in draft, with a gross tonnage of 69. The vessel was wrecked on November 5, 1910, under unknown circumstances.

Directions: The *Vita* wreckage lies close to the eastern (or inside) edge of Manitoba Ledge, off the western end of Yeo Island.

Description: The propeller shaft lies in two feet (0.6 metres) of water. Follow it down to the rest of the scattered wreckage.

Hazards: With a strong wind out of the west, this open site could be hazardous, particularly since the wreck lies within very shallow water. Huge waves pounding on this reef could prove dangerous to divers and divaeboats.

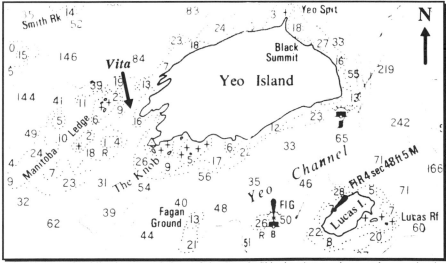

The Charts and Publications Regulations of the Canada Shipping Act require vessels operating in Canadian waters to carry the latest, best scale, corrected Canadian Hydrographic Service (CHS) charts. This document does not meet the requirements of the Act. (Portion of CHS chart 2235.)

Site 144: The *City of Cleveland*

Location:	N. of Perseverence Island, off the outlying shoal of Little Perseverence Island, 18 miles (29 kms.) north of Tobermory.
Loran Co-ordinates:	30256.2/48587.4 (see chart, p. 198).
Access:	Boat. The site is marked by a small buoy.
Skill Level:	Novice - intermediate.
Depth:	To 30 feet (9 metres).
Visibility:	8 - 25 feet (2.4 - 7.5 metres).

Background: The twin-decked, four-masted, wooden propeller, *City of Cleveland,* built in Cleveland, Ohio, by Thomas Quayle's Sons and launched on June 17, 1882, carried a length of 255' 7" (76.7 metres), a beam of 39' 5" (11.9 metres), a draft of 18' 4" (5.5 metres) and a gross tonnage of 1,609. Winter came early at the end of 1901 when, on Sept. 15, a blinding snowstorm and southwest gales forced this vessel off-course and onto the rocks. The crew rowed to the safety of Fitzwilliam Island. The *City of Cleveland,* fully loaded with 2,300 tons of iron ore from Michipicoten, Lake Superior, had been headed for the blast furnaces at Midland when she sank.

Description: The *City of Cleveland* is not only the largest shipwreck in the Tobermory area, but also the most impressive of all the shallow-water wrecks. With her bow in only 10' (3 metres) and her stern in 30' (9 metres), her decks and sides have been flattened by nature. The steam engine, massive boilers, rudder, and huge propeller are quite interesting and photogenic.

Hazards: Medical assistance is far away, so have no accident at this remote site.

The four-masted steamer, City of Cleveland, *was salvaged after this 1889 sinking; the vessel was not as lucky in 1901.* (Photo: author's collection.)

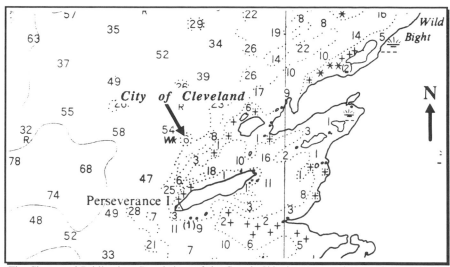

The Charts and Publications Regulations of the Canada Shipping Act require vessels operating in Canadian waters to carry the latest, best scale, corrected Canadian Hydrographic Service (CHS) charts. This document does not meet the requirements of the Act. (Portion of CHS chart 2235.)

Scuba diver Tim Philp glides in and out of the enormous engineworks on the City of Cleveland *shipwreck north of Tobermory.* (Photo by Cris Kohl)

Site 145: The *George A. Graham*

Location:	At South Baymouth, Manitoulin Island.
Access:	Boat.
Skill Level:	Novice - intermediate.
Depth:	To 15 feet (4.5 metres).
Visibility:	6 - 15 feet (1.8 - 4.5 metres).

Background: This steel bulk freight steamer was, in 1891, the first hull built
by the Chicago Shipbuilding Company, Chicago, Illinois. Launched as the
Marina and measuring 308' 3" (92.5 metres) in length, 40' (12 metres) in
beam, and 24' 6" (7.4 metres) in draft, she was renamed the *George A.
Graham* in 1912, just five years before the vessel wrecked. The ship was
named after the mayor of Fort William, Ontario (1912-1913), and he
outlived his namesake by nearly ten years. The *George A. Graham* sustained
heavy damage when she was forced ashore near South Baymouth,
Manitoulin Island, by strong winds on Oct. 7, 1917. After some machinery
salvage, she was abandoned in place by her owners, the Montreal
Transportation Company. Nature and scavenging local residents soon
removed most of this wreck from sight.

Description: Because of the salvage operation shortly after the grounding, the
gradual disappearance of the scrap metal hull, and Mother Nature doing her
normal work, the ship's remains are missing or scattered over a large area.

Hazards: Beware of local boating traffic and strong surge from westerly winds.

The steel freighter, George A. Graham, *grounded near South Baymouth,
Manitoulin Island, on Oct. 7, 1917, and was abandoned in place.* (Photo:
author's collection.)

Site 146: The *S. D. Hungerford*

Location:	East of Hungerford Pt., s.e. Manitoulin I.
Access:	Boat.
Skill Level:	Novice - intermediate.
Depth:	To 15 feet (4.5 metres).
Visibility:	8 - 15 feet (2.4 - 4.5 metres).

Background: On Nov. 25, 1883, the tug, *Gladiator,* with the lumber-laden schooner, *S. D. Hungerford,* in tow, cleared Tobermory heading for Buffalo. When the tug encountered mechanical difficulties during a severe gale, it abandoned the schooner, which soon began taking on water. Dropping her anchors near what was later named Hungerford Point in her honour, the schooner was dragged many miles towards the east by the merciless winds. The captain, William Moore, and his crew made it safely to Manitoulin Island, where they struggled for survival with only a tent and a few provisions for 19 days before an old fishing boat from Tobermory rescued them.

Description: Only small wreckage debris from the *S. D. Hungerford* can be located in the shallows of Owen Island Bank. Adventurous, experienced divers may someday locate larger portions of the hull in deeper water.

Hazards: The west wind has been known to blow up quite a breeze, making both boating and scuba diving difficult. Use discretion regarding the weather.

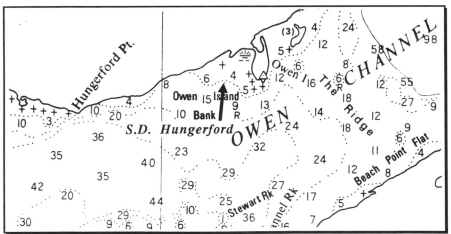

The Charts and Publications Regulations of the Canada Shipping Act require vessels operating in Canadian waters to carry the latest, best scale, corrected Canadian Hydrographic Service (CHS) charts. This document does not meet the requirements of the Act. (Portion of CHS chart 2235.)

Site 147: Rattlesnake Harbour

Location: Northern portion of Fitzwilliam Island, about 20 miles (32 kilometres) north of Tobermory, Ontario.

Access: Boat. Shore dives once on the island.

Skill Level: Novice - intermediate.

Depth: To 15 feet (4.5 metres).

Visibility: 5 - 10 feet (1.5 - 3 metres).

Description: The 180' (54-metre) schooner-barge, *Michigan,* in operation until the 1930's, lies in 10' (3 metres) of water near the abandoned fishing shanties in this well-sheltered harbour. A steel rod marks the vessel's bow. The wreck of the *Wauseda II* lies at the very eastern end of the inlet. Reports indicate that there is also a small wreck along the south shore of the bay, and another one just to the east of the *Michigan.*

Hazards: Submerged logs and tree branches clutter the clay bottom of this bay, so explore with caution. Beware of rattlesnakes on the island. Medical assistance is far away, so use caution in order to avoid an emergency situation.

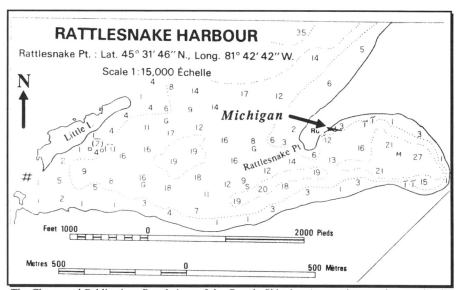

The Charts and Publications Regulations of the Canada Shipping Act require vessels operating in Canadian waters to carry the latest, best scale, corrected Canadian Hydrographic Service (CHS) charts. This document does not meet the requirements of the Act. (Portion of CHS chart 2235.)

Site 148: Club Island Harbour

Location: Club Island is located about 20 miles (32 kilometres) north of Tobermory, Ontario, and about six miles (ten kilometres) east of Rattlesnake Harbour on Fitzwilliam Island. The entrance to Club Harbour is on the island's east side.

Access: Boat. Shore access from the island.

Skill Level: Novice - intermediate.

Depth: To 15 feet (4.5 metres).

Visibility: 4 - 9 feet (1.2 - 2.7 metres).

Description: A small (57', or 17.1 metres long), unidentified, metal-sheathed shipwreck lies about 150' (45 metres) from shore opposite the bunch of fishing shanties.

Hazards: As this harbour is a popular overnight spot for boaters cruising between the North Channel and Tobermory, beware of boating traffic over this wreck site. The one night we spent here in 1981 was shared with 14 other pleasure craft.

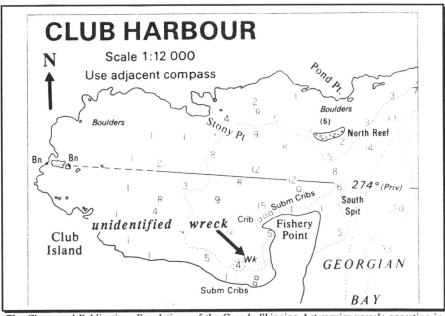

The Charts and Publications Regulations of the Canada Shipping Act require vessels operating in Canadian waters to carry the latest, best scale, corrected Canadian Hydrographic Service (CHS) charts. This document does not meet the requirements of the Act. (Portion of CHS chart 2245.)

Worth Checking Out?

The Tobermory Hyperbaric Facility offers a hyperbaric chamber, acquired in
1976, for the treatment of air embolism, decompression sickness, and other
relevant medical ailments, at the Tobermory Health Clinic. It also offers
Educational Programs, such as a Hyperbaric Dive Experience Packages, for
novice divers, sport divers, and advanced divers. Contact them for further
information or bookings at: Tobermory Health Clinic, Tobermory, Ontario,
Canada, N0H 2R0, telephone (519) 596-2305.

The schooner, *Golden West,* went ashore in 1884 at the western extremity of
Snake Island, which is due north of Flowerpot Island. Scattered wreckage is
visible in the shallows among the rocks, but to date, no large portions of
this shipwreck have been located.

*The old lighthouse and keeper's quarters on the north tip of Cove Island make an
excellent stop-over for lunch while diving the unidentified shipwrecks in the
area. The dock there is well-maintained, and items from another era, such as an
ancient capstan, dot the historic grounds.* (Photo by Cris Kohl.)

South of Tobermory

Site 149: Dyer's Bay Anchor

Location: Off the Dyer Bayside resort, Dyer's Bay, Ontario.
Access: Shore.
Skill Level: Novice - intermediate.
Depth: To 42 feet (12.6 metres).
Visibility: 8 - 15 feet (2.4 - 4.5 metres).
Description: This wooden-stock, large-fluke anchor was imported from a site further to the northwest for the convenience of the former diver training resort here. The lake bottom deepens gradually in layers from shore to the anchor site. The anchor also has 12' (3.6 metres) of huge chain attached to it. This site is usually marked with a jug during diving season.
Hazards: The only "hazard" might be missing the anchor if the diver goes underwater directly from shore and fails to locate it by means of compass navigation.

Site 150: Dyer's Bay, Devil's Face

Location: About one mile (1.6 kms.) south of Dyer's Bay.
Access: Boat.
Skill Level: Variable (depends upon depth.)
Depth: Maximum to 90 feet (27 metres).
Visibility: 10 - 22 feet (3 - 6.6 metres).
Description: Impressive rock formations, both above and below the water level, make this an exciting location. Below, there are boulders everywhere, creating canyon-like passageways, cliffs, and caves. This is also a good site to study a large crayfish population. The best depth is 20' - 30' (6 - 9 metres).
Hazards: With some care, diver disorientation in this maze of boulders can be avoided. Beware that your zeal to explore all the nooks and crannies might get you into some tight, narrow situations. Don't get stuck. Be aware of depth limitations.

A diver explores the underwater canyons, boulders, and rock formations of the "Devil's Face" site near Dyer's Bay, Ontario. (Photo by Cris Kohl.)

Site 151: Wreck of the *Gargantua*

Location: Wingfield Basin, at the end of Cabot Head, east of Tobermory. Road access is possible along the shore from Dyer's Bay. Ask permission of the lighthouse keeper for access to Wingfield Basin.

Access: Shore or boat.

Skill Level: Novice - intermediate.

Depth: To 15 feet (4.5 metres).

Visibility: 5 - 10 feet (1.5 - 3 metres).

Description: The large wooden tug, *Gargantua,* was built at the McLouth Shipyard, at Marine City, Mich., in 1919 for the U.S. Shipping Board, but shortly after the war, the contract was cancelled. In 1923, the unfinished ship was sold to, and completed by, the Lake Superior Paper Co. of Sault Ste. Marie, Ont. Measuring 130' (39 metres) by 32' 1" (9.6 metres) by 15' 4" (4.6 metres), the 381-ton *Gargantua,* under tow in Georgian Bay in 1952 after her machinery was removed, took shelter from heavy seas in Wingfield Basin, where she sat until she sank. In 1971, a mysterious fire destroyed her superstructure.

Hazards: Boat traffic and easily-disturbed silt can be problems.

The graceful lines of the steamer, Gargantua, *can still be imagined today beholding this wreck, which is mostly above water.* (Photo: author's collection).

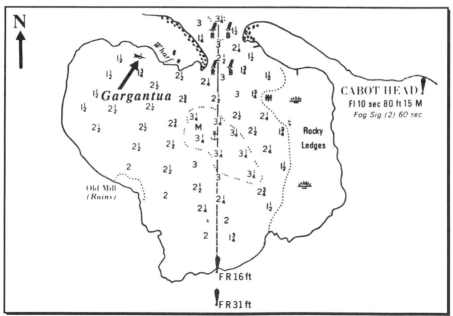

The Charts and Publications Regulations of the Canada Shipping Act require vessels operating in Canadian waters to carry the latest, best scale, corrected Canadian Hydrographic Service (CHS) charts. This document does not meet the requirements of the Act. (Portion of CHS chart 2282.)

Site 152: The *City of Chatham* Wreck

Location:	Wiarton, Ontario.
Access:	Shore or boat.
Skill Level:	Novice - intermediate.
Depth:	15 feet (4.5 metres).
Visibility:	8 - 15 feet (2.4 - 4.5 metres).

Background: Originally thought to be the remains of the steamer, *Okonra,* this wreck is likelier the oak-hulled passenger vessel, *City of Chatham,* which was built by the Polson Iron Works Company, Toronto, in 1888. Originally operating between Chatham, Ontario, and Detroit, Michigan, the *City of Chatham* was licensed to carry 627 passengers. From 1909, she operated on the St. Mary's River, between Sault Ste. Marie, Ontario, and ports on St. Joseph's Island. In 1921, the old hull was partially stripped and removed to Wiarton for rebuilding. However, the era of travel by steamship was ending, and, with roads opening up many formerly-landlocked ports, the *City of Chatham* was abandoned. Local knowledge has it that "the Wright boys worked for MacNamara [an underwater construction company], and they put the *City of Chatham* there" at the site of this wreck. The *City of Chatham* measured 136' 3" (41 metres) in length, 28' 5" (8.6 metres) in beam, and 9' (2.7 metres) in draft.

Description: These shipwreck remains lie near shore just north of the Wiarton fish hatchery, which is at the north end of town.

Hazards: Boating traffic can be heavy during the summer months.

The passenger steamer, City of Chatham. (Photo: author's collection.)

The *City of Chatham* Shipwreck

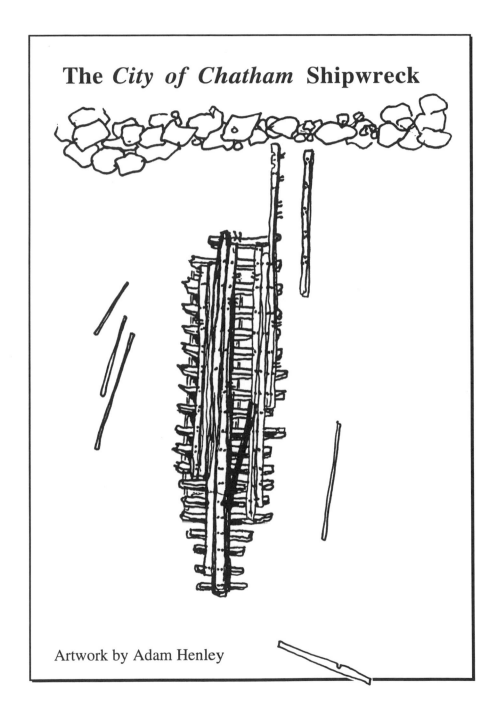

Artwork by Adam Henley

Site 153: Two More Wiarton Wrecks

Location:	Colpoy's Bay, north of Wiarton, Ontario.
Access:	Shore or boat.
Skill Level:	Novice.
Depth:	To 12 feet (3.6 metres).
Visibility:	8 - 15 feet (2.4 - 4.5 metres).

Background: The *Edward S. Pease,* a lumber barge with sails, and the Scottish-built barge, *Lothair,* were purposely sunk in their present locations, lying end-to-end, in front of Whicher's Mill, at the turn of the century to form a mill pond as protection for the log rafts. The mill company paid the Crawford Tug Company $200 each for these old vessels.

Directions: These wrecks are situated south of the pier at the small community of Colpoy's Bay, north of Wiarton.

Description: The *Lothair,* the closer wreck to the shore, is the one with the stern post reaching close to the water's surface.

Hazards: Boating traffic is probably the only concern that a diver will have at this site, which is ideal for the beginner.

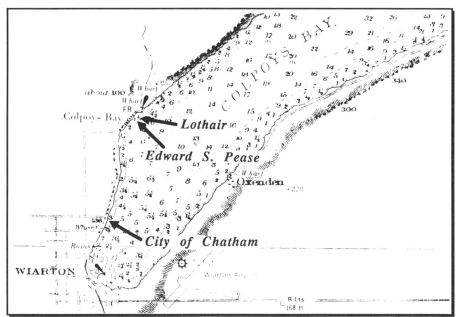

The Charts and Publications Regulations of the Canada Shipping Act require vessels operating in Canadian waters to carry the latest, best scale, corrected Canadian Hydrographic Service (CHS) charts. This document does not meet the requirements of the Act. (Portion of CHS chart 2282.)

Two Other Shipwrecks at Wiarton

Lothair

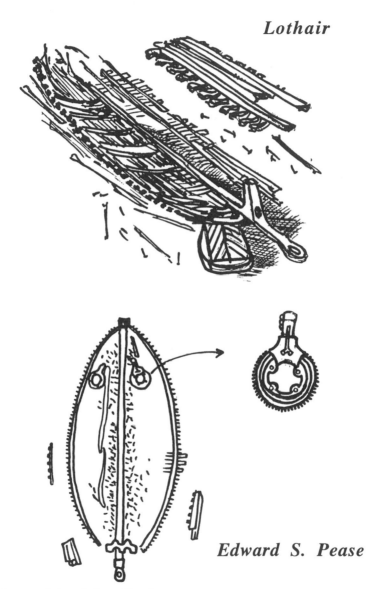

Edward S. Pease

Artwork by Adam Henley

Site 154: The Lion's Head Wrecks

Location:	Lion's Head, Ontario (Bruce Peninsula).
Access:	Shore or boat.
Skill Level:	Novice - intermediate.
Depth:	To 15 feet (4.5 metres).
Visibility:	4 - 8 feet (1.2 - 2.4 metres).

Background: Sailing vessels in the lumber industry at the beginning of this century found themselves being abandoned to age in the many Georgian Bay harbours. Two of these unidentified wrecks lie in Lion's Head harbour.

Description: The more accessible of the two wrecks lies with the remains of its bow right against the shore of a small, rounded peninsula of land to the southeast of the public beach. These skeletal remains, about 140' (42 metres) in length, are probably those of a sailing vessel, since no evidence of steam propulsion exists. A bit further east and about 200' (60 metres) offshore in 15' (4.5 metres) of water are the remains of an old tugboat.

Hazards: Boating traffic is heavy in this harbour, especially in the summer.

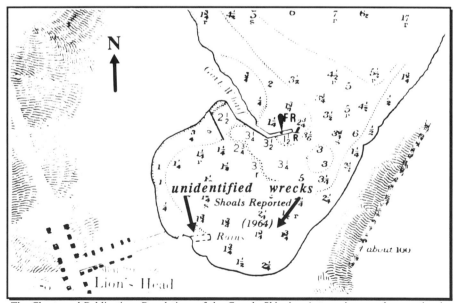

The Charts and Publications Regulations of the Canada Shipping Act require vessels operating in Canadian waters to carry the latest, best scale, corrected Canadian Hydrographic Service (CHS) charts. This document does not meet the requirements of the Act. (Portion of CHS chart 2282.)

Site 155: The *Mary Ward* Wreck

Location:	Off Craigleith, Ontario.
Access:	Boat.
Skill Level:	Novice - intermediate.
Depth:	To 15 feet (4.5 metres).
Visibility:	6 - 12 feet (1.8 - 3.6 metres).

Background: Built by A. Cantin at Montreal and launched as the wooden propeller, *North,* in 1864, this vessel burned and sank in the St. Clair River in November, 1867. Raised and rebuilt in 1870, and renamed the *Mary Ward,* she saw two more years of service before blundering into the deadly area of shallow shoals in lower Georgian Bay on November 24, 1872, while on a Sarnia-to-Collingwood run laden with freight and passengers. Just hours before a rescue party from shore saved those on board, eight members of the crew drowned while attempting to reach land in a lifeboat. Although the vessel survived the winter perched on the rocks, three salvage attempts failed the following year. By late 1873, the cargo had been removed, but the ship was abandoned. She broke up shortly thereafter.

Description: The engine, propeller, and the main portion of the wreckage lie in about 12' - 15' (3.6 - 4.5 metres) within the second reef when approaching from the open water of the north. This site, about two miles (3.2 kms.) off Craigleith, is difficult to locate, even in a calm sea.

Hazards: These shoals represent a danger for any vessel approaching them.

The steamer, Mary Ward, *built in 1864 as the* North, *spent three years (1867-70) at the bottom of the St. Clair River. She was raised, but wrecked near Collingwood in 1872 with the loss of 8 lives.* (Photo: Public Archives Canada.)

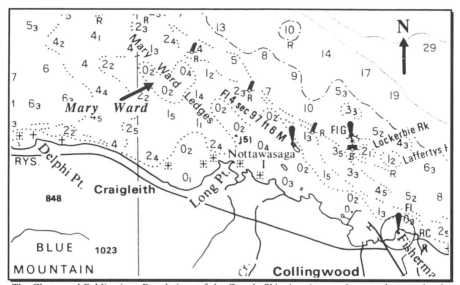

The Charts and Publications Regulations of the Canada Shipping Act require vessels operating in Canadian waters to carry the latest, best scale, corrected Canadian Hydrographic Service (CHS) charts. This document does not meet the requirements of the Act. (Portion of CHS chart 2202.)

Worth Checking Out?

The Meaford, Ontario, town dock has been explored by scuba divers, with interesting results.

The wreck of the *Shaunnon,* reputedly located by a diver from Lion's Head, apparently is scattered in 30' - 60' (9 - 18 metres) of water at Jackson Shoal, off Lion's Head.

Penetanguishene Area

Site 156: Wreck of the *Saucy Jim*

Location:	Southern portion of Christian Island.
Access:	Boat. (Shore dive from the island.)
Skill Level:	Novice.
Depth:	5 feet (1.5 metres).
Visibility:	4 - 8 feet (1.2 - 2.4 metres).

Background: Built at Meaford, Ontario, in 1887, the small steam tug, *Saucy Jim,* criss-crossed Georgian Bay performing a variety of workhorse functions. This vessel burned to a total loss at Christian Island on Nov. 18, 1910.

Directions: The wreck site is off the sandy beach just east of the government dock at Christian Island.

Description: Since this vessel burned, there is not much left to view and appreciate. Added to that information is the fact that she sank in shallow water; that means that wave and ice actions, over a period of time, have buried most of this vessel under sand. The boiler, however, rises above the water's surface to act as a location marker for those wishing to explore her.

Hazards: This site can be done on scuba, but it is better suited for snorkeling.

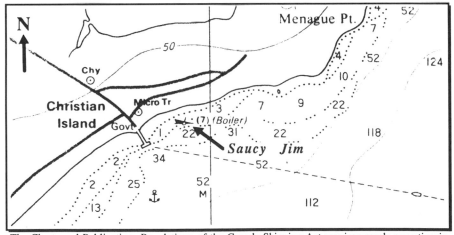

The Charts and Publications Regulations of the Canada Shipping Act require vessels operating in Canadian waters to carry the latest, best scale, corrected Canadian Hydrographic Service (CHS) charts. This document does not meet the requirements of the Act. (Portion of CHS chart 2239.)

Site 157: Wreck of the *Mapledawn*

Location:	Northwest side of Christian Island.
Loran Co-ordinates:	29655.3/48931.5
Lat./Long. Co-ordinates:	N 44 51' 52", W 80 14' 50"
Access:	Boat.
Skill Level:	Novice.
Depth:	To 30 feet (9 metres).
Visibility:	8 - 20 feet (2.4 - 6 metres).

Background: The steel freighter, *Mapledawn,* was launched as the *Manola* on Jan. 21, 1890, by the Globe Shipbuilding Company at Cleveland, Ohio. The name change took place in 1920 when the vessel was purchased by Canada Steamship Lines. On Nov. 30, 1924, the gales of November stranded the *Mapledawn,* bound for Port McNichol with a barley cargo, on Christian Island in a blinding snowstorm. Two weeks of salvage recovered 75,000 bushels of barley, but the ship was declared a total loss. Some machinery was removed then, but more of this wreck was raised for metal salvage in 1942, during the midst of World War II. In 1924, the *Mapledawn* measured 349' 1" x 40' 2" x 21' 3" (104.7 x 12 x 6.4 metres).

Description: The main sections of the twisted wreckage lie in 15' - 30' (4.5 - 9 metres), including the winch and chains, engine, and gigantic boilers. The propeller lies in 30' (9 metres) about 50' (15 metres) off the stern.

The wreck of the steel freighter, Mapledawn, *is a very popular divesite.* (Photo: Institute for Great Lakes Research, Bowling Green State University, Ohio.)

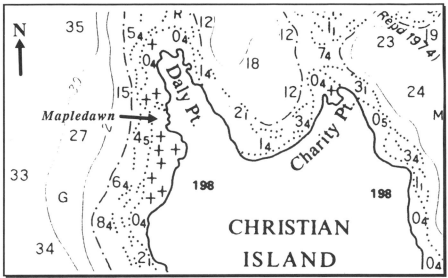

The Charts and Publications Regulations of the Canada Shipping Act require vessels operating in Canadian waters to carry the latest, best scale, corrected Canadian Hydrographic Service (CHS) charts. This document does not meet the requirements of the Act. (Portion of CHS chart 2202.)

The large steel propeller, Mapledawn, *wrecked at Christian Island in 1924, provides countless photographic opportunities.* (Photo by Cris Kohl.)

Hundreds of scuba divers, usually aboard charter boats from Penetanguishene,
visit and explore the wreck of the Mapledawn *every year.* (Photo by Cris Kohl.)

The Wreck of the *Mapledawn*

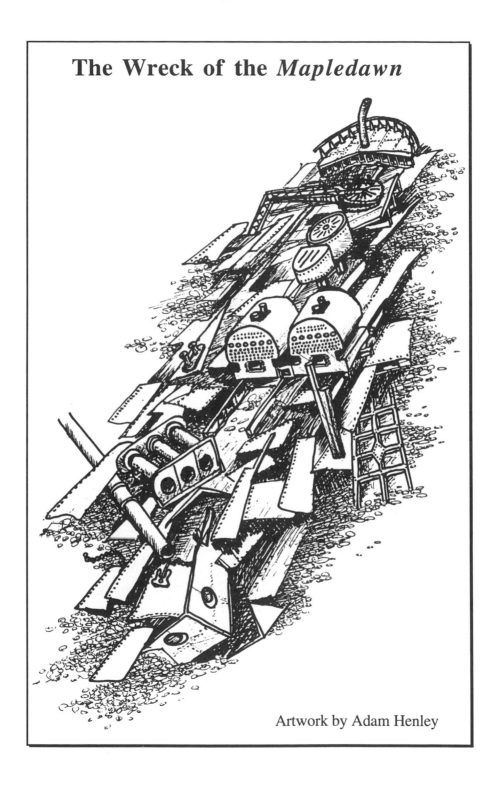

Artwork by Adam Henley

Site 158: The Wreck of the *Michigan*

Location:	Off northwest Hope Island.
Loran Co-ordinates:	29637.7/48912.7
Lat./Long. Co-ordinates:	N 44 54' 58", W 80 12' 15"
Access:	Boat.
Skill Level:	Novice.
Depth:	To 15 feet (4.5 metres).
Visibility:	8 - 20 feet (2.4 - 6 metres).

Background: The converted steel barge, *Michigan,* owned by John Harrison & Sons Company, Ltd., lightered grain from the propeller, *Riverton,* which was stranded on Hope Island, on November 24, 1943. The salvage vessel herself was blown onto the rocks and broke up in the shallows; the *Riverton* was eventually salvaged. The 1,396-ton *Michigan,* built by F. W. Wheeler & Company at West Bay City, Michigan, and launched on Oct. 30, 1890, as a railroad carferry, measured 296' 5" (89 metres) in length, 41' 3" (12.4 metres) in beam, and 15' 6" (4.6 metres) in draft.

Description: Giant gears, machinery, and metalwork offer intriguing sights.

The steel steamer, Michigan, *worked on the Great Lakes for over 50 years before her transformation into a shipwreck in Georgian Bay.* (Photo: Institute for Great Lakes Research, Bowling Green State University, Ohio.)

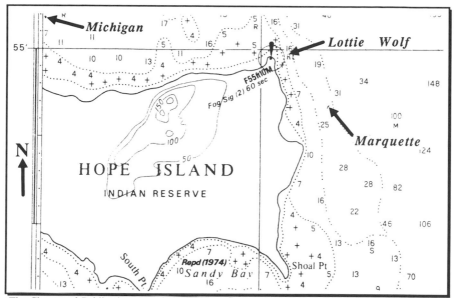

The Charts and Publications Regulations of the Canada Shipping Act require vessels operating in Canadian waters to carry the latest, best scale, corrected Canadian Hydrographic Service (CHS) charts. This document does not meet the requirements of the Act. (Portion of CHS chart 2239.)

Divers frequently explore, as thoroughly as possible, the wrecked remains of the steel steamer, Michigan. (Photo by Cris Kohl.)

The Michigan's *huge gears and scattered machinery offer opportunities galore for underwater exploration and photography.* (Photos by Cris Kohl.)

Site 159: The *Lottie Wolf* Shipwreck

Location: About 450' (135 metres) from the lighthouse dock, off the northeast corner of Hope Island, southern Georgian Bay, Ontario.

Loran Co-ordinates: 29501.9/48914.3

Access: Boat.

Skill Level: Novice.

Depth: 18 feet (5.4 metres).

Visibility: 10 - 15 feet (3 - 4.5 metres).

Description: The three-masted, 126' (37.8-metre) schooner, *Lottie Wolf,* launched at Green Bay, Wisconsin, in 1866, sailed for Midland from Chicago with a cargo of corn when she struck a rock during severe weather on Oct. 16, 1891. Purposely run aground, the vessel broke up after the crew abandoned ship. The remains lie scattered on this sandy bottom, with the sides of the hull off the south and west of the main wreckage area. Years ago, the rudder was raised and is displayed in Toronto at the Marine Museum of Upper Canada.

Hazards: This is a good site for all levels of divers.

Site 160: The Wreck of the *Marquette*

Location: Off the northeast corner of Hope Island, southern Georgian Bay, Ontario.

Loran Co-ordinates: 29620.0/48917.0

Access: Boat.

Skill Level: Novice - intermediate.

Depth: 40 feet (12 metres).

Visibility: 15 - 30 feet (4.5 - 9 metres).

Description: Located by divers in late 1975, this formerly unidentified "Hope Island Wreck" is the 139' 3" (41.8-metre) schooner, *Marquette*. Although pilfered of some of its artifacts (only one deadeye remains, on the bowsprit), this site offers excellent views and photography opportunities of two wooden-stocked bow anchors (with chains still connecting them to the windlass), a samson post, double framing, centreboard box, centreboard winch, main mast step, a capstan lying on its side in the sand inside the hull, hatch coaming, planksheers, transom, transom wing, and a portion of the rudder.

Hazards: The many divers visiting this site are likely to kick up the silt and reduce visibility, so get there early in the day.

Detail of the *Marquette's* Bow

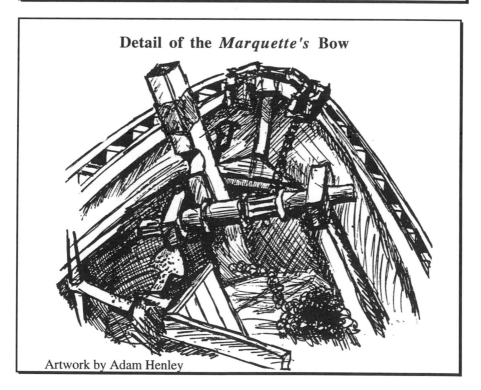

Artwork by Adam Henley

The Schooner, *Marquette*

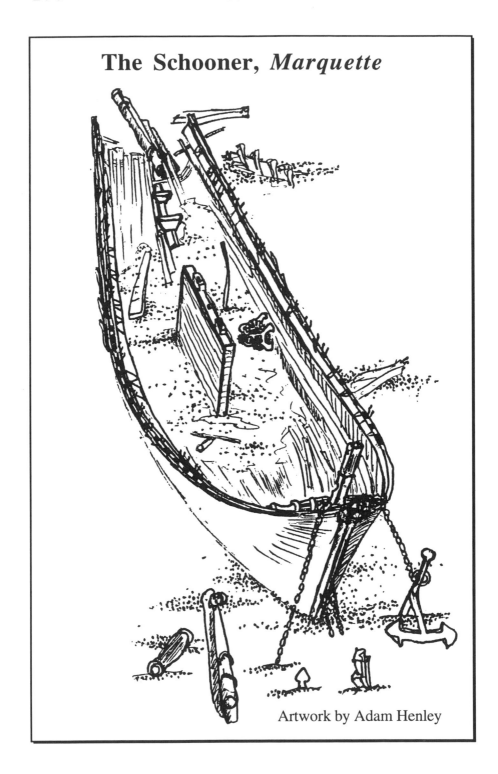

Artwork by Adam Henley

Although the deck of the schooner, Marquette, *is gone, opportunities knock for underwater photography, exploration, and appreciation.* (Photo by Cris Kohl.)

Site 161: The *Thomas Cranage* Wreck

Location:	Off "The Watchers" Islands, southern Georgian Bay, Ontario.
Loran Co-ordinates:	29593.6/48906.0
Lat./Long. Co-ordinates:	N 44 56' 39", W 80 05' 27"
Access:	Boat.
Skill Level:	Novice.
Depth:	To 25 feet (7.5 metres) maximum.
Visibility:	15 - 30 feet (4.5 - 9 metres).

Background: The 2,219.52-gross-ton wooden propeller, *Thomas Cranage,* launched proudly on July 29, 1893 by her builder, James Davidson, at West Bay City, Michigan, measured 305' (91.5 metres) in length, 43' (12.9 metres) in beam, and 20' 7" (6.2 metres) in draft. Named after a banker/businessman/transportation mogul, the vessel outlived her namesake by six months. On Sept. 25, 1911, while on a voyage from Duluth, Minnesota, to Tiffin, Ontario, with a cargo of wheat, the *Thomas Cranage* struck Watcher's Reef. Salvage efforts proved futile, and the ship broke to pieces in the early fall storms.

Description: The broken remains of this ship include the impressive triple expansion engine, the steel-reinforced rudder, and much planking. The scotch-type boilers and the propeller were likely salvaged, as they are absent.

Hazards: The site's openness makes it susceptible to adverse westerly weather.

For a while, the Thomas Cranage *was the world's largest wooden steamship.* (Photo: Institute for Great Lakes Research, Bowling Green State Univ., Ohio.)

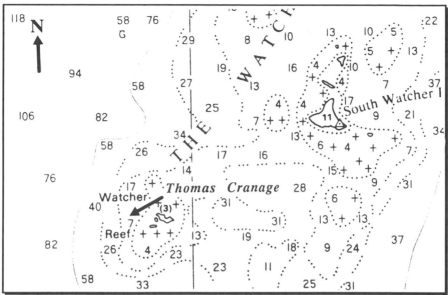

The Charts and Publications Regulations of the Canada Shipping Act require vessels operating in Canadian waters to carry the latest, best scale, corrected Canadian Hydrographic Service (CHS) charts. This document does not meet the requirements of the Act. (Portion of CHS chart 2239.)

Although broken up, the wreck of the Thomas Cranage *off The Watchers Islands offers much to curious and observant scuba divers.* (Photo by Cris Kohl.)

Site 162: Wreck of the *Reliever*

Location:	Off Methodist Point, s. Georgian Bay.
Access:	Boat (or shore through Awenda Prov. Park.)
Skill Level:	Novice.
Depth:	To 12 feet (3.6 metres).
Visibility:	5 - 12 feet (1.5 - 3.6 metres).

Background: This 1,131.44-gross-ton wooden propeller, built by James Davidson at West Bay City, Michigan, and launched originally as the *Germanic* on April 1, 1888 (perhaps in commemoration of the birthday on April 1 of Germany's statesman, Otto von Bismarck), this vessel received her name change in 1909 after she had passed to Canadian registry and been rebuilt at Midland, Ontario, in 1908-1909. As the Canadian vessel, *Reliever,* she did not last long, catching fire while taking on a load of lumber at her owner, Manley Chew's, sawmill on Methodist Point on Nov. 3, 1909. The flaming ship, cut adrift to save the mill and dock, floated to Ways Point, where she ran aground and burned to the waterline. Her machinery (a huge fire box type boiler and a fore and aft compound engine) was salvaged and placed in the new tug, *D. S. Pratt,* at Midland, Ontario, in 1911. *Reliever's* register was closed at Midland, Ontario, on March 23, 1910. She had measured 216' x 36' x 18' (64.8 x 10.8 x 5.4 metres).

Description: The *Reliever's* hull and other remains are scattered along the bottom in shallow water about 100' (30 metres) off Ways Point, Ontario.

The steamer, Reliever, *burned on Nov. 3, 1909 at Methodist Point.* (Photo: Institute for Great Lakes Research, Bowling Green State University, Ohio.)

Site 163: The *Luckport* Shipwreck

Location:	West of Sawlog Pt., s. Georgian Bay.
Access:	Boat.
Skill Level:	Novice - intermediate.
Depth:	To 25 feet (7.5 metres).
Visibility:	5 - 12 feet (1.5 - 3.6 metres).

Background: The wooden steamer, *Luckport,* launched originally as the *St. Magnus* in 1880 at Hamilton, Ontario and rebuilt (including a cut in length from 180' to 126', or 54 to 37.8 metres, and a name change to *Magnolia)* in 1898 at Midland, and again in 1919 when she received her final name, was owned by the Midland Transit Company when she caught fire, burned, and sank west of Sawlog Point in December, 1934.

Directions and Description: Only the charred hull remains about 200' (60 metres) off shore. Because this shore consists of private cottages, land access is not available. It is difficult to locate this wreck, although, in the past, the *Luckport's* rudder, placed on the beach, provided a landmark to this site.

Hazards: Beware of boating traffic from local cottagers, and occasional strong westerly winds producing difficult waves and low visibility.

The small steamer, Luckport, *tied off between the steamers* Fanny Arnold *and* Lucknow *at Midland, Ontario.* (Photo: author's collection.)

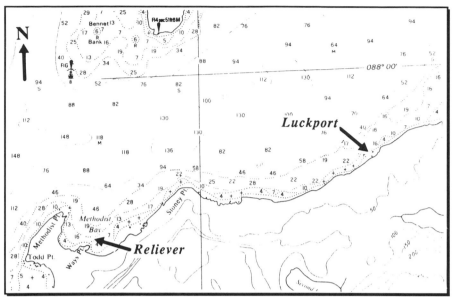

The Charts and Publications Regulations of the Canada Shipping Act require vessels operating in Canadian waters to carry the latest, best scale, corrected Canadian Hydrographic Service (CHS) charts. This document does not meet the requirements of the Act. (Portion of CHS chart 2239.)

Worth Checking Out?

Fraser Bank, just to the east of Giant's Tomb Island in lower Georgian Bay north of Penetanguishene, Ontario, has always represented a major danger to navigation. The remains of an unidentified sailing vessel, approximately the same size as the *Marquette* off Hope Island (since their centreboard boxes are the same size), lie scattered in the shallows, in 6' - 12' (1.8 - 3.6 metres) of water, about 300' (90 metres) west of the two exposed rocks at the southwest edge of Fraser Bank.

Off privately-owned Minnicognashene Island, (part of the 30,000 Islands) are the burned remains of a 28-ton gasoline launch which served the needs of local resorts and cottages during the early part of this century. Known only as "Preston's store boat," the vessel exploded and sank on August 18, 1934. A portion of the wooden hull lies twisted on a smooth, flat rock along shore, while the main segment rests in about 12' (3.6 metres) of water just off this shore.

For the adventurous, boat-owning diver, the distant Western Island Lighthouse offers a deep site just off its shore.

Site 164: The Wreck of the *Wawinet*

Location:	Off Beausoleil Pt., n. of Penetanguishene.
Loran Co-ordinates:	29501.9/48970.7
Lat./Long. Co-ordinates:	N 44 49' 30", W 79 05' 54"
Access:	Boat.
Skill Level:	Novice - intermediate.
Depth:	25 feet (7.5 metres).
Visibility:	6 - 15 feet (1.8 - 4.5 metres).

Background: The 87' (26.1-metre) private yacht, *Wawinet,* built in 1904 and purchased by Bertrand Corbeau of Penetanguishene in 1938, became one of Georgian Bay's most tragic marine accidents. On Sept. 21, 1942, returning from Honey Harbour to Penetanguishene with Corbeau and colleagues from the Midland Foundry & Machine Company, the vessel heeled over while making a sudden turn. Her lower windows were, unfortunately, open, and the ship filled and sank within two minutes, with 25 of the 42 people on board, including Corbeau, losing their lives. The survivors swam to nearby Beausoleil Island, where they were soon rescued.

Description: The *Wawinet,* intact and upright, has her bow facing southeast.

Hazards: Boating traffic can get heavy in this popular cottage area. The hull of the wreck, although intact, should be entered only while using extreme caution and safe, recognized shipwreck penetration practices. The wind and current can stir up the bottom easily and impair visibility.

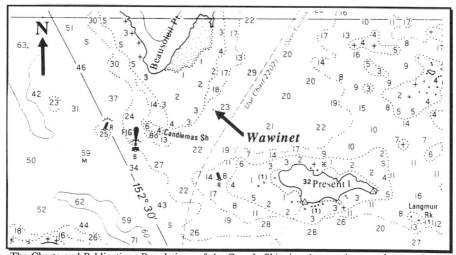

The Charts and Publications Regulations of the Canada Shipping Act require vessels operating in Canadian waters to carry the latest, best scale, corrected Canadian Hydrographic Service (CHS) charts. This document does not meet the requirements of the Act. (Portion of CHS chart 2239.)

Site 165: The *Midland City* Wreck

Location:	Tiffin Basin, at Midland, Ontario.
Access:	Shore or boat.
Skill Level:	Novice - intermediate.
Depth:	To 12 feet (3.6 metres).
Visibility:	4 - 6 feet (1.2 - 1.8 metres).

Background: This steamer, of composite construction, spent an incredible 84 years in service on the Great Lakes! Built at Kingston, Ontario, by George Thurston in 1871 (her first registry was issued there on Jan. 12, 1872), she underwent several name changes in her lifetime: *Maud* (1872-1895), *America* (1895-1921), *City of Midland* (1921), and *Midland City* (1921-1955). Rebuilt in 1895, 1899, and in 1933 as a motor vessel, the final dimensions of this 580-gross-ton vessel were 149' 2" (44.8 metres) of length, 33' 2" (10 metres) of beam, and 6' 4" (1.9 metres) of draft. Completely exhausted and worn out, the *Midland City* was dismantled at Midland, towed to the River Wye, and deliberately burned on May 7, 1955.

Description: The remains of the *Midland City*, comprising only the bottom of the hull, lie northeast of the mouth of the River Wye, bow towards shore, in about 3' to 12' (0.9 - 3.6 metres) of water. A black marker buoy is usually attached to the stern.

Hazards: Boating traffic is heavy in this harbour and marina area, while wind and current can severely limit visibility. Use caution at this site.

The popular steamer, Midland City, *underway on Georgian Bay with a load of cruising passengers.* (Photo: author's collection.)

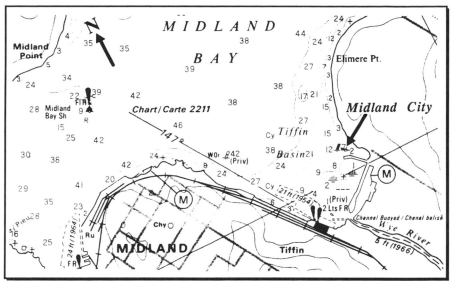

The Charts and Publications Regulations of the Canada Shipping Act require vessels operating in Canadian waters to carry the latest, best scale, corrected Canadian Hydrographic Service (CHS) charts. This document does not meet the requirements of the Act. (Portion of CHS chart 2202,

Site 166: The *Ontario* Shipwreck

Location: Musquash River, about 1.5 miles (2.4 kilometres) upstream from the southern end of Longuissa Pt., north of Penetanguishene, Ontario.

Access: Boat. (See chart portion on page 228).

Skill Level: Novice - intermediate.

Depth: To 12 feet (3.6 metres).

Visibility: 4 - 6 feet (1.2 - 1.8 metres).

Description: The old wooden barge, *Ontario* (not to be confused with the wreck of the steamer, *Ontario,* in Lake Superior; see p. 366), was built at Welland, Ontario, in 1867. After many years of service in the timber trade in and out the many Georgian Bay ports, the *Ontario* was abandoned to age at this site. Resting along the north river bank just below the second set of rapids heading upstream, the hull is 131' (39.3 metres) long and 24' (7.2 metres) in beam.

Hazards: The Musquash River poses certain navigation problems, mainly deadheads and rocks near its mouth, and getting past the first set of rapids (keep to starboard.) Beware of current and boating traffic while diving or snorkeling.

Site 167: Wreck of the *Chippewa*

Location: Musquash River, about 0.8 mile (1.3 kilometres) upstream from the extreme southern end of Longuissa Pt, north of Penetanguishene, Ontario.

Access: Boat.

Skill Level: Novice - intermediate.

Depth: 6 to 20 feet (1.8 - 6 metres).

Visibility: 4 - 7 feet (1.2 - 2.1 metres).

Description: The 94' (28.2-metre), 132-ton wooden steamer, *Chippewa,* lies very close to where she was built and launched at Muskoka Mills, at the mouth of the Musquash River, in 1874. After being a workhorse in the local Georgian Bay lumber trade for over 30 years, the vessel was abandoned to age in 1906 at her present site on the west side of the river.

Hazards: Some river current and boaters could pose problems for divers; caution must be used at this site.

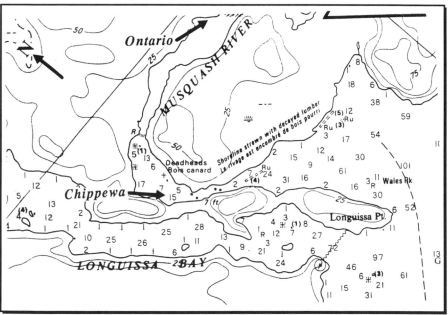

The Charts and Publications Regulations of the Canada Shipping Act require vessels operating in Canadian waters to carry the latest, best scale, corrected Canadian Hydrographic Service (CHS) charts. This document does not meet the requirements of the Act. (Portion of CHS chart 2202,

Site 168: The Galbraith Island Tug

Location:	Offshore, halfway between Penetanguishene and Parry Sound, Ontario.
Access:	Boat (shore from Galbraith Island).
Skill Level:	Novice.
Depth:	To 10 feet (3 metres).
Visibility:	4 - 7 feet (1.2 - 2.1 metres).

Background: This wooden tug remains unidentified.

Directions and Description: Lying in zero to 10' (3 metres) of water in an inlet at the northeast corner of Galbraith Island, a 53' (16-metre) portion of the keel, with remnants of framing attached to it, is of interest to divers.

Hazards: Considering the seclusion of this wreck nestled in a quiet cove, this site is very good for snorkeling or novice shipwreck diving.

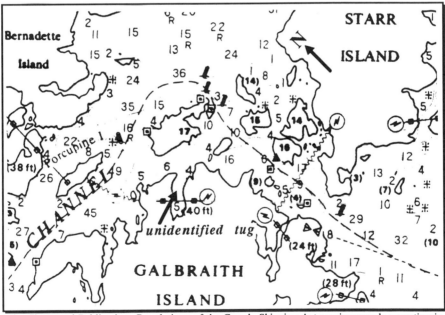

The Charts and Publications Regulations of the Canada Shipping Act require vessels operating in Canadian waters to carry the latest, best scale, corrected Canadian Hydrographic Service (CHS) charts. This document does not meet the requirements of the Act. (Portion of CHS chart 2202,

Site 169: Wreck of the *W.J. Martin*

Location:	At Middle Rock, between Ward Island and Fairlie Island, halfway between Penetanguishene and Parry Sound, Ontario.
Access:	Boat.
Skill Level:	Novice.
Depth:	5 - 20 feet (1.5 - 6 metres).
Visibility:	5 - 12 feet (1.5 - 3.6 metres).

Background: The small (75', or 22.5-metre) wooden steamer, *W. J. Martin,* existed for only two months. Launched at Midland, Ontario, in September, 1905, she burned to a complete loss in November of that year.

Description: Adjacent to the small craft channel, the boiler of this short-lived vessel acts as a focal point of interest. The remains of the hull are also appealing to snorkelers and scuba divers.

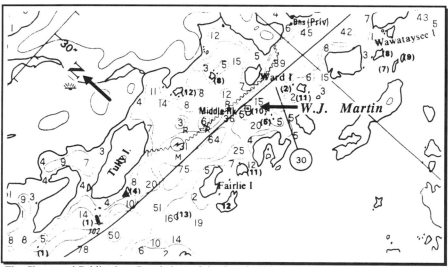

The Charts and Publications Regulations of the Canada Shipping Act require vessels operating in Canadian waters to carry the latest, best scale, corrected Canadian Hydrographic Service (CHS) charts. This document does not meet the requirements of the Act. (Portion of CHS chart 2202,

Lake Simcoe/Muskoka Area

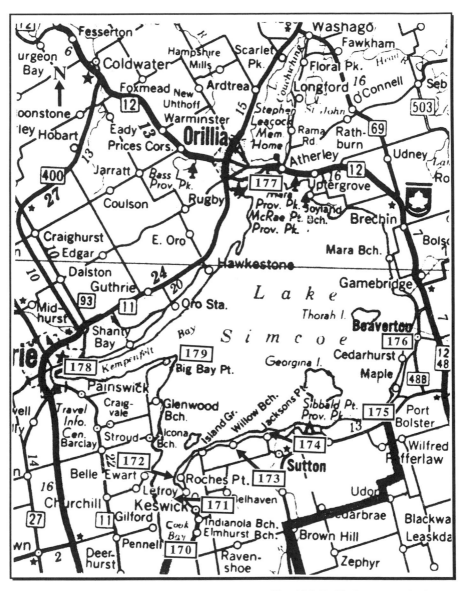

Site 170: Cook's Bay
Site 171: "Four Friends Reef", Keswick
Site 172: Roches Pt. government dock
Site 173: Willow Beach
Site 174: Jacksons Point gov't dock.

Site 175: Pefferlaw gov't dock
Site 176: Beaverton gov't dock
Site 177: Orillia dock
Site 178: Barrie government dock
Site 179: Big Bay Pt. gov't dock

Site 170: Lake Simcoe: Cook's Bay

Location: Extreme southern section of Lake Simcoe.
Access: Preferably boat.
Skill Level: Novice - intermediate.
Depth: 10 - 20 feet (3 - 6 metres) average, 40 feet (12 metres) maximum.
Visibility: 1 - 12 feet (extremely variable).
Description: This historic region of Lake Simcoe has been known to produce numerous old bottles cast away at the turn of the century.
Hazards: Extremely low visibility (frequently making this a "Braille dive") is one hazard. The large amount of pleasure boating that goes on here is another potential danger for the scuba diver. Always fly a divers down flag. Please respect the rights of property owners (hence the recommendation that you utilize a boat for dive site access.)

Site 171: "4 Friends Reef," Keswick

Location: North of the town of Keswick, Cook's Bay, southern Lake Simcoe. Line up Snake Island and Roches Pt.
Access: Boat.
Skill Level: Novice - intermediate.
Depth: 30 feet (9 metres) maximum.
Visibility: 3 - 12 feet (variable; conditions-dependent).
Description: This manmade reef, named in commemoration of four fishermen who died in a boating accident in the early 1960's, was built in 1965 under the sponsorship of the Ontario Underwater Council. Two sets of two 10' by 10' (3 metres by 3 metres) wooden crates, with the pairs set back-to-back about 10', or 3 metres, apart, and weighed down with rocks, comprise this reef, which is marked with a small buoy in the summer. This fish life on this reef is quite intense, consisting mostly of bass. A plaque explaining the reef's purpose is cleaned twice a year by local divers.
Hazards: The fishing and boating traffic can be heavy during the summer, and low visibility can plague visiting divers.

Site 172: Roches Point Dock

Location:	Northern portion of Cook's Bay, southern Lake Simcoe.
Access:	Shore.
Skill Level:	Novice - intermediate.
Depth:	20 - 30 feet (6 - 9 metres).
Visibility:	4 - 12 feet (1.2 - 3.6 metres).
Description:	This lightly-grassed underwater area off the government dock is rich in fish life, particularly bass and pike. This is a good site for night-diving.
Hazards:	Beware of boating traffic. Fly a divers down flag whenever any diver is in the water.

Site 173: Willow Beach

Location:	On the southern shore of Lake Simcoe, between the communities of Island Grove and Jacksons Point.
Access:	Shore.
Skill Level:	Novice - intermediate.
Depth:	To 25 feet (7.5 metres).
Visibility:	4 - 10 feet (1.2 - 3 metres).
Description:	In the winter, Willow Beach serves as access point for ice fisherpeople's equipment: huts, trucks, snowmobiles, etc. In early spring, some of these fisherpeople become careless, and costly equipment goes through the thinning ice. This is the ideal time to explore this area underwater.
Hazards:	Make sure any leftover ice has disappeared before venturing out from shore; the past has proven that it is all too easy for experienced divers to accidentally find themselves under a layer of retreating ice. In the warmer months, fly a divers down flag to alert boaters of your presence.

Site 174: Jacksons Point

Location: South shore of Lake Simcoe.
Access: Shore or boat.
Skill Level: Novice - intermediate.
Depth: To 20 feet (6 metres).
Visibility: 5 - 15 feet (1.5 - 4.5 metres).
Description: Submerged in about 8' to 20' (2.4 - 6 metres) of water off the concrete government dock lie the remains of the original wooden dock which served as a loading platform for, among other things, supplying the nearby Indian reservation of Georgina Island. These enormous timbers extend approximately 200' (60 metres) offshore and are in three large sections that are about 15' (4.5 metres) apart. Game fish such as bass hover in these timbers. Pike linger in the shallow, grassy area to the right of this dock. This can also be a scrounge dive, locating items lost or discarded by several generations of boaters.
Hazards: This area is one of the busiest during summer months. Swarms of people come here to enjoy the swimming and boating, so use caution and a divers down flag when scuba diving.

Site 175: Pefferlaw Dock

Location: Pefferlaw, southeast Lake Simcoe.
Access: Shore.
Skill Level: Novice - intermediate.
Depth: 30 feet (9 metres).
Visibility: 4 - 12 feet (1.2 - 3.6 metres).
Description: A good area for scrounging is off the government dock at Pefferlaw, where the depth is 30' (9 metres).
Hazards: The river running into the lake here clouds visibility; keep the diving limited to the south for the best vis. Boating traffic is heavy, since there are marinas nearby. Fly a divers down flag when diving.

Site 176: Beaverton Dock

Location:	Off Beaverton, on eastern Lake Simcoe.
Access:	Shore.
Skill Level:	Novice - intermediate.
Depth:	20 - 30 feet (6 - metres).
Visibility:	4 - 12 feet (1.2 - 3.6 metres).
Description:	Once again a good site for scrounging around for lost items on the bottom, there is the added thrill of sighting numerous fish due to the nearby fish sanctuary.
Hazards:	Boating traffic can get heavy, so use great caution and a divers down flag

Site 177: Orillia Dock

Location:	North end of Lake Simcoe.
Access:	Shore.
Skill Level:	Novice - intermediate.
Depth:	To 27 feet (8.1 metres).
Visibility:	3 - 10 feet (0.9 - 3 metres).
Description:	There is a wide range of underwater debris (beer cans, bicycles, etc.) to be located here at the Orillia town dock.
Hazards:	Extreme caution must be used because of the large number of pleasure boats in the water. Low visibility will frequently be encountered.

The *Waome* (see p.298-299)

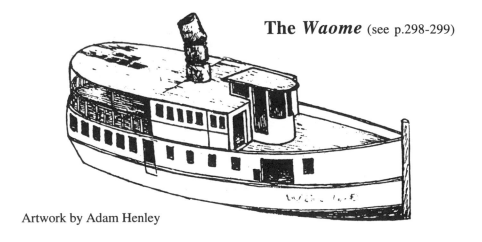

Artwork by Adam Henley

Site 178: Barrie Dock

Location:	Barrie is on the western side of Lake Simcoe.
Access:	Shore.
Skill Level:	Novice - intermediate.
Depth:	To 28 feet (8.4 metres).
Visibility:	3 - 10 feet (0.9 - 3 metres).
Description:	This is definitely a scrounge-divers heaven. Over the years, everything from bicycles, shopping carts, cars, fishing rods, milk crates, old bottles, store mannequins, and late-night party-boat drop-offs have been deposited.
Hazards:	As with any fair-size city's marina, there are hordes of boats for which divers must be on the lookout. Fly a divers down flag. Low visibility can also be a problem.

Site 179: Big Bay Point Dock

Location:	Kempenfelt Bay, on the east shore of Lake Simcoe. Two of the many good entry points are at Minet Point, which is a small provincial parkland area across the bay from Barrie, and the government dock at Big Bay Point, at the mouth of Kempenfelt Bay.
Access:	Shore.
Skill Level:	Intermediate - advanced.
Depth:	To 140 feet (42 metres) at the deepest spot.
Visibility:	4 - 15 feet (1.2 - 4.5 metres).
Description:	The drop-off to very deep water sometimes begins quite close to shore (about 100', or 30 metres, offshore). The marine life is at its best in this deep, dark, cold bay, including the legendary "Kempenfelt Kelly" sea monster. Numerous small-vessel shipwrecks are also located in this area.
Hazards:	The darkness and depth of this bay are hazards. Bring a dive light if going deep. Plan your dive carefully.

The Muskoka Lakes

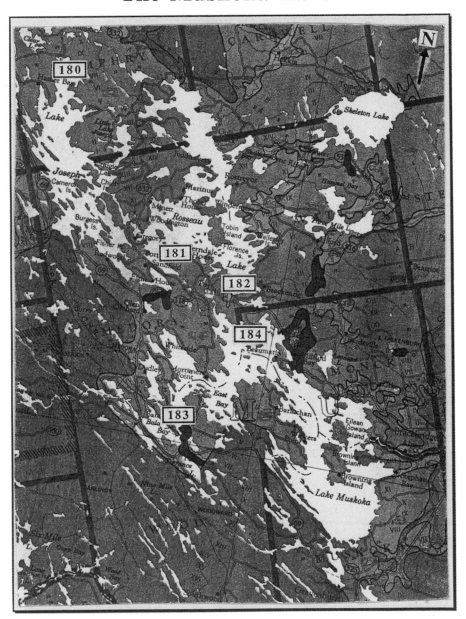

Site 180: The Wreck of the *Nipissing* Site 183: Bala Falls/ Moon River
Site 181: Port Sandfield channel Site 184: The Wreck of the *Waome*
Site 182: Port Carling dock

Site 180: Lake Joseph: *Nipissing*

Location:	Off Blueberry Island, northern part of Lake Joseph. Access is from a gravel road connected to Highway 69 just past Hamer Bay.
Access:	Boat.
Skill Level:	Novice - intermediate.
Depth:	10 - 23 feet (3 - 6.9 metres).
Visibility:	8 - 25 feet (2.4 - 7.5 metres).
Description:	The broken up remains of the inland steamer, *Nipissing,* lie just off Blueberry Island. The rock and sand bottom prevents silting, so good visibility is almost always guaranteed. Much fish life abounds, especially bass. This site is excellent for underwater photography.
Hazards:	The occasional bit of boating traffic is the only real hazard. Fly a divers down flag when you dive here.

Site 181: Port Sandfield Channel

Location:	Between Lake Rosseau and Lake Joseph.
Access:	Shore or boat.
Skill Level:	Intermediate - advanced.
Depth:	To 20 feet (6 metres); much deeper on the Lake Rosseau side, around the bend (to about 120', or 36 metres).
Visibility:	8 - 25 feet (2.4 - 7.5 metres).
Description:	The Port Sandfield Channel links Lake Joseph and Lake Rosseau. If you drift dive, you can allow the current to sail you down the channel into the deeper hole on the Lake Rosseau side. Here you will find remains of a majestic old hotel which used to sit on the point of land. More experienced divers can swim around that point of land and explore the wall which plunges straight down to over 100' (30 metres).
Hazards:	There is usually a mild current running in the channel. The main problem will be the heavy boating traffic during weekends and summers.

Site 182: Port Carling Dock

Location:	Historic Port Carling sits between Lake Rosseau and Lake Muskoka.
Access:	Shore.
Skill Level:	Novice - intermediate.
Depth:	To 30 feet (9 metres).
Visibility:	5 - 15 feet (1.5 - 4.5 metres).
Description:	Good scrounge diving in quest of old bottles and other items is possible right in the harbour by the government dock.
Hazards:	This being a harbour, the boating traffic can be quite heavy. Always fly a divers down flag and use constant caution.

Site 183: Bala Falls/Moon River

Location:	At the western side of Lake Muskoka.
Access:	Shore or boat.
Skill Level:	Variable, novice to advanced, depending upon depth.
Depth:	22 - 100 feet (6.6 - 30 metres).
Visibility:	8 - 25 feet (2.4 - 7.5 metres).
Description:	There are three levels of underwater cliffs just off the site of the old hotel, one to 22' (6.6 metres), another to 40' (12 metres), and the third to 100' (30 metres). Many pices of pottery and china have been located here and appreciated by divers. Adjacent to the Foodland grocery store near the waterfalls, a gentle drop to about 35' (10.5 metres) to the falls barrier provides an interesting dive. In the Moon River below the waterfalls, the constant, cleansing current creates good visibility, as well as a variety of large game fish finding the base of the falls an ideal feeding spot.
Hazards:	At the waterfalls, there is, of course, a certain amount of current. Approach with caution and according to the level of your experience.

Site 184: The Wreck of the *Waome*

Location:	North Lake Muskoka, near Milford Bay.
	This shipwreck lies off Keewaydin Island.
Access:	Boat.
Skill Level:	Intermediate - advanced.
Depth:	50 - 74 feet (15 - 22.2 metres).
Visibility:	4 - 8 feet (1.2 - 2.4 metres).

Background: Originally launched as the steamer *Mink* at Gravenhurst in 1912, this steel-framed, 60.18-ton vessel measured 78' (23.4 metres) in length and 14' (4.2 metres) in beam. On May 28, 1928, new owners registered this ship, renamed the *Waome* (pronounced "Way-OH-mee," an Ojibwa word meaning "water lily.") at Toronto. On October 6, 1934, on her last run of the season (hasn't that so often been the case?), and carrying the captain, five crew members, and one passenger (an old-fashioned minister who preferred to travel by ship rather than on the new busline), the *Waome* headed from the upper lakes towards Beaumaris. Off Keewaydin Island, a sudden "dirty-looking piece of weather" from the west caught the vessel unprepared and, without warning, a powerful gust of wind knocked the ship onto her port side and water gushed into her holds. In about one minute, the *Waome* was out of sight, taking with her one crew member and the minister. There had not even been time to launch the solitary lifeboat. The elderly skipper of the vessel succumbed to a heart attack as he swam for his life on the surface. The other four crewmen, swimming in bitterly cold water, were fortunate in reaching Keewaydin Island in about an hour. With a total loss of three lives, the *Waome* passed into history as Muskoka's worst marine disaster.

Description: The *Waome* is considered the premier wreck of the Muskoka Lakes. Sitting upright and intact in dark, tea-coloured water, the vessel 's original white paint still clings to her wood in places. The subtle glow of the bit of light that makes it to this depth reflects eerily off the *Waome's* oak. Entering the vessel is possible; from the upper deck past the wheelhouse, the diver can descend the stairway to the lower deck or head towards the fantail. The interior of the *Waome* can be explored, with a touch of reverence, as well as perhaps with disgust at the sight of wall panels destroyed when divers attempted to pry them loose for use in their own rec rooms. In the engine room, the vessel's permanent inhabitant, a large burbot, or ling, will greet you with a watchful gaze. A brass plaque on the wheelhouse reminds visitors that the *Waome* is part of our marine heritage.

Hazards: The windows on this wreck are gone, and thus offer emergency exits, but one diving fatality at this site (summer, 1989) indicated that the victim had problems getting through one of these windows (see the Ontario Underwater Council's Fatalities Report for further details). Boating traffic can be heavy on summer weekends, so use of a dive flag is wise. Since this water is dark to begin with, take a dive light with you.

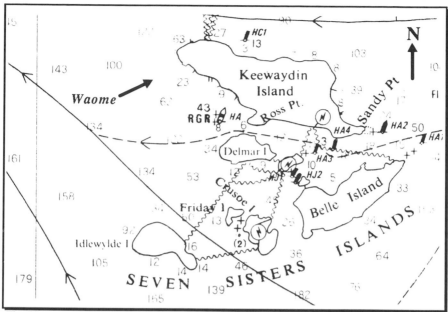

The Charts and Publications Regulations of the Canada Shipping Act require vessels operating in Canadian waters to carry the latest, best scale, corrected Canadian Hydrographic Service (CHS) charts. This document does not meet the requirements of the Act. (Portion of CHS chart 6021.)

The steamship, Waome, *sank on Lake Muskoka on October 6, 1934, with the loss of three lives. She is a popular divesite today.* (Photo: author's collection.)

Worth Checking Out?

There are reportedly two Royal Canadian Air Force jets somewhere in Lake Muskoka that would make interesting divesites. Check out local knowledge about these potential places to explore.

There is a wealth of another generation's garbage lying on the bottom of Lake Muskoka. At the turn of the century, the many luxurious resorts that existed in this area catered to the endless whims of multitudinous well-heeled clients. Since roads were at a premium then, many of these resorts could be reached only by water. Hence, their provisions had to be brought in by boat, and any garbage had to be similarly removed, or, as was likelier the case in those environmentally worry-free times, pitched into a certain, pre-ordained "garbage area" of the lake. With dozens of resorts in operation at the time, scores of old bottle sites have been located, and scores more remain to be found in these lakes.

Sites worth checking out near Peterborough, Ontario, are Young's Point on the Otonobee River (to a depth of 20', or 6 metres), Sturgeon Lake's 20-foot (6-metre) depths, Buckhorn Rapids on the Trent Canal (depth to 20', or 6 metres), and, for advanced divers, a dunk under Fenelon Falls. Please check these out first.

The long-running annual Peterborough Ice Floe Race, sponsored by the Trident Underwater Club of Peterborough, attracts clubs and groups from many provinces and states wishing to get costumed and to push a block of ice a couple of miles down a cold, swift-moving (Otonobee) river. A great way to wake up!

March's annual Peterborough Ice Floe Race offers competition, camaraderie, and individuality, as bag-piping Todd Shannon attests. (Photo by Cris Kohl.)

The Parry Sound Area

Site 185: Harold Pt., Killbear Park

Location:	Due west of Parry Sound, Ontario, but the road access takes one north first, then west, then south again, to Killbear Provincial Park. It's a bit of a walk from the nearest parking lot to Harold Point.
Access:	Shore or boat.
Skill Level:	Variable (depends upon depth).
Depth:	To 40 feet (12 metres); drops off beyond 90' (27 metres) from the ledge.
Visibility:	10 - 25 feet (3 - 7.5 metres).
Description:	This natural, rocky setting within a provincial park is used on occasion as a dive checkout site. Underwater boulders and fish highlight the attractions here.
Hazards:	Beware of boating traffic; fly a divers down flag. Also beware of your depth limitations, and don't accidentally sink too deep!

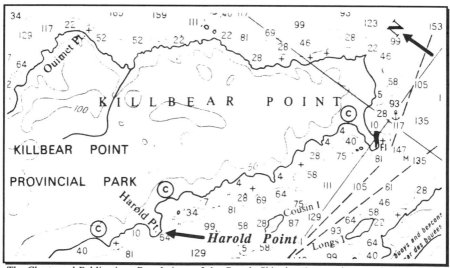

The Charts and Publications Regulations of the Canada Shipping Act require vessels operating in Canadian waters to carry the latest, best scale, corrected Canadian Hydrographic Service (CHS) charts. This document does not meet the requirements of the Act. (Portion of CHS chart 2202,

Site 186: Wreck of the *Waubuno*

Location:	In an inlet on the southern tip of Bradden Island, just north of Wreck Island, halfway between the Musquash River to the south and Parry Sound, Ontario, to the north.
Co-ordinates:	N 45 07' 15", W 80 09' 58"
Access:	Boat; keep off the private island!
Skill Level:	Novice - intermediate.
Depth:	Maximum 15 feet (4.5 metres).
Visibility:	6 - 15 feet (1.8 - 4.5 metres).

Background: The 185-gross-ton, wooden, sidewheel steamer, *Waubuno,* built by John Simpson at Port Robinson, Ontario, in 1865, enjoyed 14 years of service on Georgian Bay before becoming a mystery vessel. On Nov. 22, 1879, the ship left Collingwood with passengers and freight heading for Parry Sound. Another vessel saw the heavily-laden *Waubuno* pass north on the protected east side of Christian Island, while, later, a logging crew on shore near the Moon River heard the vessel's whisle sounding distress signals in a blinding snowstorm. Then she simply disappeared with all 30 hands. The following spring, this washed-up hull was located, but no bodies were ever found. The *Waubuno* had measured 135' (40.5 metres) in length, 18' 3" (5.5 metres) in beam, and 7' (2.1 metres) in draft. There is some speculation that these shipwreck remains are not those of the *Waubuno.*

Description: The hull lies in shallow water (maximum 15', or 4.5 metres), providing a safe habitat for numerous pike, perch, and bass.

Hazards: Sudden westerly winds can be strong and threatening to boats and divers at this wreck site. It is also easier to simply snorkel this location.

The steamer, Waubuno, *mysteriously disappeared.* (Photo: author's collection.)

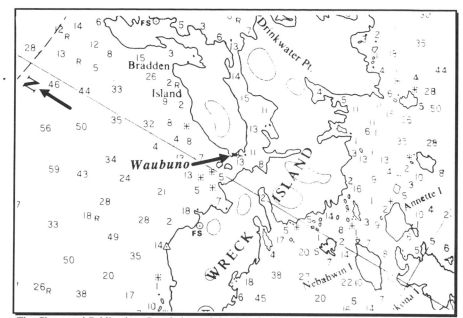

The Charts and Publications Regulations of the Canada Shipping Act require vessels operating in Canadian waters to carry the latest, best scale, corrected Canadian Hydrographic Service (CHS) charts. This document does not meet the requirements of the Act. (Portion of CHS chart 2202,

At the bow of the Waubuno, *diver Kathy Hoey descends for a closer inspection of these historic remains.* (Photo by Cris Kohl.)

Site 187: The *Emma* Shipwreck

Location:	In the Boyd Group of the Thirty Thousand Islands, west-southwest of Parry Sound, Ontario.
Access:	Boat.
Skill Level:	Novice - intermediate.
Depth:	4 - 20 feet (1.2 - 6 metres).
Visibility:	6 - 15 feet (1.8 - 4.5 metres).

Background: Robert J. Morrill of Collingwood, Ontario, constructed the 75-ton, wooden, Canadian, steam yacht, *Emma,* and launched her there on May 1, 1894. Rebuilt in 1901 at Parry Sound, Ontario, she measured 89' 3" (26.8 metres) in length by 18' (5.4 metres) in beam by 6' 6" (2 metres) in draft, with her gross tonnage increased to 146. Bound from Parry Sound to Owen Sound to take advantage of some of the busy, summer tourism, the *Emma* caught fire and burned to a complete loss on the Fourth of July, 1912.

Description: Only the bottom portion of the hull remains of this fire-ravaged vessel. Her engine and boiler were salvaged shortly after her loss.

Hazards: This shipwreck lies in a sheltered cove; there are far more navigational hazards to overcome in getting to this site than there are scuba diving hazards.

The Canadian steam yacht, Emma, *plied the Parry Sound waters at the turn of the century before burning in 1912.* (Photo: Public Archives Canada.)

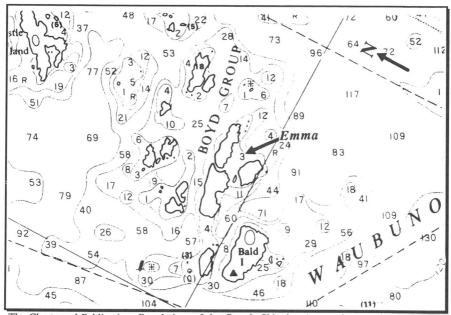

The Charts and Publications Regulations of the Canada Shipping Act require vessels operating in Canadian waters to carry the latest, best scale, corrected Canadian Hydrographic Service (CHS) charts. This document does not meet the requirements of the Act. (Portion of CHS chart 2202, Sheet 3.)

The broken, wooden timbers of the steamer, Emma, *lie hidden in the shallows of a distant, secluded cove.* (Photo by Cris Kohl.)

Site 188: The Wreck of the *Ella Ross*

Location:	Parry Sound, Ontario, harbour..
Access:	Shore or boat.
Skill Level:	Novice - intermediate.
Depth:	20 feet (6 metres) maximum.
Visibility:	4 - 8 feet (1.2 - 2.4 metres).

Background: The iron steamer, *Ella Ross,* built at Montreal by William Webster in 1873, and launched as the *Gypsy,* measured 99' 2" (29.8 metres) in length, 27' 8" (8.3 metres) in beam, and 6' 4" (1.9 metres) in draft, with an original gross tonnage of 325. A subsequent rebuild at Kingston, Ontario, in 1880 left her with a gross tonnage of 228. The name change from *Gypsy* to *Ella Ross* occurred in 1887. On June 5, 1912, the *Ella Ross* burned to a complete loss at her dock in Parry Sound. Her register was closed at Deseronto, Ontario, on Feb. 11, 1913.

Description: Most of the hull remains are buried at the bottom of the harbour, and the superstructure completely burned off. For those reasons, this is not an expecially popular divesite.

Hazards: Boating traffic can be heavy in Parry Sound harbour; always fly a divers down flag and utilize great caution. Low visibility can also hamper a diver's exploration of this site.

The iron steamer, Ella Ross, *burned at Parry Sound in 1912.* (Photo: author's collection.)

The Wreck of the *Ella Ross*

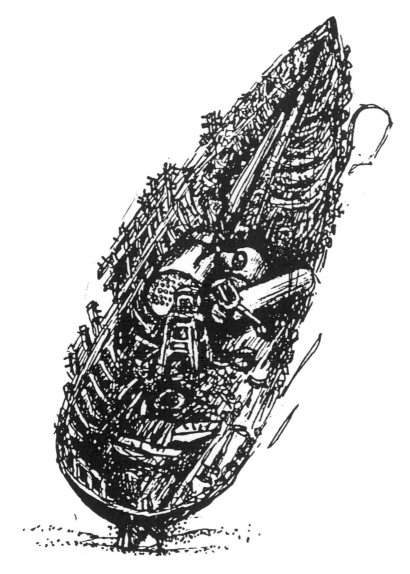

Artwork by Adam Henley

Site 189: The Wreck of the *Atlantic*

Location:	Near the Spruce Rocks, south of Spruce Island, a fair distance west of Parry Sound.
Co-ordinates:	N 45 20' 02", W 80 15' 39"
Access:	Boat.
Skill Level:	Novice - intermediate.
Depth:	5 - 40 feet (1.5 - 12 metres).
Visibility:	8 - 20 feet (2.4 - 6 metres).

Background: Flames fanned by the fierce gale of November 10th, 1903, destroyed, for the second and last time, the combination passenger/package freight steamer, *Atlantic*. No lives were lost, although in her first incineration on May 18, 1882, when she was named the *Manitoulin,* about 30 people perished. Her relatively new hull at that time was raised and the vessel was rebuilt and renamed. Built originally by John Simpson at Owen Sound, Ont., in 1880, this 706-ton wooden propeller measured 147' (44.1 metres) in length, 30' (9 metres) in beam, and 11' (3.3 metres) in draft.

Description: Easily located are the propeller and huge rudder in less than 10' (3 metres) of water. The superstructure totally burned off or caved in on the hull, and, lying there with the stern in the shallows and the bow in the deeper water, the seascape of tangled debris that includes chain, capstan, gears, boiler, engine, and other machinery proves irresistible to divers.

Hazards: Boating hazards are many, as the site lies in the shoal-strewn, island-dotted "30,000 Islands." A west wind can prove dangerous at this open site.

The steamer, Atlantic, *burned twice in her lifetime, in 1882 and 1903.* (Photo: Institute for Great Lakes Research, Bowling Green State University, Ohio.)

The steamer Atlantic's *bow was frequently heavy with excursionists enjoying the natural wonders of a day on Georgian Bay.* (Photo: Archives of Ontario).

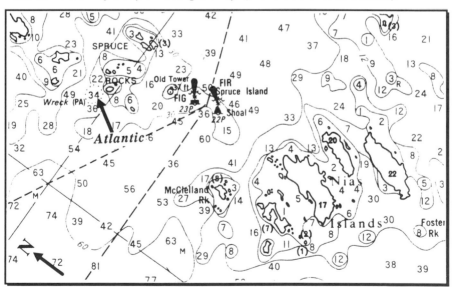

The Charts and Publications Regulations of the Canada Shipping Act require vessels operating in Canadian waters to carry the latest, best scale, corrected Canadian Hydrographic Service (CHS) charts. This document does not meet the requirements of the Act. (Portion of CHS chart 2203, Sheet 1.)

The Wreck of the Steamer, *Atlantic*

Artwork by Adam Henley

The massive steam engine and boiler at the Atlantic *site are certain to impress visiting divers such as Shari Müller. A modern snowmobile lies at the bottom of the shipwreck just off the bow, but the visibility usually diminishes at that depth (about 45', or 13.5 metres) and a thermocline is noticeable. The best shipwreck sights are up in the shallows.* (Photo by Cris Kohl.

Site 190: Blackmore Island Wreck

Location:	30,000 Islands, west of Parry Sound, Ont.
Access:	Boat.
Skill Level:	Novice - intermediate.
Depth:	10 - 20 feet (3 - 6 metres).
Visibility:	7 - 15 feet (2.1 - 4.5 metres).

Background: The background of this unidentified wreck is unknown, although speculation is that this vessel, seemingly not of rugged construction, may have been used as a scow in the timber trade of this area.

Directions: Boating caution must be used in reaching this remote part of the Thirty Thousand Islands. The wreck lies in the shallows just to the south of Schade Island and just to the west of the northern portion of Blackmore Island.

Description: The remains of this vessel measure approximately 85' (25.5 metres) in length and about 20' (6 metres) in beam.

Hazards: There are far greater boating hazards in reaching this site than there are scuba diving hazards once you get there. This is a safe dive site, although the usual vigilance must be maintained.

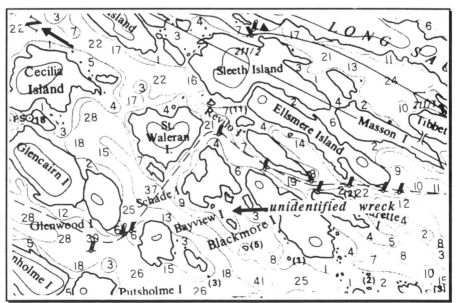

The Charts and Publications Regulations of the Canada Shipping Act require vessels operating in Canadian waters to carry the latest, best scale, corrected Canadian Hydrographic Service (CHS) charts. This document does not meet the requirements of the Act. (Portion of CHS chart 2202,

Site 191: The *Dolphin* Shipwreck

Location:	West of Parry Sound, Ontario, just off the mainland northwest of Snug Harbour.
Access:	Boat.
Skill Level:	Novice - intermediate.
Depth:	30 feet (9 metres).
Visibility:	3 - 10 feet (0.9 - 3 metres).

Background: The locals refer to this small tug as the wreck of the *Dolphin*. If it is, as it seems likely to be the case, this 49' (14.7-metre) vessel was built in 1900 and was owned by James Playfair, a lumber merchant from Midland, Ontario.

Directions: The wreck was moved in recent years from its original location in a quiet backwater area between the mainland and the northern tip of the small, unnamed island to the east of Westyle Island, a short distance to the northwest of Snug Harbour. It is reportedly out in slightly deeper water.

Description: This small ship is broken up and sits on a silt bottom in 30' (9 metres) of water. Her propeller adorns a cottage front on Westyle Island.

Hazards: Adverse weather should be no problem at this site, since it is protected by land from all sides. Divers must use caution not to stir up the silt bottom, as this will result in sudden and enormous loss of visibility.

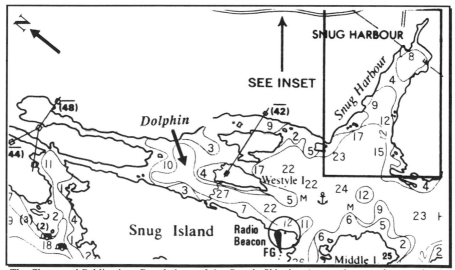

The Charts and Publications Regulations of the Canada Shipping Act require vessels operating in Canadian waters to carry the latest, best scale, corrected Canadian Hydrographic Service (CHS) charts. This document does not meet the requirements of the Act. (Portion of CHS chart 2203, Sheet 1.)

Site 192: Wreck of the *Jane McLeod*

Location:	Off the south part of McLeod Island, in the Thirty Thousand Islands, west of Parry Sound, Ontario.
Access:	Boat.
Skill Level:	Novice - intermediate.
Depth:	20 - 25 feet (6 - 7.5 metres).
Visibility:	6 - 16 feet (1.8 - 4.8 metres).

Background: The 117' (35.1-metre) schooner, *Jane McLeod,* built at St. Catharines, Ontario in 1868, left Parry Sound on Nov. 4, 1890, light after delivering a grain-and-hay cargo. Anchored for the night off what later became known as McLeod Island, she parted her anchor chain and the wind ran her aground. Captain and crew camped, island captives fighting for survival until rescue arrived five days later. The autumn winds battered the schooner until she became totally wrecked.

Description: Lying about 100' (30 metres) from the island's south shore, the bow rests in 20' (six metres) of water with the stern slightly deeper in 25' (7.5 metres). Scattered portions of this vessel cover a wide area.

Hazards: This area is susceptible to sudden, adverse westerly wind conditions.

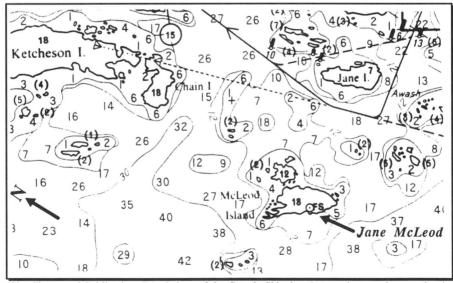

The Charts and Publications Regulations of the Canada Shipping Act require vessels operating in Canadian waters to carry the latest, best scale, corrected Canadian Hydrographic Service (CHS) charts. This document does not meet the requirements of the Act. (Portion of CHS chart 2203,

The Schooner, *Jane McLeod*

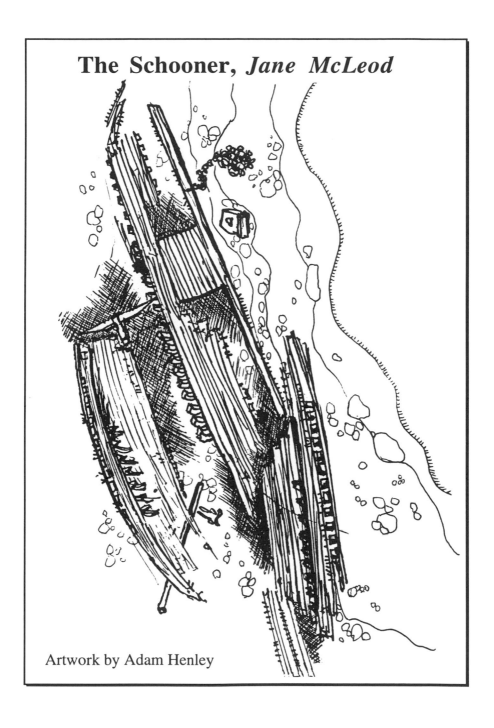

Artwork by Adam Henley

The rocky, almost treeless shoreline seems inhospitable even on a good day, but this is where the survivors of the Jane McLeod *shipwreck set up camp and survived. The wreck lies at the base of these rocks.* Below: *The ships' frames lay exposed on the rocky bottom.* (Photos by Cris Kohl.)

Anchor chain from the schooner, Jane McLeod, *lies tumbled across rocks at the base of the wall that is the island. Diver Shari Müller investigates closely the huge links.* (Photo by Cris Kohl.)

Site 193: Wreck of the *Seattle*

Location:	Just west of Green Island, in the Mink Islands, Georgian Bay, considerably west of Parry Sound, Ontario.
Loran Co-ordinates:	29735.6/48706.8
Access:	Boat.
Skill Level:	Novice - intermediate.
Depth:	15 - 20 feet (4.5 - 6 metres).
Visibility:	10 - 25 feet (3 - 7.5 metres).

Background: The 498-gross-ton, wooden propeller, *Seattle,* built by H. Still in Oscoda, Michigan, in 1892, lasted eleven years on the Great Lakes. The failure of her steeple compound engine in the winds and heavy Georgian Bay seas of Nov. 11, 1903 grounded her on granite at this remote, desolate shoal, where she quickly became a total loss. The *Seattle* measured 160' 7" (48.2 metres) in length, 36' 5" (11 metres) in beam, and 9' 9" (2.9 metres) in draft. No lives were lost.

Description: With calm weather conditions, the boiler (a fire box type, built in Detroit, Mich., by the Dry Dock Engine Works in 1885, measuring 7' by 14', or 2.1 by 4.2 metres) may be easily located. The wreck lies scattered.

Hazards: Since this site is both distant and open, it is susceptible to delays in case of an accident, as well as severe weather from westerly winds.

The steamer, Seattle, *laboured in the Georgian Bay lumber industry.* (Photo: Institute for Great Lakes Research, Bowling Green State University, Ohio.)

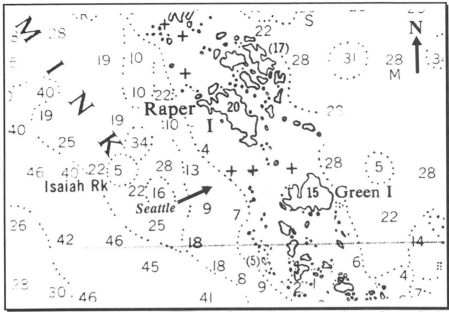

The Charts and Publications Regulations of the Canada Shipping Act require vessels operating in Canadian waters to carry the latest, best scale, corrected Canadian Hydrographic Service (CHS) charts. This document does not meet the requirements of the Act. (Portion of CHS chart 2203,

Shari Müller hovers above one of the large propeller blades that for many years moved the steamer Seattle *from port to port.* (Photo by Cris Kohl.)

Site 194: Wreck of the *Metamora*

Location:	In Shawanaga Inlet, Ontario.
Access:	Boat.
Skill Level:	Novice - intermediate.
Depth:	To 15 feet (4.5 metres).
Visibility:	7 - 16 feet (2.1 - 4.8 metres).

Background: The *Metamora* was a large, 239-gross-ton, wooden tug that measured 115' (34.5 metres) in length, 39' 3" (11.8 metres) in beam, and 10' 8" (3.2 metres) in draft. Built by Peck & Masters at Cleveland, Ohio, in 1864, she was sold to Canadian interests the following year, and served there until her demise over 40 years later. Armour plating and cannon became part of her rigging when she was used in the defense of the Great Lakes against the Fenians, fanatical Irish nationalists attacking from the northern United States in efforts to take Canada hostage to secure Ireland's independence. Later, hauling both passengers and freight on Georgian Bay at the turn of the century, the *Metamora* burned to a complete loss at the east end of Nadeau Island (at the northeast corner of Shawanaga Island) in Shawanaga Inlet 25 miles (40 kms.) from Parry Sound, on September 29, 1907.

Description: Since this vessel burned, there is not much left intact. The stern section is the most alluring portion, since it contains the rudder, steam engine, and propeller. The boiler, which protrudes above water, serves as the foundation for the navigational daymark.

The wooden tug, Metamora, *enjoyed a long and varied career in Canadian waters before burning on Georgian Bay in 1907.* (Photo: Public Archives Canada.)

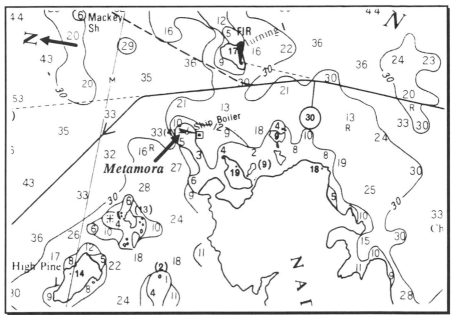

The Charts and Publications Regulations of the Canada Shipping Act require vessels operating in Canadian waters to carry the latest, best scale, corrected Canadian Hydrographic Service (CHS) charts. This document does not meet the requirements of the Act. (Portion of CHS chart 2203, Sheet 2.)

You won't need Loran C or G.P.S to locate the wreck of the Metamora. *The boiler acts as a base for a navigation daymark.* (Photo by Cris Kohl.)

The Metamora's *huge, four-bladed propeller is one of the more interesting shipwreck sights studied by diver Shari Müller.* (Photo by Cris Kohl.)

Site 195: Wreck of the *Midland*

Location: On the east side of the Mink Islands, southeast of the site of the *Seattle* wreck.

Loran Co-ordinates: 29708.4/48718.5

Access: Boat.

Skill Level: Intermediate.

Depth: 50 feet (15 metres).

Visibility: 10 - 25 feet (3 - 7.5 metres).

Description: Built by Robert J. Morrill at Midland, Ontario in 1896 and launched as the *D.L. White,* this 56-ton wooden tug measured 62' (18.6 metres) in length, 13' (3.9 metres) in beam, and 6' 8" (2 metres) in draft. In 1908, her name was changed to the *Midland.* She foundered on Georgian Bay in 1923. Today, the vessel lies on a clay bottom in 50' (15 metres) of water. The propeller and the rudder can be found a bit off the wreck, while the stern is virtually intact. Other items of interest to divers include the bilge pump and the steeple compound engine (built by the John Doty Engine Company in Toronto in 1894).

Hazards: The remoteness of this site, so far away from medical and other aid, makes it potentially hazardous.

The steamer, Midland, *offers many investigative opportunities. Here, diver Shari Müller takes a good look at a valve atop the boiler.* (Photo by Cris Kohl.)

The *Midland* Shipwreck

Artwork by Adam Henley

Site 196: The *Northern Belle* Wreck

Location:	In Byng Inlet, halfway between French River to the north and Shawanaga Inlet to the south.
Access:	Boat.
Skill Level:	Novice - intermediate.
Depth:	10 feet (3 metres).
Visibility:	5 - 12 feet (1.5 - 3.6 metres).

Background: This wooden propeller, launched as the *Gladys* on May 21, 1875, by builder David Lester at Marine City, Michigan, was sold in 1877 to Canadian interests, the Great Northern Transit Company, which renamed her *Northern Belle*. For over twenty years, she served the tiny lumbering communities between Sault Ste. Marie and Collingwood, before burning to a total loss in the narrows at Byng Inlet on Nov. 6, 1898. This 513-gross-ton vessel measured 129' by 22' 6" by 9' 5" (38.7 by 6.7 by 2.8 metres).

Description: The burned remains of this vessel can be located from the surface, resting against the south shore of the inlet, west of Old Mill Island.

Hazards: Beware of the current and occasional boating traffic at this site.

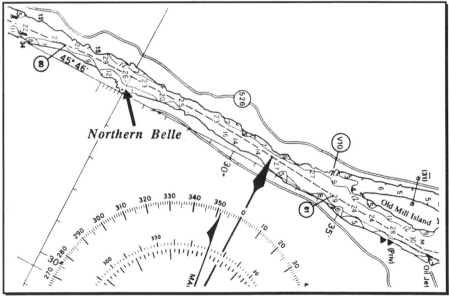

The Charts and Publications Regulations of the Canada Shipping Act require vessels operating in Canadian waters to carry the latest, best scale, corrected Canadian Hydrographic Service (CHS) charts. This document does not meet the requirements of the Act. (Portion of CHS chart 2203,

North Georgian Bay

Site 197: French River Rapids

Location: There are several sets of rapids in the French River, including Recollet Falls, Five Finger Rapids, and Little and Big Pine Rapids.
Access: Shore or boat.
Skill Level: Advanced.
Depth: Usually 10 - 30 feet (3 - 9 metres), but holes can be 65' (19.5 metres) or deeper.
Visibility: Zero to 6 feet (1.8 metres).
Description: Be aware that the French River is a designated Ontario Heritage Site, and as such, nothing may be removed. Ancient Indian pottery, fur trade goods, and any other items must not be disturbed. Recollet Falls is a fun place that is popular with scuba divers. Depth can vary by as much as 15' (4.5 metres), depending on the time of the year (spring run-off can be dangerous.) The visibility can be relatively good, except when there is foam on the water.
Hazards: Diving in rapids must be like being in a toilet when it is flushed. Depth in rapids varies from 10' (3 metres) to 30' (9 metres), and is also dependent upon the time of year. There are deep holes in some parts of this dam-controlled French River, dropping to 65' (19.5 metres) and beyond; supposedly there is one hole 180' (54 metres) deep! An abandoned logging village at the mouth of the river has interesting underwater views. Diving the French River is for advanced divers only.

Site 198: Mattawa River Rapids

Location: East of North Bay, running to the town of Mattawa.
Access: Boat.
Skill Level: Advanced.
Depth: 10 -30 feet (3 - 9 metres).
Visibility: zero to 6 feet (to 1.8 metres).
Description: The Mattawa River Provincial Park is a Heritage Site. Do not disturb or remove anything from this area. The main rapids areas are outlined in the Ministry of Natural Resources brochure on this park.
Hazards: This is for advanced, rapids divers only.

Site 199: L. Nipissing, *John Fraser*

Location: Just east of Goose Island, in the centre of Lake Nipissing.

Access: Boat.

Skill Level: Advanced.

Depth: 50 feet (15 metres).

Visibility: 2 - 6 feet (0.6 - 1.8 metres).

Description: The oak-hulled steamer, *John Fraser,* built in 1888 at Sturgeon Falls on Lake Nipissing, was making its final run of the year across Lake Nipissing on Nov. 7, 1893. Seven crewmembers and 17 lumbermen were aboard. In the middle of the lake, fire broke out near the coal-fueled boiler. Some people sought refuge on a scow which the *John Fraser* was towing, while others resorted to a lifeboat which, unfortunately, overturned, drowning its occupants. Of the total of 24 people on the *John Fraser,* only seven survived. The burned-out hull of the *John Fraser*, along with the steam engine, boiler, and piping, was discovered in 1972 by members of the North Bay Scuba Club. Many artifacts from this site were raised and conserved, and are on display at the small *John Fraser* exhibit in the Nipissing Room of the North Bay Area Museum.

Hazards: Visibility in Lake Nipissing being extremely poor due to the silty bottom, this wreck requires two boats, compasses, and, sometimes, side-scan sonar, to relocate it every year. There are floats attached to it, but people sometimes remove them. The underwater tangle of twisted pipes and rails can also be dangerous to divers who might get snagged on them.

Site 200: Trout Lake

Location: Just east of North Bay, Ontario.

Access: Shore or boat.

Skill Level: Novice - intermediate.

Depth: To 40 feet (12 metres). Do not go deeper.

Visibility: 12 - 25 feet (3.6 - 7.5 metres).

Description: This lake is clear and cold, but pleasant for sightseeing, although there is very little to see.

Hazards: Be aware of submerged trees and branches, and do not get snagged in them.

Site 201: The Wreck of the *India*

Location:	Off West Mary Island, about three miles (5 kms.) northeast of Strawberry Light, North Channel, about 8 miles (13 kms.) from Little Current, Ontario.
Access:	Boat.
Skill Level:	Novice - intermediate.
Depth:	20 - 30 feet (6 - 9 metres).
Visibility:	7 - 25 feet (2.1 - 7.5 metres).

Background: The 976-ton, wooden propeller, *India,* built by Calvin & Company at Garden Island, Ontario, in 1899, burned to a complete loss on September 4, 1928. The vessel had measured 215' 9" (64.7 metres) by 36' 4" (10.9 metres) by 15' (4.5 metres).

Directions: This site is a relatively short jaunt from Killarney, Ontario.

Description: The vessel's keel, mast, boiler, and propeller are the highlights of a visit to this popular site. Schools of sunfish and bass swim between boilers and protruding spikes, while lazy ling lie between the beams.

Hazards: This is a relatively safe site for all levels of divers.

The steamer, India, *ablaze near Little Current on Sept. 4, 1928.* (Photo: Institute for Great Lakes Research, Bowling Green State University, Ohio.)

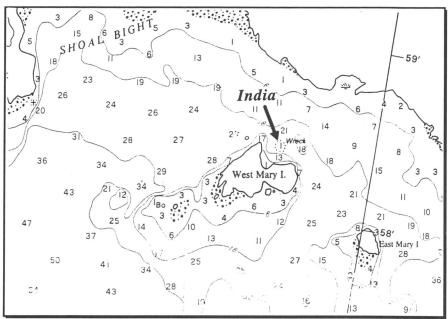

The Charts and Publications Regulations of the Canada Shipping Act require vessels operating in Canadian waters to carry the latest, best scale, corrected Canadian Hydrographic Service (CHS) charts. This document does not meet the requirements of the Act. (Portion of CHS chart 2205.)

Diver Sean Moore examines the braided steel cables attached to a short mast lying off the starboard side of the steamer, India. *(Photo by Cris Kohl.)*

Site 202: Wreck of the *Wilma Ann*

Location:	Adjacent to the Kokanongwi Shingle, southwest of Killarney, Ontario.
Access:	Boat.
Skill Level:	Intermediate - advanced.
Depth:	65 - 80 feet (19.5 - 24 metres).
Visibility:	10 - 20 feet (3 - 6 metres).

Description: It is 65' (19.5 metres) to the top deck of this wooden fishing tug. Built in Owen Sound by Killarney builders in 1932, the *Wilma Ann,* after longtime service as a commercial fishing vessel, was converted for use as a fuel barge, supplying remote communities on Georgian Bay. Abandoned in Parry Sound, the vessel was purchased by the Sportsman's Inn of Killarney in 1983 and scuttled as a dive site. The ship sits upright in mud, intact, including open holds, the wheelhouse, and the after superstructure.

> **NOTE:** The *Wilma Ann* is the property of the Sportsman's Inn and removal of anything from the vessel constitutes theft under the law.

Hazards:	Beware of depth and bottomtime limitations.

Site 203: The *M. J. Low* Shipwreck

Location:	Killarney Bay, northeast of Killarney, Ontario.
Access:	Boat.
Skill Level:	Intermediate - advanced.
Depth:	65 feet (19.5 metres).
Visibility:	10 - 15 feet (3 - 4.5 metres).

Description: The *M.J. Low* was a wooden fishing vessel, built in Killarney and utilized there for many years by a prominent, local fisherman. Scuttled in 1951 by this fisherman, who is still the owner of the sunken vessel, the *M.J. Low* was located by the Sportsman's Inn in 1984 using sidescan sonar. The highlights of a diving visit to this historic site are the wheelhouse, boilers, and steam engine. Unfortunately, a scuba thief has taken the ship's spoked wheel; please leave all items there for future divers to appreciate!

Hazards:	Since this is considered a deep dive, plan it carefully and regulate your bottom time.

Site 204: The *Dove* and the *Branch II*

Location:	Just past the Killarney east light at Red Rock Point, in a protected channel, Killarney, Ontario.
Access:	Boat.
Skill Level:	Novice.
Depth:	23 feet (6.9 metres).
Visibility:	15 - 20 feet (4.5 - 6 metres).
Description:	The 28' (8.4-metre) *Dove* and the 32' (9.6-metre) *Branch II* are two classic Chris Craft double-planked cabin cruisers, purposely scuttled in the 1980's. The sandy bottom makes for excellent visibility. This site is ideal for the new diver, underwater photography, or snorkeling.

Site 205: The "Parking Lot"

Location:	Near the Killarney east light at Red Rock Point, north Georgian Bay, Ontario.
Access:	Boat.
Skill Level:	Novice - intermediate.
Depth:	40 feet (12 metres).
Visibility:	15 - 30 feet (4.5 - 9 metres).
Description:	Labelled "an underwater curiousity that you're not likely to find anywhere else," this manmade site consists of three antique automobiles, two old half tons, and an enormous International truck cab, complete with dual tractors, a fifth wheel, and the doors removed so that divers have no problems getting behind the wheel and "driving" it.
Hazards:	Look out for traffic and don't get caught speeding!

Site 206: The "Silica Wall"

Location:	Near the Indusmin Silica Mine, not too far away from Killarney, Ontario.
Access:	Boat.
Skill Level:	Intermediate - advanced.
Depth:	Sheer drop to 80' (24 metres); rubble to 120' (36 metres).
Visibility:	15 - 30 feet (4.5 - 9 metres).
Description:	This wall dive offers the underwater enthusiast rocks covered with white silica (silica is a hard, glassy mineral found in quartz and sand).
Hazards:	Depth and bottom times must be carefully considered and gauged.

Site 207: The "Boat Rock Wall" Dive

Location:	Close to Badgeley Island, near Killarney, Ontario.
Access:	Boat.
Skill Level:	Advanced.
Depth:	To 110 feet (33 metres).
Visibility:	15 - 30 feet (4.5 - 9 metres).
Description:	This is a vertical wall dive.
Hazards:	Use caution on this deep dive. Watch your depth and bottom time.

Worth Checking Out?

Large, pink, granite boulders and an interesting stone wall with multitudes of crayfish are the sights offered to divers who check out Red Rock Point, just west of the Killarney, Ontario, east light. With a depth to 55' (16.5 metres) and visibility averaging 15' (4.5 metres), this would be considered a novice-intermediate divesite.

Site 208: Collins Inlet Ghost Town

Location:	Collins Inlet, six miles (ten kilometres) east of Killarney, Ontario.
Access:	Shore or boat.
Skill Level:	Intermediate.
Depth:	To 30 feet (9 metres).
Visibility:	8 - 15 feet (2.4 - 4.5 metres).

Background: The town of Collins Inlet was created in the 1880's, and soon boasted a sawmill, boarding house, several privately-owned homes, a store, and a school. The community, however, came to a grinding halt in 1917 when the mill burned down and lumber operations were rerouted to Midland. One building in the "ghost town" of Collins Inlet is still in use as a fish camp, while the rest are in ruins and history.

Directions: Access is either by boat or by car. By car, procede west on Highway 637 from Highway 69 for about 21 miles (35 kms.). Turn onto the old, unsurfaced Pike Road down to the present-day fish camp at Collins Inlet. Boaters can launch at Killarney and head into Philip Edward Channel to Mill Lake and on to Collins Inlet.

Description: Ruins of docks and pilings where the lumber-laden schooners and steamers once tied up can easily be seen. Exploring this area underwater is of interest because turn-of-the-century cast-offs or losses lie here.

Hazards: Beware of sunken logs, trees, and branches and avoid getting snagged on them. Visibility is easily disturbed when rummaging on the bottom.

The schooner, Sephie, *was only one of numerous vessels that loaded lumber at Collins Inlet at the turn of the century.* (Photo: Archives of Ontario)

Site 209: The *Hiawatha* Shipwreck

Location: Little Current, Ontario, at the northeast edge of Low Island, which is, in fact, connected to Manitoulin Island. This wreck is clearly marked on the CHS chart, "Little Current and Approaches" (#2294).

Access: Shore or boat. You can drive close to this site.

Skill Level: Intermediate.

Depth: 5 - 30 feet (1.5 - 9 metres).

Visibility: 3 - 10 feet (0.9 - 3 metres).

Description: The propeller steamer, *Hiawatha,* built at Dresden, Ontario, in 1874, measured 93' (28 metres) in length and 163 tons. She was abandoned at Little Current, Ontario, in about 1930. The wreck of the *Hiawatha* has the remains of a small barge beside it. There are a couple of pulleys and braces at this site that make it interesting.

Hazards: Beware of the usual boating traffic, as well as the fact that, at this site, the silt stirs up quite quickly and severely limits visibility.

For many years, the small steamer, Hiawatha, *plied the waters of the St. Clair River at Sarnia. She was abandoned at Little Current around 1930.* (Photo: The Great Lakes Marine Collection of the Milwaukee Public Library.)

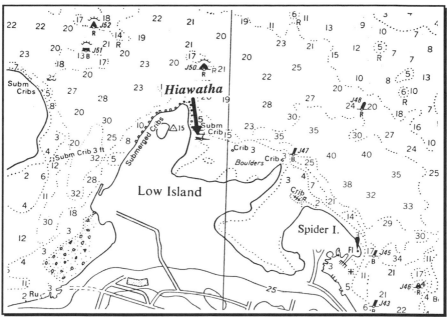

The Charts and Publications Regulations of the Canada Shipping Act require vessels operating in Canadian waters to carry the latest, best scale, corrected Canadian Hydrographic Service (CHS) charts. This document does not meet the requirements of the Act. (Portion of CHS chart 2294.)

Site 210: Wreck of the *Alexandria*

Location:	East end of the government dock at Little Current, Ontario.
Access:	Shore or boat.
Skill Level:	Novice - intermediate.
Depth:	22 - 24 feet (6.6 - 7.2 metres).
Visibility:	5 - 20 feet (1.5 - 6 metres).
Description:	Resting on this rock bottom are the remnants of the small, wooden steamer, *Alexandria,* 91' (27.3 metres) long with a 25' (7.5-metre) beam. The prominent feature identifying this as a shipwreck is the boiler. In fact, most divers would likely pass over the rest of the wreck, namely a bit of bow deadwood with a few hull strakes, without recognizing it as vessel remains. The *Alexandria,* launched in Chatham, Ontario, in 1902, burned at Little Current in 1927.
Hazards:	Due to the enormous amount of boating traffic during the months of June, July, and August, do not dive this site during those times.

Site 211: Killarney Channel

Location: At Killarney, Ontario.

Access: Shore.

Skill Level: Novice - intermediate.

Depth: To 30 feet (9 metres) maximum.

Visibility: 6 - 15 feet (1.8 - 4.5 metres).

Description: The Killarney Channel has historically been a place of refuge for vessels since the last century, and the community of Killarney also stems from that time. Burned and abandoned vessels, as well as garbage from over the years, clutter the bottom of the Killarney Channel. In the 1970's, two scuba colleagues borrowed a total of 17 scuba tanks (this was before there was a dive shop or compressed air available at remote Killarney) and explored the area for several days. Their finds from the channel included hundreds of antique bottles (including entire sets of Quench pop bottles from Owen Sound, with the year of production embossed in the bottom of each bottle) and a brass ship's compass, still mounted on a wooden base, that was found lying in muck on the bottom, looking like garbage -- in fact, the diver cast it aside as junk on his first dive! He was somewhat more observant on his second dive.

Hazards: The voluminous boating traffic in the late spring and entire summer is absolutely hazardous nowadays. Use extreme caution and gauge your diving times well, ideally when boaters are least likely to be active.

Site 212: Sudbury, Windy Lake

Location: At Windy Lake, go straight across the lake and dive in the bay just below the forestry tower.

Access: Shore or boat.

Skill Level: Variable, dependent upon depth (novice to advanced).

Depth: To 60+ feet (27+ metres).

Visibility: 8 - 20 feet (2.4 - 6 metres).

Description: With fish galore in Windy Lake, approach with a sense of piscatory appreciation. There is a steep, sloping, sand and mud bottom. Diving off the old golf course will yield souvenirs from frustrated swingers.

Hazards: Beware of depth limitations, as well as submerged trees onto which divers should not become snagged.

Site 213: Wreck of the *Wanipitee*

Location:	Next to the rock in the middle of Little Detroit Passage, Spanish, Ontario. This rock has an old iron ring (which was used for log booms) in it.
Access:	Boat.
Skill Level:	Novice - intermediate.
Depth:	20 - 30 feet (6 - 9 metres).
Visibility:	4 - 12 feet (1.2 - 3.6 metres).
Description:	This was a general purpose, mail/passenger/freight, tug made of wood.
Hazards:	This is an area of heavy, dangerous boating traffic. The visibility is nothing impressive either; the water is coffee-coloured to begin with, and the silt at the site stirs up easily.

Site 214: Wreck of the *Winona*

Location:	South shore of the entrance to Spragge Harbour.
Access:	Shore or boat.
Skill Level:	Novice - intermediate.
Depth:	10 - 12 feet (3 - 3.6 metres). The upper part is awash sometimes. You may want to snorkel this one!
Visibility:	3 - 6 feet (0.9 - 1.8 metres).
Description:	The passenger and oackage freight steamer, *Winona*, built in 1902 at Port Stanley, Ontario, and burned at Spragge, Ontario, on Nov. 13, 1931, measured 110' (33 metres) in length and 21' (6.3 metres) in beam, with a tonnage of 231.
Hazards:	Beware of boating traffic and low visibility.

Site 215: Wreck of the *North Wind*

Location:	East of Robertson Rock, near Clapperton Island. A two-gallon can, placed every spring by the Dolphin Club of Sudbury, marks the site.
Loran Co-ordinates:	30343.3/48293.4
Access:	Boat.
Skill Level:	Advanced.
Depth:	80 - 110+ feet (24 - 33+ metres).
Visibility:	15 - 35 feet (4.5 - 10.5 metres).

Background: The 2,476-ton steel freighter, *North Wind,* built by the Globe Iron Works, Cleveland, Ohio, and launched on July 31, 1888, measured 299' 5" (89.9 metres) in length, 40' 8" (12. 1 metres) in beam, and 21' 6" (6.4 metres) in draft. She saw six years of service (1917-1923) in the Atlantic Ocean out of Boston; for this location change, she had been cut in half and taken to the coast in two pieces in 1917. Two hours after being stranded on Robertson Rock on July 1, 1926, the *North Wind* slid off into deep water. No lives were lost.

Description: Tie your boat off on the can marker. The name, *North Wind,* is faint on this shipwreck, while two bow anchors and a main anchor winch can be found on the bow. Portholes exist at 80' - 100' (24 - 30 metres). A four-bladed propeller rests on the deck at 110' (33 metres). The wheelhouse, unfortunately, is missing, blown off when the ship sank.

Hazards: This steel shipwreck is starting to cave in; do not attempt to penetrate this shipwreck! Be aware of your depth and bottom time as well.

The steel propeller, North Wind, *ran aground and slide into deep water.* (Photo: Institute for Great Lakes Research, Bowling Green State University, Ohio.)

Site 216: The Tug *Clarence E.*

Location:	Northwest tip of wharf, Providence Bay, Manitoulin Island, Ontario.
Access:	Shore or boat.
Skill Level:	Intermediate.
Depth:	25 feet (7.5 metres).
Visibility:	4 - 12 feet (1.2 - 3.6 metres).
Description:	This tug sank in 1936.
Hazards:	Be cautious of boating traffic.

Site 217: *Thomas J. Cahoon* Wreck

Location: Southwest side of Innes Island, at Kenny Point, inside Kenny Shoal, near Manitoulin Island.

Loran Co-ordinates: 30398.1/48286.1

Access: Boat.

Skill Level: Novice - intermediate.

Depth: Maximum 20 feet (6 metres).

Visibility: 8 - 20 feet (2.4 - 6 metres).

Description: Get to the shallowest spot on Kenny Shoal, then look around on the inside of the reef. Search for straight lines (planking); you can usually see this shipwreck from the surface. Launched in 1881 at Saginaw, Michigan and measuring 166' (50 metres) in length, the 431-ton lumber schooner-barge went ashore here in a storm on Oct. 11, 1913. This vessel was a centreboarder, and the wreckage includes the centreboard, plus bow and stern deadwood.

Hazards: Be cautious about boating traffic in this area.

Site 218: The *Michipicoten* Wreck

Location:	Cook's Dock, or Silverwater Dock, Gore Bay County, Ontario.
Access:	Shore or boat.
Skill Level:	Novice - intermediate.
Depth:	25 feet (7.5 metres).
Visibility:	4 - 10 feet (1.2 - 3 metres).

Background: Built by the Detroit Dry Dock Company of Wyndotte, Michigan, in 1883 and launched as the tug, *E.K. Roberts,* this oak-hulled steamer was renamed the *City of Windsor* in 1890 and given her last name, *Michipicoten,* in 1910. The ship caught fire and was destroyed on Oct. 10, 1927.

Description: The burned-out hull is all that remains of this vessel.

Hazards: Low visibility and occasional boating traffic must be considered when planning this dive.

The steamer, Michipicoten, *a year before she burned.* (Photo: author's collection)

Site 219: The Wreck of the *Winslow*

> **Location:** In the harbour opposite the Net Shed Museum, Meldrum Bay, western end of Manitoulin Island, Ontario.
> **Access:** Shore.
> **Skill Level:** Novice - intermediate.
> **Depth:** 20 feet (6 metres).
> **Visibility:** 4 - 12 feet (1.2 - 3.6 metres).
> **Description:** The tug, *Winslow,* built in 1865 at Cleveland and sunk in 1911, measured 120' (36 metres) in length and 19' (5.7 metres) in beam. The *Winslow* burned at Meldrum Bay on August 21, 1911. The remains lie about 200' (60 metres) from shore.

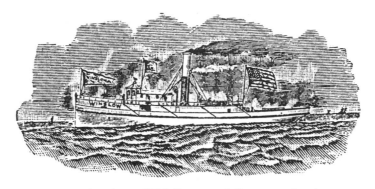

The tug, *Winslow,* in an 1896 Grummond Company advertisement.

Site 220: The *Jacqueline* Wreck

> **Location:** North tip of Clapperton Island, north Georgian Bay, Ontario. There is only one real bay on the north shore of Clapperton Island. The *Jacqueline* lies on the west side of that bay between the first and second stone beaches.
> **Access:** Boat.
> **Skill Level:** Novice.
> **Depth:** 5 - 12 feet (1.5 - 3.6 metres).
> **Visibility:** 15- 25 feet (4.5 - 7.5 metres).
> **Description:** The double-ender car ferry, *Jacqueline,* was abandoned here in the mid-1930's. The hull and some machinery can be seen. This wreck can be seen from the surface.
> **Hazards:** The water drops off quite deep just beyond this point, and that part is for advanced divers only.

Site 221: The Wreck of the *Iroquois*

Location:	East Rock, McBean Channel, about ten miles (16 kilometres) northeast of Spanish Mills, Ontario.
Access:	Boat.
Skill Level:	Novice - intermediate.
Depth:	25 - 30 feet (7.5 - 9 metres).
Visibility:	12 - 25 feet (3.6 - 7.5 metres).

Background: The wooden steamer, *Iroquois,* was destroyed by flames on Oct. 24, 1908. Built by Gregory Fitchner of Wiarton, Ontario, in 1902, and measuring 112' (33.6 metres) in length, 20' (6 metres) in beam, and 8' 7" (2.6 metres) in draft, this passenger and package freighter was owned by the Goderich Engine and Bicycle Company at the time of her demise.

Directions: The green channel marker is about 650' (200 metres) away.

Description: This vessel's superstructure was destroyed by the flames, so only the burned-out hull remains.

Hazards: Beware of the occasional bit of boating traffic.

The steamer, Iroquois, *served for a scant six years.* (Photo: author's collection.)

The St. Mary's River

Site 222: The "Old Schooner" Site

Location: St. Mary's River, west of Sault Ste. Marie, Ontario, off Pointe aux Pins, downstream from the dock and the navigation buoy, abreast of two new cottages.

Access: Shore or boat.

Skill Level: Intermediate - advanced.

Depth: To 43 feet (12.9 metres).

Visibility: 5 - 20 feet (1.5 - 6 metres).

Description: This 120' (36-metre) wooden centreboard schooner, believed to be the *J. Farwell,* which was built in the 1850's and which stranded and sank in the St. Mary's River in August, 1863, lies just off the drop-off, with one end quite close to the sandy, underwater embankment in a bit more than 30' (9 metres) of water, and the opposite end sloping to a depth of 43' (12.9 metres). Local divers discovered this shipwreck in 1961. The ship's rudder, which had been "recovered" by divers in the late 1970's, was returned to the site on Aug. 7, 1989, by the Sault Ste. Marie chapter of Save Ontario Shipwrecks.

Hazards: The current is fast at this site, so have some river diving experience. Boating traffic can also get heavy, so use a divers down flag.

Site 223: The Beechcraft Airplane

Location: The St. Mary's River, west of the Sault, off Pointe aux Pins, about 1100' (330 metres) downstream from the "old schooner" site.

Access: Shore or boat.

Skill Level: Intermediate - advanced.

Depth: 42 feet (12.6 metres).

Visibility: 6 - 15 feet (1.8 - 4.5 metres).

Description: Local scuba divers purposely planted this vintage Beechcraft 18 airplane in the river on June 5, 1982 about 75' (22.5 metres) upstream from the old schooner, but a huge "seiche" (inland lake tidal-like wave) swept the plane downstream on July 15, 1988, leaving a trail of scattered wreckage. The plane finally came to rest upside down.

Hazards: The current can pose a problem for inexperienced river divers. Boating traffic can also be heavy, so use a divers down flag.

Worth Checking Out

On August 28, 1991, an unusual commemorative gesture occurred near Sault Ste. Marie, Ontario. A 2,400 pound concrete block with an engraved brass plaque was lowered over the side of the 65-foot (19.5-metre) tugboat, *Tolsma Bay,* and placed about ten feet (three metres) off the bow of the "old schooner" (see preceding page) in the St. Mary's River.

The memorial is dedicated to the memory of David Eric Peer, a Master SCUBA Instructor who had been in the business in the Sault for many years, and who had passed away exactly a year, to the day, of the placing of this marker.

The underwater memorial, the first in the Great Lakes dedicated to a diver, sits in 42' (13 metres) of clear, blue Lake Superior water near Pointe aux Pins, west of Sault Ste. Marie.

The Loran co-ordinates are 31030.4/47820.5. Dive in some time, and pay the memorial a visit!

The David Eric Peer Underwater Memorial was placed, mainly, by (from left to right) Hugh Wyatt, Mark Iskrowicz, Ken Wyatt, and Norm McLaren. (Photo by Bonnie Shelly.)

Site 224: The Schooner *B. F. Bruce*

Location:	Lower St. Mary's River, at Sailor's Encampment, channel marker C "15".
Access:	Shore or boat.
Skill Level:	Advanced.
Depth:	30 feet (9 metres).
Visibility:	3 - 10 feet (0.9 - 3 metres).
Description:	The wooden schooner, *B.F. Bruce,* sank in October, 1895. It was located on August 8, 1969 by five divers from the Sault area.
Hazards:	The incredibly low visibility sometimes and the fast speed of the current make this location an advanced dive site. Beware of boating traffic also.

Site 225: Pointe aux Pins

Location:	A few kilometres west of Sault Ste. Marie, Ontario.
Access:	Shore or boat.
Skill Level:	Intermediate - advanced.
Depth:	To 45 feet (13.5 metres).
Visibility:	4 - 12 feet (1.2 - 3.6 metres).
Description:	Pointe aux Pins is famous as being the first shipyard on Lake Superior, being used by early explorers from 1730 to 1836. One can drift dive from Pointe Louise to Furkey's Marina searching for antique bottles.
Hazards:	The diver should have some experience in current diving. Since boating traffic is heavy, a dive flag is strongly recommended.

Site 226: Garden River Drift Dive

Location: The community of Garden River is located east of
Sault Ste. Marie, Ontario, on the St. Mary's River.
Access: Shore.
Skill Level: Novice - intermediate.
Depth: To 30 feet. (9 metres).
Visibility: 4 - 12 feet (1.2 - 3.6 metres).
Description: This scavenge dive site is usually done along the steep
underwater clay bank, or the "drop-off." Many antique bottles, including an
embossed infants' nursing bottle and patent medicine bottles, have been seen here,
just downstream from the village of Garden River. Near the former site of a late
19th century cookhouse is the underwater area known as the "bone yard" where
cattle bones and horns lie in abundance. Divers can also appreciate discarded
cooking utensils, axes, saws, and other broken garbage.
     Hazards: There is a bit of a current at this site, and caution
should be used regarding boating traffic. Fly a divers down flag.

Site 227: St. Joseph's Island

Location: Southeast of Sault Ste. Marie, Ontario.
Access: Shore or boat.
Skill Level: Novice - intermediate.
Depth: To 30 feet (9 metres).
Visibility: 6 - 20 feet (1.8 - 6 metres).
Description: St. Joseph's Island is rich with history, beginning
with the strategic fort at Old Fort St. Joe Point on the southern portion of the
island during the War of 1812. Most island communities on the waterfront had
their own docks, and exploring around these areas can be rewarding.
     Hazards: Beware of boating traffic. Fly a divers down flag.

Worth Checking Out?: Squirrel Island, just east of Garden River, is a good
antique bottle site. A boat is necessary to get to the island, but once there,
virtually any area offers rewards. Among the many recent finds was a green, blob
top, soda bottle, embossed "James E. Eaton, Mineral Water, Whitewater Wisc."

Lake Superior
Site 228: Wreck of the *Columbus*

Location:	Gargantua Bay, in Lake Superior Prov. Park.
Access:	Shore or boat.
Skill Level:	Novice.
Depth:	To 30 feet (9 metres) maximum.
Visibility:	15 - 30 feet (4.5 - 9 metres).

Background: This large, 328.34-ton, wooden tug, launched as the *John Owen* on March 7, 1874 by the Detroit Dry Dock Company, measured 136' 2" (40.9 metres) in length, 25' 2" (7.5 metres) in beam, and 11' 8" (3.5 metres) in draft. Sold to Canadian interests who changed her name to the *Columbus* in 1907, the vessel worked hauling supplies to Canadian backports on Lake Superior. On Sept. 10, 1909, the *Columbus* caught fire while at dock at Gargantua Harbour, and was cut loose to prevent damage to the dock.

Directions: There is a rough, adventurous road about ten miles (16 kms.) long that runs from the Trans-Canada Highway to within two miles (3.2 kms.) of the abandoned fishing community. At the parking area, launch an inflatable from the rock-strewn shore, or haul your scuba gear along a trail to the site.

Description: The top of the engine shows conspicuously above water in the harbour. The deck and superstructure burned off, but the hull and machinery are interesting and quite photogenic. The *Columbus,* which lies on her port side, had her bow sheathed for light ice work. A capstan, spikes, propeller etc., can be seen in debris. The boiler has toppled over from its firebed.

Hazards: Avoid over-exertion if hauling your equipment to this remote site.

The Columbus *burned to a total loss in 1909 at Gargantua Harbour.* (Photo: Institute for Great Lakes Research, Bowling Green State University, Ohio.)

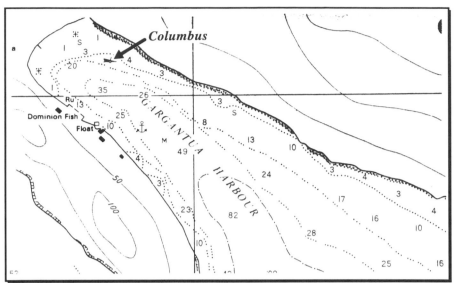

The Charts and Publications Regulations of the Canada Shipping Act require vessels operating in Canadian waters to carry the latest, best scale, corrected Canadian Hydrographic Service (CHS) charts. This document does not meet the requirements of the Act. (Portion of CHS chart 2315.)

The rough road to Gargantua Harbour from the Trans-Canada Highway is nine miles (14 kms.) long, and crosses several rickety bridges. (Photo by Cris Kohl.)

Diver Gary Gentile approaches the Columbus' *propeller, while* (below) *diver Shari Müller marvels at the size of the ship's boiler.* (Photos by Cris Kohl.)

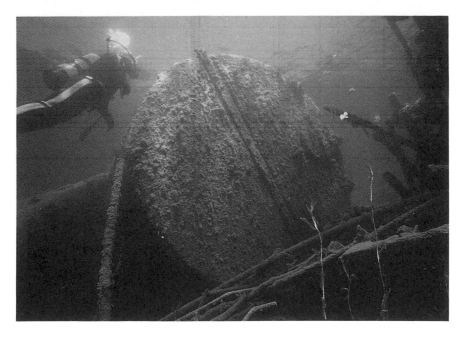

The wreck of the Columbus *offers divers many opportunities to go exploring, particularly in the dramatic engineworks.* (Photo by Cris Kohl.)

Site 229: Cribs and Dredge

Location:	Gargantua Harbour, Lake Superior Provincial Park, just south of Wawa, Ontario.
Access:	Shore.
Skill Level:	Novice.
Depth:	To 30 feet (9 metres).
Visibility:	10 - 25 feet (3 - 7.5 metres).
Description:	On the shore opposite the wreck of the *Columbus* lie the remains of half a dozen submerged cribs and an abandoned flatbed workbarge with cleats and an interesting winch at its stern. Fishing community cast-offs, such as teapots, can be found near the cribs.
Hazards:	Don't get entangled in the branches of any of the submerged trees near the cribs.

An abandoned barge along this former fishing community's shore displays huge cleats and an interesting winch at the stern. (Photo by Cris Kohl.)

Site 230: The *Hiram R. Dixon*

Location: Extreme east end of Quebec Harbour, on the south
                     side of Michipicoten Island.
Skill Level: Novice.
Depth: 10 - 15 feet (3 - 4.5 metres).
Visibility: 8 - 15 feet (2.4 - 4.5 metres).
Description: The 156-ton wooden propeller, *Hiram R. Dixon,* built
at Mystic, Connecticut in 1883, measured 147' 2" x 20' 6" x 9' (44.1 x 6.1 x 2.7
metres) when she burned to a total loss on August 18, 1903. Her machinery was
salvaged, but the process damaged the hull and stern. Nearby along the shore,
beavers are living in the firebox of another shipwreck. The two submerged cribs
and old dock areas marked on the chart of this harbour contain mid-to-late-19th-
century artifacts.

The Hiram R. Dixon *burned to a total loss in 1903 in Quebec Harbour on the
south side of Michipicoten Island.* (Photo: author's collection.)

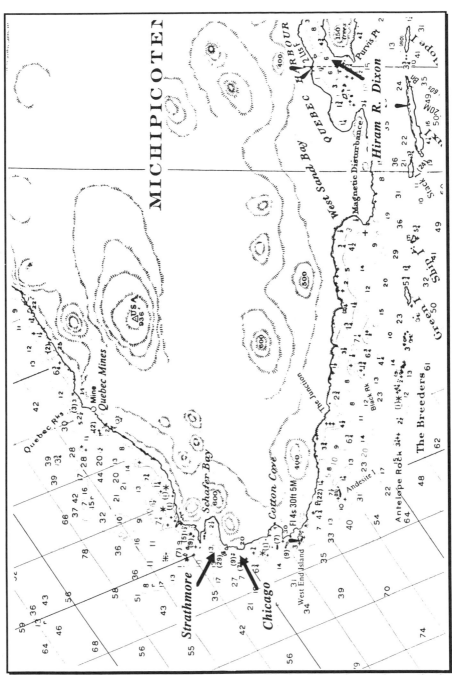

The Charts and Publications Regulations of the Canada Shipping Act require vessels operating in Canadian waters to carry the latest, best scale, corrected Canadian Hydrographic Service (CHS) charts. This document does not meet the requirements of the Act. (Portion of CHS chart 2309.)

Site 231: The *Chicago* Shipwreck

Location:	At Shaffer Bay, western Michipicoten Island, a short distance south of the wreck of the *Strathmore*.
Co-ordinates:	N 47 43' 84", W 85 57' 91"
Depth:	5 - 70 feet (1.5 - 21 metres).
Visibility:	20 - 45 feet (6 - 13.5 metres).
Skill Level:	Intermediate - advanced.

Background: Stranded on October 23, 1929, on the western shores of distant Michipicoten Island, the 3,195-ton, 324' 2" (97.4-metre) steel propeller, *Chicago,* slid into deep water during salvage operations on December 19, 1929. No lives were lost from the 31 people that were on board at the time of the stranding.

The *Chicago* was launched at Buffalo, New York, on Sept. 28, 1901, by the Buffalo Ship Building Company; her first owners was the Western Transit Company.

Description: This wreck lies on her side and offers good visibility and views of a capstan on stern deck, the cargo of zinc ingots, two chains running down a stern hawsepipe, a chain locker, a propeller with a hub, and a "stream anchor".

The bow in the shallows is badly broken up, but still displays a windlass and a popped-out hawsepipe (with the chain still in the pipe).

The huge, steel steamer, Chicago, *plied the waters of the Great Lakes for almost 30 years,* above. (Photo: The Great Lakes Marine Collection of the Milwaukee Public Library.). Below: *Fortunately, no lives were lost from the 31 on board when the* Chicago *stranded on Michipicoten Island on Oct. 23, 1929.* (Photo: The Great Lakes Historical Society, Vermilion, Ohio.)

Site 232: Wreck of the *Strathmore*

Location: In Shaffer Bay, western Michipicoten Island, off an island a short distance north of the wreck of the *Chicago*.
Co-ordinates: N 47 44' 64", W 85 57' 36"
Skill Level: Novice - intermediate.
Depth: 5 - 35 feet (1.5 - 10.5 metres).

Description: Launched in 1871 at Detroit, Michigan, as the *Gordon Campbell*, she was given her last name in 1906. On Nov. 14, 1906, while downbound with a grain cargo, the *Strathmore* ran onto the rocks. She had measured 207' x 33' x 21' (62.1 x 9.9 x 6.3 metres). An engine head comes to within about 5' (1.5 metres) of the surface. An underwater photographer's delight resting on a rock and sand bottom, she displays big eccentric rods, and a complete propulsion system with shafts running off, fading into the distance, to the propeller. At Quebec Harbour, a pair of *Strathmore* bollards stand on a dock, and a *Strathmore* rudder reclines on a lawn.

The Strathmore *was one of the three famous commercial vessels to be lost at Michipicoten Island in this century.* (Photo: author's collection.).

Site 233: The *William O. Brown*

Location:	At Mamainse Point, about 50 miles (80 kilometres) north of Sault Ste. Marie, Ontario.
Access:	Shore or boat.
Skill Level:	Novice - intermediate.
Depth:	30 feet (9 metres).
Visibility:	10 - 25 feet (3 - 7.5 metres).
Description:	The 400-ton, two-masted, wooden schooner, *William O. Brown,* lost in a ruthless west-southwest snow-battering gale which sank three other ships, on Nov. 28, 1872, carried an 18,000-bushel cargo of wheat at the time of her loss. A portion of engine machinery from the wreck of a tug can be seen just offshore the middle of the eastern side of Mamainse Island. This is also an interesting site.
Hazards:	Since this is close to a public harbour, beware of boating traffic around this divesite. Always fly a divers down flag.

Site 234: Montreal River Harbour

Location:	Montreal River Harbour, just south of Lake Superior Provincial Park.
Access:	Boat.
Skill Level:	Novice - intermediate.
Depth:	24 - 35 feet (7.2 - 10.5 metres).
Visibility:	10 - 20 feet (3 - 6 metres).
Description:	Two unidentified, broken-up tugboats lie in shallow water just off the mouth of the harbour.
Hazards:	There is the occasional bit of boating traffic on the surface that divers and boat operators will have to watch.

Site 235: The *Rappahannock*

Location:	Jackfish Bay, near Schreiber, Ontario.
Access:	Boat (shore dive from Jackfish Bay).
Skill Level:	Intermediate - advanced.
Depth:	35 - 85 feet (10.5 - 25.5 metres).
Visibility:	12 - 25 feet (3.6 - 7.5 metres).

Background: The 2,380.8-gross-ton, wooden propeller, *Rappahannock,* built by James Davidson at West Bay City, Michigan, was launched on June 6, 1895. For 16 years, she pursued a normal Great Lakes freighter lifestyle, until, on July 25, 1911, during a severe gale, the *Rappahannock* was manoeuvred into Jackfish Bay and grounded in order to save her. However, she soon filled with water and sank on the steep, underwater incline.

Directions: Launch an inflatable at Jackfish Lake and, heading towards Lake Superior, follow an extremely narrow channel under the Jackfish Bay railway culvert into Jackfish Bay. You may have to get out and pull or push the boat through (a large inflatable is a perfect size; anything bigger won't fit). The wreck is marked with a plastic jug placed by local S.O.S. divers.

Description: The *Rappahannock* is in excellent shape. The hull is intact, with a capstan on display, as well as the ship's wheel, which was returned to the wreck site (and chained to it!) in August, 1989, by members of the Lake Superior chapter of Save Ontario Shipwrecks. Several intact glass windows can be gazed into by the diver as s/he swims along the covered walkway, held up by carved, wooden supports. Below, there is a carpenter's bench, a stove with a pan on it, and much machinery, including a triple expansion steam engine built in Detroit in 1895 by the Frontier Iron Works.

Hazards: This wreck site has a current (a "seiche") divers should be aware of.

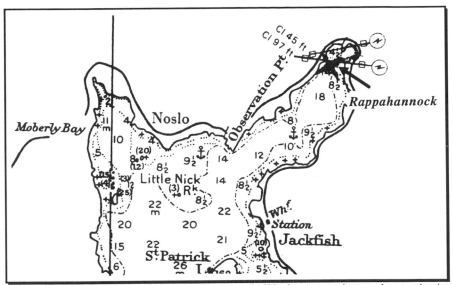

The Charts and Publications Regulations of the Canada Shipping Act require vessels operating in Canadian waters to carry the latest, best scale, corrected Canadian Hydrographic Service (CHS) charts. This document does not meet the requirements of the Act. (Portion of CHS chart 2304.)

The wooden steamer, *Rappahannock,* underway. (Photo: author's collection.)

This photograph was taken in 1989 the day after the long-missing ship's wheel was returned and chained to the Rappahannock *by Ryan LeBlanc (who originally located the shipwreck in 1978) and members of the Lake Superior chapter of Save Ontario Shipwrecks. Unfortunately, in the early summer of 1995, someone stole the wheel again from the site. (Photo by Cris Kohl.)*

Site 236: The *Mary E. McLachlan*

Location:	One mile (1.6 kilometre) offshore, 35 miles (55 kilometres) west of Schreiber, Ontario.
Loran Co-ordinates:	31454.5/46053.0
Access:	Boat.
Skill Level:	Novice - intermediate.
Depth:	15 - 35 feet (4.5 - 10.5 metres).
Visibility:	12 - 30 feet (3.6 - 9 metres).

Description: The huge four-masted schooner, *Mary E. McLachlan,* was hull number 96 built by Frank Wheeler & Company at West Bay City, Michigan, and launched on March 2, 1893. Named after the owner's mother (who never saw her namesake by the time she died in 1899), the impressive vessel measured 251' (75.3 metres) in length, 41' (12.3 metres) in beam, and 16' 2" (4.8 metres) in draft. In October, 1913, when the steamer, *Lackawanna,* lost her rudder gear, the engineless *Mary E. McLachlan* came to the rescue and, lashed to the bigger boat, steered for them both while the steam of the *Lackawanna's* engines furnished the motive power. From 1916 on, the *Mary E. McLachlan* served under Canadian registry, until she foundered on Nov. 7, 1921. The hull is intact, with the decks in 15' (4.5 metres) of water. Artifacts abound here. This wreck was located by Ryan LeBlanc in 1981.

Hazards: Visibility is poor sometimes, since two rivers, namely the Gravel River and the Little Gravel River, flow into the wreck. Algal bloom later in the summer reduces visibility also.

The Mary E. McLachlan *was an enormous, four-masted schooner.* (Photo: The Great Lakes Marine Collection of the Milwaukee Public Library.)

Site 237: *Whaleback Barge 115*

Location:	Seven miles offshore, off the middle of the west end of Pic Island, off Neys Provincial Park.
Access:	Boat.
Skill Level:	Intermediate - advanced.
Depth:	30 - 75 feet (9 - 22.5 metres).
Visibility:	20 - 60 feet (6 - 18 metres). Best in May.

Description: The 256' (76.8-metre), 1,169-ton, ore-laden *Whaleback Barge 115,* towed by the whaleback, *Colgate Hoyt,* broke away during a severe snowstorm on Dec. 13, 1899. For five days, the ship and her crew were pitched around northern Lake Superior before grounding on Pic Island. It took four more days of fighting for survival before the nine crewmen were rescued.

This shipwreck was located by Ryab LeBlanc in 1980. Wreckage from *Whaleback Barge 115* can be located as distant as 50' up on the cliffside, amongst the delicate rock flowers and other plants groping for a foothold on the cliff-face. Underwater, only the bow is intact and sits on a rock bottom. The forward section with the deckhouse is a good dive. Artifacts such as the bell are on display at the nearby provincial park visitors' centre.

Hazards: This is a very weather-dependent dive site. Be prepared for sudden changes in weather that could have an effect upon your access to, or departure from, Pic Island. Two of us were once "trapped" for over two hours when the weather suddenly worsened and the wind and waves picked up. Fortunately, the inflatable boat was relatively safe in a small, protected cove, and we gathered some dry firewood before the rain started, and built a small, heat-radiating campfire beneath one of the cliff overhangs which kept us dry. The bad weather did not last long, fortunately, and we were able to find a break in the weather and return quickly to the mainland.

After storms, the rivers and streams flowing into Lake Superior at Pic Island carry an incredible amount of natural debris, such as logs and mud. This could easily affect diving visibility and turn it into pea soup at the shipwreck site, even though Pic Island is several miles offshore, and, depending upon how fast you are used to cruising in your boat, an abundance of logs or "deadheads" could also have a detrimental effect upon a trip.

Whaleback Barge 115 *was of a quite unique design.* (Photo: author's collection.)

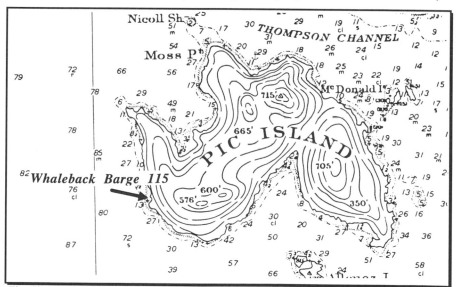

The Charts and Publications Regulations of the Canada Shipping Act require vessels operating in Canadian waters to carry the latest, best scale, corrected Canadian Hydrographic Service (CHS) charts. This document does not meet the requirements of the Act. (Portion of CHS chart 2304.)

A very small cove on Pic Island offers small boat sanctuary at the site of the Whaleback Barge 115. (Photo by Cris Kohl.)

Bits and pieces of the steel Whaleback Barge 115 *ended up a fair distance inland on Pic Island due to the forces of nature.* (Photo by Cris Kohl.)

Site 238: Wreck of the *Ontario*

Location:	At the east end of Battle Island, seven miles (11 kms.) offshore from Rossport, Ontario.
Loran Co-ordinates:	31426.7/46178.0
Lat./Long. Co-ordinates:	N 48 45' 20", W 87 31' 99"
Access:	Boat.
Skill Level:	Novice - intermediate.
Depth:	10 - 40 feet (3 - 12 metres).
Visibility:	13 - 40 feet (4 - 12 metres); best in August.

Background: The wooden passenger/freight steamer, *Ontario,* rebuilt as a 723-gross-ton bulk carrier the year before her career ended, smashed onto the rocks in the shallows just off the eastern end of Battle Island on August 10, 1899, while bound for Nipigon, Ontario, with a cargo of coal. No lives were lost. The *Ontario* had been constructed by Simpson & Chisholm at Chatham, Ontario, in 1874, and measured 181' (54.3 metres) in length, 35' (10.5 metres) in beam, and 12' 2" (3.6 metres) in draft.

Description: This shipwreck was originally located by Ryan LeBlanc of nearby Schreiber in 1977. A landmark to the site of this wreck is one of *Ontario's* huge boilers on shore. The other boiler lies in about 10' (3 metres) of water just offshore. The wreck is broken up and scattered, lying on a rock and sand bottom, with timbers extending around the point to the north of the land boiler. The Superior chapter of Save Ontario Shipwrecks placed marker tags on this wreck so visiting divers could identify parts.

Hazards: Visibility can be low due to algal blooms and other natural growth.

The steamer, Ontario, *sank in a storm in the summer of 1899.* (Photo: The Great Lakes Marine Collection of the Milwaukee Public Library.)

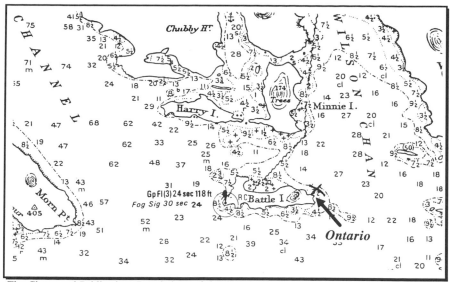

The Charts and Publications Regulations of the Canada Shipping Act require vessels operating in Canadian waters to carry the latest, best scale, corrected Canadian Hydrographic Service (CHS) charts. This document does not meet the requirements of the Act. (Portion of CHS chart 2303.)

Joyce Hayward and Ryan LeBlanc explore the huge Ontario *boiler that Mother Nature beached on the rocky shore adjacent to the site.* (Photo by Cris Kohl.)

Site 239: Wreck of the *Neebing*

Location:	Off the north tip of Moss Island, in the Nipigon Straits, Ontario.
Access:	Boat.
Skill Level:	Intermediate - advanced.
Depth:	60 - 100 feet (18 - 30 metres).
Visibility:	6 - 20 feet (1.8 - 6 metres).
Description:	The *Neebing,* launched as the *John B. Ketcham II* on

May 21, 1892, at Toledo, Ohio, by the builder, the Craig Shipbuilding Company, passed into Canadian registry in 1913, had her name changed to the *Coalhurst* in 1927 and, finally, to the *Neebing* in 1928. Converted to a 1,109-gross-ton gravel carrier in 1937, she foundered in Nipigon Straits on Sept. 24, 1937, while hauling a load of gravel from Paradise Island bound for Red Rock, Ontario, with the barge *Coteau* in tow. Five lives were lost. Her measurements were 193' (57.9 metres) of length, 40' 5" (12.1 metres) of beam, and 12' 3" (3.7 metres) of draft. This wreck is not badly broken up at all. There is a huge crane worth seeing, and the missing wheelhouse, with the wheel, may be nearby.

Hazards: The wind and the river combine, from out of Nipigon Bay, to chew up the visibility, which is usually under 10' (3 metres). A north wind is bad, because it pushes the dirty water out into the lake.

The Neebing *sank in 1937 with five lives lost.* (Photo: author's collection.)

Site 240: The *St. Andrew* Shipwreck

Location: Off tiny St. Andrew's Island, north shore of Lake Superior, Ontario.

Access: Boat.

Skill Level: Intermediate - advanced.

Depth: 40 - 60 feet. (12 - 18 metres).

Visibility: 25 - 40 feet (7.5 - 12 metres).

Description: Launched originally as the *W. B. Hall* at the Louis Shickluna Shipyard at St. Catharines, Ont., in 1885, the *St. Andrew* received her name change, as well as 35' (10.5 metres) of length, in 1897, the year she was sold by W.B. Hall of Toronto to James Playfair & Company of Midland, Ontario. Her engine came from the tug, *W.T. Robb.* The ship ran hard onto the rocks of Blanchard Island on Sept. 21, 1900, while enroute from Jackfish Bay to Port Arthur, Ontario. The crew escaped unharmed, but the vessel slid off the rock ledge into deeper water the next day. Her final dimensions were 193' by 21' by 12' (57.9 by 6.3 by 3.6 metres). The *St. Andrew's* machinery was salvaged, and she lies broken, littered with many small artifacts, blocks, carts, metal strapping around part of her hull, etc. In 1975, the first divers at the site picked up, among other goodies, the ship's bell (it's gone now.) The small, nearby island is named after the wreck. The forward pilot house will likely be located soon.

Hazards: The site's sheer openness makes it weather-hazardous.

The Canadian wooden propeller, St. Andrew, *was wrecked in 1900.* (Photo: Institute for Great Lakes Research, Bowling Green State University, Ohio.)

Site 241: Wreck of the *A. Neff* (?)

Location:	Just off Porphryr Island, northern Lake Superior.
Access:	Boat.
Skill Level:	Intermediate - advanced.
Depth:	5 - 70 feet (1.5 - 21 metres).
Visibility:	10 - 30 feet (3 - 9 metres).
Description:	This wreck may not be that of the small steamer, *A. Neff,* which, according to records, went ashore on the rocks of Edward Island, but had her hull salvaged and reused as the barge, *Butcher's Maid.* The identity of this particular shipwreck may be elusive.

Site 242: The *Gray Oak* Shipwreck

Location:	About two miles (3.2 kms.) beyond the Welcome Islands, near Thunder Bay, Ontario.
Loran Co-ordinates:	31800.7/45915.7
Access:	Boat. The site is usually marked with a jug.
Skill Level:	Advanced.
Depth:	Maximum 108 feet (32.4 metres).
Visibility:	10 - 30 feet (3 - 9 metres).
Description:	This flat-bottomed, blunt-nosed, scow-schooner was scuttled in 1911 along with several other boats. The hull is intact, but penetration is not advised. Glass in the windows is also intact. White letters on the wooden hull clearly spell out the name, *GRAY OAK,* as well as *BU,* the first two letters of "Buffalo", the home port. The rest of the letters are obliterated. The ship's wheel is located at the 75' (22.5-metre) level.
Hazards:	Dirty water sometimes diminishes the visibility at this site.

Site 243: The *Gordon Gauthier*

Location:	On St. Mary's Island, off Silver Harbour, near Thunder Bay, Ontario.
Access:	Boat.
Skill Level:	Novice - intermediate.
Depth:	15 feet (4.5 metres).
Visibility:	15 - 30 feet (4.5 - 9 metres).
Description:	Located at the present-day land site of a rock with red paint on it, the 26-ton, wooden tug, *Gordon Gauthier,* burned at the dock of a rock quarry at Port Arthur harbour on Oct. 8, 1911. Built in 1884, the vessel was owned by the Lake Superior Tug Company at the time of loss. The ship's propeller was removed to a dive shop.
Hazards:	Beware of occasional boating traffic at this site.

The propeller from the Gordon Gauthier *was removed in 1974 by divers who would have received $25 for its scrap metal value; instead, they sold it to an appreciative diver for the same amount* (Photo by Cris Kohl.)

Site 244: The *Robert L. Fryer* Wreck

Location:	At "B" Island, in the Welcome Islands, near Thunder Bay, Ontario.
Access:	Boat.
Skill Level:	Novice - intermediate.
Depth:	To 35 feet (10.5 metres).
Visibility:	10 - 25 feet (3 - 7.5 metres).

Description: The bulk freight steamer, *Robert L. Fryer,* built in 1888 by F.W. Wheeler & Company at West Bay City, Michigan, and having the hull measurements of 290' (87 metres) by 41' 6" (12.4 metres) by 20' (6 metres), was declared a total loss after a fire at Marine City, Michigan, on April 28, 1914. The following year, purchased by Canadian interests, she became a transfer vessel at Fort William-Port Arthur, Ontario (present-day Thunder Bay). As a display of spectacular entertainment, the ship was towed to the Welcome Islands and set on fire in 1930, burning part of the island as well. With a section of the hull breaking the water surface, the site, up against "B" Island, is easily located. The remains include the boiler, propeller, and rudder. A small unidentified wreck lies beside the *Robert L. Fryer,* while portions of three other scuttled wrecks lie nearby. The four islands in the Welcomes are unimaginatively named after the first four letters of the alphabet. "A" Island is big, with a lighthouse on it. "B" Island is the second largest, with most of the shipwrecks.

Hazards: This is considered a safe dive site.

The Robert L. Fryer *had a long history scanning over 40 years on the Great Lakes before the vessel's ignoble end.* (Photo: author's collection.)

SPECIAL EXCURSION
to Silver Islet
and the burning of the
Str. Robert L. Fryer

The steamer Fryer will be burned tomorrow evening, July 29, in the bay.

By going to Silver Islet tomorrow you may spend the day at the Islet and witness the burning of the ship on the way in. The Islet Prince will stop alongside the burning vessel and you may have a broadside view.

Round trip fare, including the burning $1.00 return.
Children Half Fare.

Islet Prince leaves Fort William tomorrow morning at 9.30

This will be a Sight of a Lifetime

DAILY MAIL SERVICE

This newspaper advertisement ran in the July 28, 1930, edition of *The Daily Times-Journal* (Fort William, Ontario). On July 30th, the same newspaper reported that "The Robert L. Fryer, hospital ship which cruised the harbor for many years,...was burned last night, moored six miles out, on the land side of the Welcome Islands. It was a most spectacular fire, and gave to thousands of citizens, who viewed the awe-inspiring sight with great interest, some idea of a ship afire at sea. For the past two or three weeks, the Fryer has been lying in the yards of the Sin-Mac Lines, at the foot of Manitou street, Port Arthur. On Monday the tug Whalen towed her out to her moorings and the hatches were filled with kindling and coal oil was being poured over the wood. At nine o'clock last evening a match was put to her and she blazed away merrily until one o'clock this morning. More than seven hundred persons went out on a steamer to view the spectacle. Officials of the Sin-Mac Lines went out to the scene of the burning ship this morning to see if the ruins needed any further attention."

Site 245: The Wreck of the *Puckasaw*

Location:	Off the Welcome Islands, about 450' (135 metres) northeast of the wreck of the *Green River*.
Access:	Boat.
Skill Level:	Intermediate - advanced.
Depth:	55 - 80 feet (16.5 - 24 metres).
Visibility:	10 - 25 feet (3 - 7.5 metres).
Description:	The steam tug, *Puckasaw*, built in 1889 to a length

of 96' (28.8 metres), was scuttled in 1911 off "B" Island of the Welcome Islands. The hull is intact, although her upper cabins were damaged by fire. During scuttling, the hull was weighted down with several old boilers (which distracts from the integrity of the *Puckasaw* as an archaeological site!) Divers can explore the galley, forward decks, and companionways. Penetration is possible, but take a dive light and use it. The deck sits at 55' (16.5 metres), with a maximum depth at this site of 80' (24 metres).

Hazards:	Beware of boating traffic at this site. The silt stirs up quite easily; procede with caution.

The tug, Puckasaw, *was one of several vessels scuttled at the Welcome Islands.*
(Photo: The Great Lakes Marine Collection of the Milwaukee Public Library.)

Site 246: The *W.J. Emmerson*

Location:	Off distant Bennett Island, at the old Number 10 Light, northern Lake Superior.
Access:	Boat.
Skill Level:	Intermediate.
Depth:	30 feet (9 metres).
Visibility:	10 - 25 feet (3 - 7.5 metres).
Description:	The small, 19-ton tug, *W.J. Emmerson,* 70' (21 metres) long and built in 1900, sank on Oct. 11, 1933. An upright, two-piston, steam-engine stack remains at this site.
Hazards:	The plankton growth in late June affects visibility. Generally, this is not considered a very satisfying dive site.

Site 247: Wreck of the *Green River*

Location:	At "B" Island, in the Welcome Islands, near Thunder Bay, Ontario, about 450' (135 metres) north of the *Robert L. Fryer* wreck.
Access:	Boat.
Skill Level:	Intermediate - advanced.
Depth:	50 - 80 feet (15 - 24 metres).
Visibility:	10 - 30 feet (3 - 9 metres).

Description: Launched by F.W. Wheeler & Company at West Bay City, Michigan, on Oct. 1, 1887, as the 1,680.71-gross-ton wooden propeller, *Gogebic,* this vessel was sold to Canadian interests in 1921, renamed the *Green River,* and reduced to a barge measuring 275' (82.5 metres) in length, 40' (12 metres) in beam, and 22' (6.6 metres) in draft, with a new gross tonnage of 1,750. The *Green River* was dismantled and scuttled at "B" Island in the Welcome Islands group on Nov. 5, 1932. The deck and rudder are intact, penetration is possible, but use dive lights, and there are lots of ling (burbots; those ugly "lawyer fish") at this site. The deck is at 50' (15 metres), with the wreck sitting in a maximum of 80' (24 metres). Experienced divers that are good on air and navigation could possibly do both the *Puckasaw* and the *Green River* on the same dive.

Hazards: Beware of boating dangers and silted visibility.

NOTE: All five or six of the Welcome Island wrecks near Thunder Bay, Ontario, are buoyed by the beginning of the summer, thanks to local initiative.

Site 250: Silver Islet

Location:	To the east of Thunder Bay, Ontario.
Loran Co-ordinates:	31750.0/46010.0
Access:	Boat.
Skill Level:	Intermediate - advanced.
Depth:	10 - 60 feet (3 - 18 metres), or deeper.
Visibility:	20 - 40 feet (6 - 12 metres).
Description:	The townsite of Silver Islet, active in the 1860's to the 1880's, is on the mainland, at the end of the Sibley Peninsula (the "Sleeping Giant"), while the islet is a mile offshore. This area is an old mine site. Drive to this site and dive off the main pier, where torpedo bottles have been found in the past.
Hazards:	Keep out of the mine shaft at the islet. Not only is it quite dangerous, as it has been caving in, but it is privately-owned. Please respect private property.

Some Post-Divebook Thoughts

With the incredible proliferation of people in Ontario learning how to scuba dive, and with more and more shipwreck, and other, sites being located in our expansive Great Lakes waters, I truly believe that this book will make people much more aware of what is in our own back yard than ever before. Now, that certification card they earned in Ontario won't be used only during that annual winter trip down south to the tropics.

Some brief, general notes on Ontario scuba diving, past, present, and future, seem appropriate.

The past is a foreign country; they do things differently there. It's fun to research the past in terms of shipwrecks, but I wouldn't want to live there.

Here's to the present. Today, this book is finished. Today, there are thousands of scuba dive sites within the province of Ontario. Unfortunately, it is impossible to adequately describe all of these sites within the confines of a 408-page (plus viii) book. The good news is that the 250 sites described in this finished product are a happy compromise that covers the best and most popular scuba locations available to today's divers in Ontario.

Here's to the future. Hundreds more divesites in the province of Ontario will be located and enjoyed by underwater adventurers within the next few years. Electronic means of scanning the lakes will become even more affordable and prevalent. Many shipwrecks not yet located in Ontario waters are presently awaiting the moment when excited scuba divers will descend and marvel at these long-hidden remains, man's first modern visit to symbols of a distant era, frozen in time. Many interesting, submerged geological sites, such as caves or walls or boulder fields, or the remnants of ancient rivers now submerged by larger bodies of water will also be discovered. Likely, too, is an increase in the introduction of immigrant shipwrecks (also termed "artificial wrecks"), such as the steel ferry, *Wolfe Islander II,* at Kingston in 1985, the wooden schooner, *Caroline Rose,* moved from Owen Sound and scuttled just outside the boundary of Fathom Five National Marine Park in 1990, and countless smaller toys (boats, cars, planes) dropped into flooded quarries and other underwater locations.

Keeping up with new dive locations (or old ones missed!) will be more of a challenge than a problem. If you can help, please write to me, Cris Kohl, at 16 Stanley Ave., Chatham, Ontario, Canada, N7M 3J2, or telephone (519) 351-1966, or fax me at (519) 351-1753. New dive site information is welcome and will be appreciated!

This book, hopefully, has described many underwater locations that new divers can enjoy for a long time to come after they first get certified and gradually become more experienced. Maybe it will arouse the curiosities of certified divers who dropped out, but need a reason or two to resume the sport. Perhaps it will revitalize the old pro's who thought they had done it all.

Whatever this book does, may your favourite dive site be a source of joy to you forever, free of frets, pollution, intrusion, and destruction.

APPENDIX A

Ontario Underwater Council (O.U.C.)

The Ontario Underwater Council represents and serves the Ontario sport diving community. This unique organization, the largest of its kind in the world today, was formed in 1958 to promote diving safety and develop diving opportunities for scuba enthusiasts. Membership has grown from 18 dive clubs and a handful of diveshops to over 4,000 divers, 75 dive clubs, and 125 commercial businesses.

The O.U.C. supports the major Canadian certifying agencies in attracting new participants into our sport. Once certified through a recognized program, the new diver's enjoyment of this activity is increased through the O.U.C.'s programs: ensuring that the air divers consume is safe; that charter boats operate at a high standard; that on-going educational programs are available; that open channels of communication are maintained between all segments of the diving community; and that scuba divers' interests and needs are represented to all levels of government and the public (Author's note: don't underestimate the value of these points just because they seem to put nothing into your pocket!)

The aims of the Ontario Underwater Council are to support the activities of member divers, clubs, and business affiliates; to encourage co-operation in the interests of good conservation; to promote safe diving and the safe use of approved diving equipment; and to provide up-dates on safety, medical, technical, and research data to all member clubs and individuals.

The O.U.C. annually produces "Underwater Canada," which has earned the enviable reputation as being the #1 consumer dive show in North America.

Benefits of becoming a member of the Ontario Underwater Council include receiving the quarterly *Dive Ontario* magazine, a copy of the *Diving Industry Index,* a discount for a subscription to *DIVER* magazine, Canada's most respected diving publication, a discount to the annual Underwater Canada show and the Treasure Hunt (see p. 89 of this book), and many other benefits. Scuba clubs can obtain additional special benefits by joining the O.U.C.

The Ontario Underwater Council deserves the support of every scuba diver and scuba dive club in the province. Become a member of the O.U.C. Telephone (416) 426-7033, or fax them at (416) 426-7336, or write to: Ontario Underwater Council, 1185 Eglinton Ave. East., NORTH YORK, Ontario M3C 3C6.

APPENDIX B
Save Ontario Shipwrecks (S.O.S.)

In 1980, a group of Ontario divers became concerned by the wholesale stripping of shipwrecks and consequent destruction of some of the best heritage diving sites in the province. They formed an organization called Save Ontario Shipwrecks (S.O.S.) to combat this situation through a program of diver and public education. S.O.S. was incorporated in 1981 to further public knowledge and appreciation of Ontario's marine heritage by assisting museums and public archives in acquiring information about our maritime heritage, educating divers and the public of the need for conservation, and encouraging diver and non-diver involvement in marine archaeological projects of our shipwrecks.

Chapter activities include local shipwreck research, surveying of submerged resources, public information and education, individual projects, archival research, pictorial collections, computer data bases, publishing, and para-professional archaeological activities.

Membership in S.O.S. is open to all individuals who have an interest in the preservation of Ontario's marine heritage.

For more information, contact Save Ontario Shipwrecks, 2175 Sheppard Ave. East, Suite 310, WILLOWDALE, Ont. M2J 1W8, or telephone (416) 491-2373.

Preserve Our Wrecks (P.O.W.)

Preserve Our Wrecks (P.O.W.) was formed in the Kingston area in 1981 by divers upset at the unauthorized salvage and damage done to a popular local shipwreck. P.O.W. is a group of concerned individuals who volunteer their time towards the preservation of shipwrecks in the Kingston area for the benefit of all. They install permanent moorings adjacent to the wreck sites in order to prevent anchor damage by visiting boats, and they work with charter boat operators in maintaining these moorings. They also perform volunteer underwater archaeological surveys on Kingston shipwrecks and help educate divers about the histories and non-renewabilities of these shipwrecks. For more information, write to Preserve Our Wrecks, c/o Marine Museum of the Great Lakes at Kingston, 55 Ontario St., Kingston, Ont. K7L 2Y2.

Shipwrecks and Scuba: The Ethics and the Law

by *Cris Kohl*

Our Great Lakes waters hold the most unique and the richest resource of inland marine heritage in the world. Visiting scuba divers from as far away as Australia are aware of these rare treasures, so beautifully preserved in our cold freshwater seas, to which we have such easy access and which so many of us, unfortunately, take for

Much is being written and spoken about the removal of items from shipwrecks. All in all, it is an activity that is loaded with too much temptation for some divers to resist. Scuba diving is, unfortunately, still looked upon by some as a macho activity, and as such, some divers are of the primitive mentality that anything they see underwater is theirs for the taking, or that the retrieval of a "token of accomplishment" (to quote David Trotter) will prove to their friends what excellent

In Ontario, there are many laws governing not only the removal of items from shipwrecks, but also our very presence on these museum pieces. Unless otherwise proven, all shipwrecks are the property of the province of Ontario, and as such, no individual may legally take, for his own use or disposition, any portion of a shipwreck in Ontario waters, regardless of its country of origin. The Criminal Code contains legal mechanisms to prevent and punish the stripping of shipwrecks, numerous acts of both summary and indictable types, including "the removal of object from wreck, value under (or over) $200," "the possession of objects illegally removed from wreck," "wilful damage or destruction of wreck," violations under the "Trespass to Property Act," and, as a Provincial Offence under the Ontario Heritage Act, "archaeology without a licence," including sidescan sonar searches for

Since it is impossible to police all of our Great Lakes shipwrecks all of the time, the removal of items from them is one of the easiest and least detectable crimes being commissioned. It speaks little of human nature, ranking about as low, and requiring about as much courage, as slashing a rival's automobile tires when it is known for certain that he won't show up to protect his property.

Education and consideration are the keys. Every person who ventures underwater onto these unwatched candy stores of the deep must be aware that this public property has irreplacable historic value, and that items removed from the historic setting lose their value considerably. A rusty spike or a wooden plank or deadeye has far greater appreciation value when it is seen *in situ* on its shipwreck rather than when it has been translocated to someone's personal den, or, even worse, relegated to deterioration and the collecting of dust in a basement, an attic or a garage. Once removed from the original site, the artifact loses a great deal of value; the awe is gone, much like visiting Arizona to view the original London Bridge. It's

Shipwrecks and all their trappings are the mainstays of scuba diving in the Great Lakes. Their removal or destruction deteriorates our recreational dive sites, much to the detriment of the entire diving community.

The real treasure of our Great Lakes shipwrecks is that they are there for all of us who venture into the watery world to enjoy and appreciate. In spite of the actions of some irresponsible divers, we have not been legislated off these time capsules. We must not betray that trust.

The ethics alone are enough to stop wreckstripping. The laws exist only as a formality.

APPENDIX C

Ontario Dive Shops and Air Stations

This diveshop listing follows the order of the regions as described in this book. Please call the dive shop to verify services or hours of operation, or, for much more information on each dive shop, buy the inexpensive booklet entitled "Diving Industry Index," published by the Ontario Underwater Council, 1185 Eglinton Avenue East, NORTH YORK, Ontario, M2C 3C6, (416) 426-7033.

OTTAWA AREA
Adventures in Diving, 5360 Canotek Rd., Unit 2, GLOUCESTER, Ont. K1J 9E3. (613) 745-7211

Alpha Dive Centre Ltd., 518 Bank St., OTTAWA, Ont. K2P 1Z6. (613) 567-1402; fax (613) 230-8825

Barryvale Lodge, R. R. #2, CALABOGIE, Ont. K0J 1H0. (613) 752-2392

Burton's Dive Service, 1161 Cyrville Rd., GLOUCESTER, Ont. K1J 7S6. (613) 745-6444; fax (613) 746-5426

Discover Scuba Ltd., 1383 Clyde Ave., NEPEAN, Ont. K2G 3H7. (613) 723-3483; fax (613) 723-3299

Dive Quest II, Bancroft Rental, Box 628 - 236 Hastings St. N., BANCROFT, Ont. K0L 1C0. (613) 332-4100; fax (613) 332-0399

Diver's Wearhouse, 6 - 210 Colonnade Rd., NEPEAN, Ont. K2E 7L5. (613) 723-3055 and (613) 797-0877; fax, call first (613) 723-3055

Kanata Diving Supply, 215 Terence Matthews Cres., Unit #2, KANATA, Ont. K2M 1X5. (613) 592-9169; fax (613) 592-1832

Scuba Consultants, 37 Bentley Ave., NEPEAN, Ont. K2E 6T7. (613) 226-8805

Sea-Dive Scuba Centre, 482 Boundary Rd., PEMBROKE, Ont. K8A 6L5. (613) 732-9518

Smith Falls Diving Supply, 52 George St. N., SMITH FALLS, Ont. K7A 1Y9. (613) 283-1962; fax: same.

ST. LAWRENCE RIVER
E & T Fire Protection, P. O. Box 1494, BROCKVILLE, Ont. K6Y 5Y6. (613) 342-1234

Ron's Scuba Shop, 13-11th St. West, CORNWALL, Ont. K6J 3A8. (613) 933-1362

Sea 'N Sky, #102 - 197 Water St., PRESCOTT, Ont. K0E 1T0. (613) 925-0308; fax (613) 284-1696

KINGSTON AREA AND LAKE ONTARIO (includes Toronto)
Aqua Systems Scuba Centre, 1730 Dundas St. E., MISSISSAUGA, Ont. L4X 1L8. (905) 277-3483

Aquarius Scuba & Sport, 4020 Dundas St. W., Unit 2, TORONTO, Ont. M6S 4W6. (416) 604-4203; fax: same.

Below H2O, 5293 Hwy #7 East, Unit #6, MARKHAM, Ont. L3P 7M7. (905) 472-2000; fax (905) 472-6385

Blakey Diving Services, 78 Elwood Blvd., TORONTO, Ont. M5N 1G8. (416) 977-2244

Bottom Dwellers Diving, R. R. #1, BELLEVILLE, Ont. K8N 4Z1. (613) 967-6135

Canadian Sport Divers, 133 Yeomans St., BELLEVILLE, Ont. K8P 3X9. (613) 967-4734.

Canadian Sport Subs Ltd., 59 Dundas St. E., BELLEVILLE, Ont. K8N 1B7. (613) 966-8903; fax (613) 962-0049

Dave's Aquatic Services, 2338 Wyecroft Rd.,OAKVILLE, Ont.L6L 6M1.(905) 827-3843; fax: same

Dive Quest Canada, 61 Yonge St., KINGSTON, Ont. K7M 1E4. (613) 547-3483

Divemasters, 105 St. Lawrence St. W., MADOC, Ont. K0K 2K0. (613) 473-4642

Diver Down Underwater Services, 1182 Eglinton Ave.W., TORONTO, Ont. M6C 2E3. (416) 787-0264; fax (416) 787-6201

Happy Divers Den Inc., 2 - 70 Delta Park Blvd., BRAMPTON, Ont. L6T 5E9. (905) 792-7473; fax (905) 799-3554

Innerspace Dive & Marine, 1848 Liverpool Rd., Unit 10, PICKERING, Ont. L1V 1W3. (905) 420-8331; fax: same

Irie Irie, 267 Parkhome Ave., WILLOWDALE, Ont. M2R 1A1

Kingsdive Ltd.,121 Princess St.,KINGSTON, K7L 1A8.(613) 542-2892

Kingston Diving Centre Inc., 786 Bath Rd., KINGSTON, Ont. K7M 4Y2. (613) 634-8464; fax (613) 384-9383

L.T.C. Scuba Centre, 270 Pennsylvania Ave., #6, CONCORD, Ont. L4K 3Z7. (905) 660-6359; fax: same

Oakville Divers, 12 Lakeshore Rd. W., Unit 4, OAKVILLE, Ont. L6K 1C5. (905) 842-8881

Prince Edward Pt. Resort/The Ducks Dive Shop (Pt. Traverse), R.R. #3, PICTON, Ont., K0K 2T0. (613) 476-3764

Scubamasters Diving Academy, 1132 The Queensway, ETOBICOKE, Ont. M8Z 1P7. (416) 255-3483; fax (416) 503-3500

Stouffville Scuba, 117 Ringwood Dr., STOUFFVILLE, Ont. L4A 8C1. (905) 642-3483

Tam Dive Ltd., 246 King St. E., TORONTO, Ont. M5A 1K1. (416) 861-1664; fax (416) 861-0610

The Air Supply Scuba & Snorkeling Centre, 800 Dundas St. E., Unit G, MISSISSAUGA, Ont. L4Y 2B6. (905) 281-2100

The Water Sports Store Ltd., 444 Eglinton Ave. W., TORONTO, Ont. M5N 1A5. (416) 488-1000; fax (416) 488-1302

The Wet Shop, 10077 Yonge St., RICHMOND HILL, Ont. L4C 1T7. (905) 884-7951; fax (905) 884-7984

The Wet Shop Metro East, 1645 Dundas St. W., WHITBY, Ont. L1N 5R4. (905) 666-4152

Water Adventures, 855 O'Connor Dr., TORONTO, Ont. M4B 2S7. (416) 757-6935; fax (416) 757-5342

Waterline, 1953 Avenue Rd., TORONTO, Ont. M5M 4A3. (416) 488-6000; fax (416) 488-6026

Wreck Ventures Inc., 1101 Hickerywood Cres., KINGSTON, Ont. K7P 1Y4. (613) 389-2319

NIAGARA RIVER

Bob's Sport & Dive, 222 Kenilworth Ave. N., HAMILTON, Ont. L8H 7J3. (905) 549-1043

CEA Canucks, 1104 Fennell Ave. E., HAMILTON, Ont. L8T 1R9. (905) 385-3064

Dan's Dive Shop Inc., 329 Welland Ave., ST. CATHARINES, Ont. L2R 2R2. (905) 984-2160; 1-800-268 DANS; fax (905) 984-2167

Ed's Pro Dive, 19 Main St., ST. CATHARINES, Ont. L2N 4T5. (905) 646-1481; fax (905) 646-8216

Float N' Flag Sport & Dive Inc., 564 Plains Rd. E., BURLINGTON, Ont. L7T 2E5. (416) 333-DIVE; fax (905) 3483

LAKE ERIE

B.C. Dive Centre, 67 Tillson Ave., Box 191, TILLSONBURG, Ont. N4G 4H5. (519) 842-4144; fax (519) 688-2470

Big Ed's Watersports, 27 Ontario St., STRATFORD, Ont. N5A 3G7. (519) 272-2070

Booth's Harbour Developments Ltd., R.R. #1, P.O. Box 50, ST. WILLIAMS, Ont. N0E 1P0. (519) 586-2731; fax (519) 586-2192

Brant Dive Shop, R. R. #1, BURGESSVILLE, Ont. N0I 1C0. (519) 424-2351

Cambridge Divers, 1648 King St. E., CAMBRIDGE, Ont. N3H 3R7. (519) 653-7722

Dean's Sport & Dive, 1769 Victoria Rd., NORTH BRESLAU, Ont. N0B 1M0. (519) 648-3121

Deep Three Scuba, 262 Richmond St., LONDON, Ont. N6B 2H7. (519) 672-9180; fax (519) 672-9994

Dive Bell, 78 Icomm Dr., BRANTFORD, Ont. N3S 2X5. (519) 759-3483; fax (519) 753-1682

Divers Down, 864 Dundas St. East, LONDON, Ontario N5W 2Z7. (519) 434-7258

Good Guy's Scuba Service, 212 Horton St., LONDON, Ont. N6B 1K8. (519) 432-0886; fax (519) 432-3084

Ground Hog Divers, 194 Victoria St. W., KITCHENER, Ont. N2H 5C6. (519) 742-5415; fax (519) 742-4330

Ken's Dive Locker, 724 Dundas Street, LONDON, Ont. N5W 2Z4. (519) 434-5349

MMI (Leamington), 17 Robson Rd., LEAMINGTON, Ont. N8H 2M8. (519) 322-9916

Neptune's Divers, 692 Dundas St., WOODSTOCK, Ont. N4S 1E6. (519) 421-4031

Pelee Passage Dive Centre, 9 Robson Rd., LEAMINGTON, Ont. N8H 2M8. (519) 326-3483; fax (519) 326-8655

Red Devil Scuba Supplies, 2 Grand Ave. E., CHATHAM, Ont. N7L 1V5. (519) 358-1988

Royal City Scuba, 95 Crimea Street, GUELPH, Ontario N1H 2Y5. (519) 763-3483

Scuba Plus, R.R. #5, SIMCOE, Ontario N3Y 4K4. (519) 428-3125

Simcoe Dive Centre, 54 Robinson Street, SIMCOE, Ont. N3Y 1W6. (519) 426-3996

Southwest Scuba Centre, 25 King St. E., CHATHAM, Ont. N7M 3M6. (519) 354-9110; fax (519) 354-3992

Sub Surface, 892 Warwick, WOODSTOCK, Ont. N4S 8X8.

The Dive Shop II, 122 Division St. S., KINGSVILLE, Ont. N9Y 1P6. (519) 733-5141.

The Gas Station, 614 Dundas Street East, LONDON, Ont. N5W 2Y8. (519) 434-DIVE

Travel Sports Equipment, 67 Wharncliffe Rd. N., LONDON, Ont. N6H 2A5. (519)

Trout Lake Air Station, P.O. Box 57, INNERKIP, Ont. N0J 1M0. Summer: (519) 469-3363 Winter: (519) 469-3431

DETROIT RIVER
Aqua Ventures, 6 Sylvester Cres., Box 116, ST. JOACHIM, Ont., N0R 1S0. (519) 972-5615
MMI Scuba Centre, 65 Victoria St., Box 97, ESSEX, Ont. N8M 2Y1. (519) 776-6060; fax (519) 776-9282

ST. CLAIR RIVER
Bluewater Dive & Marine, 101 Michigan Ave. POINT EDWARD, Ont. N7V 1E5. (519) 337-3483
Bridgeview Watersports, P.O. Box 309, 1 Marina Rd., POINT EDWARD, Ont. N7T 7J7. (519) 337-8033; fax (519) 332-4181

LOWER LAKE HURON
Ground Hog Divers II, Box 1405 - 582 Gustavus St., PORT ELGIN, Ont. N0H 2C0. (519) 389-3629; fax (519) 389-3883

TOBERMORY AREA
Big Tub Harbour Resort, P.O. Box 239, TOBERMORY, Ont. N0H 2R0. (519) 596-2219; fax (519) 793-4083
G & S Watersports, Box 21, Little Tub Harbour, TOBERMORY, Ont. N0H 2R0. (519) 596-2200; fax (519) 596-2833
Divers Den, P.O. Box 87, TOBERMORY, Ontario N0H 2R0. (519) 596-2363; fax: same

SOUTH OF TOBERMORY
Bill Dowkes Scuba, 764 3rd Avenue West, OWEN SOUND, Ont. N4K 4P3. (519) 376-1921
Downunder Dive & Scuba Centre, R.R. #2, Hwy. #26, COLLINGWOOD, Ont. L9Y 3Z1. (705) 444-0041
Owen Sound Dive Centre, 2503-8th Ave. E., OWEN SOUND, Ont. N4K 6W5
Wiarton Auto Marine, P.O. Box 846, 678 Berford St., WIARTON, Ont. N0H 2T0. (519) 534-0160

LAKE SIMCOE/MUSKOKA AREA
Discovery Dive Services, Box 2481, 289 Hunter St. W., PETERBOROUGH, Ont. K9J 7Y8
Dive Muskoka, (Campbell Sports), 7 Manitoba St., Box 2039, BRACEBRIDGE, Ont. P0B 1C0. (705) 645-3131
Huronia Sport & Dive, 32 Eccles St. N., BARRIE, Ont. L4N 3V7. (705) 737-3560
Lett's Dive!!, 16995 Yonge St., Unit #4, NEWMARKET, Ont. L3Y 5Y1. (905) 836-7234; fax: same
Northern Scuba, 58 Emerson Way, NEWMARKET, Ont. L3Y 7M3. (905) 853-6101
Rock Bottom Enterprises, Box 276, R.R. #6, BURKES FALLS, Ont. P0A 1C0. (705) 382-2625
Scuba Shack, 141 Hotchkiss St., GRAVENHURST, Ont. P1P 1H6. (705) 687-5879; fax (705) 687-8251

Scuba Shack - Bala, Hwy. #169, BALA, Ont. (705) 762-0988

The Dive Shop (Newmarket), 161 Davis Dr., NEWMARKET, Ont. L3Y 2N3. (905) 898-0988; fax: same.

The Diving Locker, 315 Maitland Ave., PETERBOROUGH, Ont. K9J 5G6. (705) 743-5143

The Wet Shop (Barrie), 75 Cedar Point Dr., Unit 6, BARRIE, Ont. L4N 5R7. (705) 722-5859

Tim's Place/CANDI (Canadian Association of Nitrox Divers Inc.) R.R. #2, MINESING, Ont. L0L 1Y0. (705) 721-9797; fax (705) 721-1924

Undersea Ventures Dive Centre, Lamers Rd., NEW LOWELL, Ont. L0M 1N0. (705) 424-5234

Wilrob Lodge, Moon River Marina, MACTIER, Ont. (705) 375-2342

PARRY SOUND
Divers Nook, 55 Bowes St., PARRY SOUND, Ont. P2A 2L4. (705) 746-9757

NORTH GEORGIAN BAY
Diver Double, 50 Mary St., Box 1264, NEW LISKEARD, Ont. P0J 1P0. (705) 647-5642; fax (705) 647-6624

Ed's Pro Dive 2, 144 Wilson Cres., Box 1944, ESPANOLA, Ont. P0P 1C0. (705) 869-2695

Island Divers Ltd., 33 Vankonghnet, LITTLE CURRENT, Ont. P0R 1K0. (705) 368-3648

Rainbow Camp (air station), R.R. #1, NOELVILLE, Ont. P0M 2N0. (705) 898-2356

Sportsman's Inn, 37 Channel St., KILLARNEY, Ont. P0M 2A0. (705) 287-2411; fax (705) 287-2691

Underwater Fantacies, 226 Duke St. West, NORTH BAY, Ont. P1B 6E7. (705) 474-

Water Ways, 485 Frood Rd., SUDBURY, Ont. P3C 5A2. (705) 670-9009

ST. MARY'S RIVER
Bowfin Diving Services, 366 Korah Rd., SAULT STE. MARIE, Ont. P6C 4H3. (705) 942-1840; fax: same

Great Lakes Divers, 17 Linstedt St., SAULT STE. MARIE, Ont. P6B 3H8. (705) 942-2342

Sault S.C.U.B.A. Centre Ltd., 358 Lake St., SAULT STE. MARIE, Ont. P6B 3L1. (705) 256-8015

LAKE SUPERIOR
Thunder Country Diving Supply Ltd., 448 North May St., THUNDER BAY, Ont. P7C 3R5. (807) 623-6550

NOTE: If we missed you, please contact the author, Cris Kohl, at 16 Stanley Ave., Chatham, Ontario N7M 3J2, telephone (519) 351-1966, fax (519) 351-1753 for inclusion in any future edition.

APPENDIX D

Scuba Charter Boats

According to new Canadian Coast Guard shipping regulations, all boats functioning as passenger vessels (and this includes scuba charters) should, by now, have been inspected and be conforming to the regulations, which place much greater emphasis on seaworthiness and overall safety. The reader takes the full risk involved in contacting and booking any of these charter vessels. The author offers only the connection, without any endorsement or approval. Following each vessel's name, in brackets, is the number of passengers the ship can take.

ST. LAWRENCE RIVER (Cornwall):
Manta-Ray (10), Bob's Dive Charters, 552 Jase St., Cornwall, Ont. K6H 7G4.(613) 932-6435

ST. LAWRENCE RIVER (Prescott):
Lisa Jane Diver (8), Sea & Sky, R.R. #2, Kemptville, Ont. K0G 1J0. (613) 258-3550

ST. LAWRENCE RIVER (Brockville):
Deb Ring Dive Charters, P.O. Box 414, Brockville, Ont. K6V 5V6. (613) 345-0521
Little Diver (18), Ron's Scuba Shop, 13 Eleventh St. W., Cornwall, Ont. K6J 3A8. (613) 933-1362
25' Rampage (8), Diver's Wearhouse, 6-210 Colonnade Rd., NEPEAN, Ont. K2E 7L5. (613) 723-3055 or (613) 797-0877

LAKE ONTARIO (Kingston):
Brooke-Lauren (16), Kingston Diving Centre Inc., 786 Bath Rd., Kingston, Ont. K7M 4Y2. (613) 634-8464
Southern Diver (14), Southern Nights Dive Charters, 1161 Cyrville Rd., Gloucester, Ont. K1J 7S6. (613) 745-6444
Southern Princess (20), Southern Nights Dive Charters, 1161 Cyrville Rd., Gloucester, Ont. K1J 7S6. (613) 745-6444
Wreck Hunter I (14), Kingsdive Ltd., 121 Princess St., Kingston, Ont. K7L 1A8. (613) 542-2892

LAKE ONTARIO (Point Traverse):
M.R. Ducks (14), Ducks Dive Shop, R.R. #3, Picton, Ont. K0K 2T0. (613) 476-3764

LAKE ONTARIO (Toronto):
"Coral" Arrow Glass (7), Aquarius Scuba, 4020 Dundas St. W., Toronto, Ont. M6S 4W6. (416) 604-4203

TRANSPORTABLE (from Toronto):
Princess II (4-6), Carl Vincente, c/o 59 Charlemont Cres., Scarborough, Ont. M1T 1M3. (905) 946-5635

LAKE ONTARIO (Niagara River Area):
31' Hinterholler (10), Dan's Dive Shop, 329 Welland Ave., St. Catharines, Ont. L2R 2R2. (905) 984-2160 or 1-800-268-DANS

LAKE ERIE:
Divewell Dive Charters, R.R. #7, Dunnville, Ont. N1A 2W6. (905) 774-4792
32' Luhrs (10), Waruwanago Boat Charters, R.R. #1, Wheatley, Ont.. N0P 2P0. (519) 825-4758

Harbourcraft (6), Waruwanago Boat Charters, R.R. #1, Wheatley, Ont.. N0P 2P0. (519) 825-4758

Offshore Diver Scuba Charters, P.O. Box 943, Blenheim, Ont. (519) 676-2136

Pearl Dive Charters, 35' Chris Craft. John Schertzer, St. Catharines, Ont. (905) 684-0294

Vida-C (16), Art Vermette, P.O. Box 5, Kingsville, Ont. N9Y 2E8. (519) 733-5141

ST. CLAIR RIVER (Sombra):

T.J. Dive Charters, 164 Water St., P.O. Box 63, Sombra, Ont. N0P 2H0. (519) 892-3474

LOWER LAKE HURON:

Huron Explorer (8-10), Bluewater Dive, 101 Michigan Ave., Sarnia, Ont. N7V 1E5. (519) 337-3483

Jo-Chaney (4-6), Deep Three Enterprises, 262 Richmond St., London, Ont. (519) 672-9180

Marius (6), Candive Charter, R.R. #1, Port Elgin, Ont. N0H 2C5. (519) 832-5970

TOBERMORY AREA

Anzac K. (30) Scuba Charters, 19 Mandarin Cres., Bramalea, Ont. (905) 791-7830; fax (905) 791-2869, or P.O. Box 176, Tobermory, Ont. N0H 2R0. (519) 596-2492

B.T.X. (10), Big Tub Harbour Resort, Tobermory, Ont. N0H 2R0 (519) 596-2219

Bullet (6), G & S Watersports, Box 21, Tobermory, Ont. N0H 2R0 (519) 596-2200

Bruce Isles (15-20) Dive Charters, 135 Sutherland Dr., Toronto, Ont. M4G 1H8. (416) 421-7502

Danmark (10-12), G & S Watersports, Box 21, Tobermory, Ont. N0H 2R0 (519) 596-2200

Earl D. (18), Harbourdive Charters, P.O. Box 208, Tobermory, Ont. N0H 2R0. (519) 596-2608

Gone Fishing (6), G & S Watersports, Box 21, Tobermory, Ont. N0H 2R0 (519) 596-2200

Jacqueline (18), Harbourdive Charters, P.O. Box 208, Tobermory, Ont. N0H 2R0. (519) 596-2608

Lark (18), G & S Watersports, Box 21, Tobermory, Ont. N0H 2R0 (519) 596-2200

Let's Go (10), Harbourdive Charters, P.O. Box 208, Tobermory, Ont. N0H 2R0. (519) 596-2608

Mamie (24), G & S Watersports, Box 21, Tobermory, Ont. N0H 2R0 (519) 596-2200

Nolan D. (12), G & S Watersports, Box 21, Tobermory, Ont. N0H 2R0 (519) 596-2200

R. G. Berry (24), Harbourdive Charters, P.O. Box 208, Tobermory, Ont. N0H 2R0. (519) 596-2608

W. A. Spears (18-30), G & S Watersports, Box 21, Tobermory, Ont. N0H 2R0 (519) 596-2200

GEORGIAN BAY (Penetanguishene Area):

Argonaut Diver (18), Capt. Ken Hisey, General Delivery, Penetang, Ont. L0K 1P0. (705) 549-8721

Bacchus Diver (18), Capt. Ken Hisey, General Delivery, Penetang, Ont. L0K 1P0. (705) 549-8721

Highlander (6), David Holding (formerly Great Lakes Adventures), 319 Champlain Rd., Box 1848, Penetanguishene, Ont. L0K 1P0. (705) 549-6317

Candi Diver (12), Tim's Place, R.R. #2, Minesing, Ont. L0L 1Y0. (705) 721-9797

LAKE SIMCOE/MUSKOKA AREA:
Bottom Tymes (10), Scuba Shack, 141 Hotchkiss St., Gravenhurst, Ont. P0C 1G0.
    (705) 687-5879
Northern Shark (10), Northern Scuba, 58 Emerson Way, Newmarket, Ont. L3Y 7M3.
    (905) 853-6101
Valiant (10), Lett's Dive!!, 16995 Yonge St., Unit 4, Newmarket, Ont. L3Y 5Y1
    (905) 836-7234

GEORGIAN BAY (Parry Sound):
Cambrian (25), Kennedy Marine Services, R.R. #1, Parry Sound, Ont. P2A 2W7.
    (705) 746-5579

GEORGIAN BAY (Killarney):
Cyjack II (15), The Sportsman's Inn, Killarney, Ont. P0M 2A0. (705) 287-2411
Killarney Queen (12), The Sportsman's Inn, Killarney, Ont. P0M 2A0. (705) 287-
    2411
Sportsman's Express (4), The Sportsman's Inn, Killarney, Ont. P0M 2A0. (705) 287-
    2411

LAKE SUPERIOR:
Aqua Tech Dive Charters, 366 Korah Rd., Sault Ste. Marie, Ont. P6C 4H3. (705) 942-
    1840
J. A. Diver (6), Thunder Country Diving, 448 N. May St., Thunder Bay, Ont. P7C
    3R5. (807) 623-6550
Superior Dive Tours, 90 Chartwell Dr., Sault Ste. Marie, Ont. P6A 6A2. (705) 946-
    3929

For more detailed information on dive charter boats in Ontario, obtain the latest
copy of the *Diving Industry Index* from the Ontario Underwater Council, 1185
Eglinton Avenue East, NORTH YORK, Ontario, M2C 3C6, (416) 426-7033.

APPENDIX E

Scuba Dive Clubs in Ontario

This dive club listing follows the order of the regions as described in this book. For further information, contact the Ontario Underwater Council, 1185 Eglinton Avenue East, NORTH YORK, Ontario, M2C 3C6, (416) 426-7033, fax (416) 426-7336.

OTTAWA AREA

Bancroft Scuba Diving Club, 236 Hastings St. N., Box 628, BANCROFT, Ont. K0L 1C0
Barracudas Scuba Club (B. Laing), Dundonald Hall, CRB Petawawa, PETAWAWA, Ont. K8H 2X3
Beavers Scuba Club, P.O. Box 8874, Main Terminal, OTTAWA, Ontario K1G 3J2
Bottomtimers Scuba Club, P.O. Box 30041, 250 Greenbank Rd., NEPEAN, Ont. K2H 8X0
CFB Ottawa Scuba Club/Aqua Ducks, P.O. Box 398, OTTAWA, Ontario K1A 0K5
CFB Petawawa Scuba Club (R. Lang/B. Therens), Canadian Forces Base Petawawa, PETAWAWA, Ont. K8H 2X3
Delta Minor Aquatic Association, 278 Stone Quarry, #95129, OTTAWA, Ont. K1K 3Y2
Diver's Wearhouse Dive Club, 6-210 Colonnade Rd., NEPEAN, Ont. K2E 7L5
Forces Sub-Aqua Club, Main Plaza, P.O. Box 70006, 160 Elgin St. (N), OTTAWA, Ont. K2P 2M3
National Capital Scuba Advocates, 3 Desjardins Ave., Unit #51, OTTAWA, Ontario K1N 5N8
Ottawa Beavers Scuba Club, Box 8874 Terminal, OTTAWA, Ont. K1G 3J2
Valley Diver Association, 482 Boundary Rd., PEMBROKE, Ont. K8A 6L5
Wet Owls Scuba Club, 1161 Cyrville Rd., GLOUCESTER, Ontario K1J 7S6

ST. LAWRENCE RIVER

St. Lawrence Dive Club, 8 Pearl St. E., BROCKVILLE, Ont. K6V 2N1
Seaway Valley Divers, c/o Vern Solowy, 13 Eleventh St. West, CORNWALL, Ontario K6J 3A8

KINGSTON AREA AND LAKE ONTARIO (including Toronto)

Ajax Scuba Club, P.O. Box 152, AJAX, Ontario L1S 3C3
Canadian Sport Divers, 133 Yeomans St., BELLEVILLE, Ont. K8P 3X9
Canadian Sub-Aqua Club, 300 John St., Thornhill Sq., Box 87501, THORNHILL, Ontario L3T 7R3
Club Challenge, 23 Leacroft Cres., NORTH YORK, Ont. M3B 2G5
Devonian Divers of Canada (Fred Harley), 2073 Kawartha Crescent, MISSISSAUGA, Ontario L5H 3P8
Diver Down Sea Rays, 1182 Eglinton Ave. W., TORONTO, Ontario M6C 2E3
Dolfin Divers of Oshawa (Robert Morrison), 1033 Lavender Court, OSHAWA, Ontario L1G 3H2

Down Under Club of Kingston (D.U.C.K.S.), (K. Fuller), 34 Sydenham St., KINGSTON, Ont. K7L 3G9

Downsview Denizens Dive Club, 1433 Sheppard Ave. W., DOWNSVIEW, Ont.,M3M 2W8

Etobicoke Underwater Club, 1530 Albion Rd., P.O. Box 47542, ETOBICOKE, Ontario M9V 5H4

Flying Frogmen Scuba Club, C/o Box 279, CFB Trenton, ASTRA, Ontario K0K 1B0

Georgetown Depth Chargers, 41 Mill Street, GEORGETOWN, Ontario L7G 2H6

Hart House Underwater Club, RAC Office, Room #101, Hart House, 7 Hart House Circle, Univ. of Toronto, TORONTO, Ontario M5S 1A1

I.B.M. Canada Scuba Club, c/o Carl Vicente, 3600 Steeles Ave. E., Module A4, Dept. 626, MARKHAM, Ont. L3R 9Z7

Innerspace Divers, 569 King St. E., OSHAWA, Ont. L1H 1G3

Intrepid Divers (N. Semmler), R.R. #4, English Settlement Rd., TRENTON, Ont. K8V 5P7

Metropol Underwater Club, 112 Colbeck St., TORONTO, Ontario M6S 1V4

Mississauga Scuba Club (G. Cunliffe), 1931 Balsam Ave., MISSISSAUGA, Ont. L5J 1L3

Mud Puppies Underwater Club, Inc., 3 Benstanton Blvd., SCARBOROUGH, Ont. M1H 1N4

Nautilus Sub-Aqua Club (R. Johns), R.R. #5, COBOURG, Ontario K9A 4J8

Northern Rays Scuba Club (W. Butt), 101 Prudential Dr., #1204, SCARBOROUGH, Ont. M1P 4S5

Northern Telecom Diving Club, 30 Fontaine Court, BRAMPTON, Ontario L6T 3J2

Olympium Scuba Club 109 Mercury Rd., REXDALE, Ontario M9W 3H7

Ont. U/W Hockey Assoc.(C. Conner), 200 James S., #302A, HAMILTON, Ont. L8P 3A9

Ontario Underwater Explorers, (A. Remeika-Janeway), 60 Dennis Ave., TORONTO, Ont. M6N 2T8

Phoenix Scuba Club, 1531 Asgard Dr., MISSISSAUGA, Ont. L5E 2C1

Pisces U/W Club (W. Newhall), 30 Vonda Ave., WILLOWDALE, Ontario M2N 5E9

Port Hope Dive Club (L. Caswell), 79 Shelbourne St., PORT HOPE, Ont. L1A 1H3

Ryenauts Scuba Club, (G. Cormack), 259 Neal Dr., RICHMOND HILL, Ontario L4C 3L3

Scarborough Snorkel & Rescue Aquatics Club, 8 Fairglen Ave., AGINCOURT, Ont. M1T 1G7

Scarborough Underwater Club, P.O. Box 114, SCARBOROUGH, Ontario M1K 5C1

Stouffville Underwater Divers Society, 41 Cedar St. N., UXBRIDGE, Ont. L9P 1B1

The Scuba Club, 43 Stave Cres., RICHMOND HILL, Ontario L4C 9K1

Toronto Mantarays, 490 A Jane St., TORONTO, Ontario M6S 4A2

Toronto Superturtles Dive Club, 70 Clipper Rd., #1303, WILLOWDALE, Ont. M2J 4E3

Wet Shop Dive Club, 10077 Yonge Street, RICHMOND HILL, Ontario L4C 1T7

NIAGARA RIVER

Aqua Knights of Hamilton, P.O. Box 73018, Limeridge Mall, HAMILTON, Ontario L9A 5H7

Barra Scuba U/W Club, Hamilton YMCA, 79 James St. South, HAMILTON, Ontario L8P 2Z1

Brock University Scuba Club, c/o Brock U. Student Union, Glenridge Ave., ST. CATHARINES, Ontario L2S 3A1

Burlington Sub-Aqua Scuba Club, 3341 Rexway Dr., BURLINGTON, Ontario L7N 2L2

Halcyon Divers, Box 32006, Stone Church Postal Outlet, HAMILTON, Ontario L8W
    3L3
Hamilton Sea Devils, Inc., 144 Erie Ave S., HAMILTON, Ont. L8N 2W8
Hamilton Sub-Mariners, P.O. Box 57446, Jackson Station, HAMILTON, Ontario L8P
    4X2
Hamilton Tiger Sharks U/W Diving Club, c/o 87 Brentwood Drive, HAMILTON,
    Ontario L8T 3W4
Hamilton-Wentworth Police Scuba Club, 555 Upper Wellington St., HAMILTON,
    Ontario L9A 3P8
Laurier Divers, c/o Rick Browning, 39 Norwich Rd., STONEY CREEK, Ont. L8E 1Z7
McMaster Univ. Scuba Club, c/o 249 Sutherland St.W., P.O.Box 825, CALEDONIA,
    Ont. N0A 1A0
Niagara Divers Association, (J. Grice), 6176 Collins Dr., NIAGARA FALLS, Ont.
    L2G 2S2
Northern Aquatic Recreational Club, BURLINGTON, Ont.
Not Another Diving Association (K. Kissman), 4646 Miller Rd., WELLAND, Ont.
    L2R 6Z4
Seaway Scuba Club, R.R. #2, LOWBANKS, Ontario N0A 1K0
Steel City Sport Divers of Hamilton, 6 Priscilla Lane, HAMILTON, Ont. L8E 2K9

LAKE ERIE
Club S.W.O.D.A., c/o Howie Moore, 460 Southdale Rd., Unit 11, LONDON, Ont. N6E
    1A4
Golden Triangle Aquanauts, (J. Bennett), Box 1234, KITCHENER, Ontario N2G 4G9
Great Lakes Explorers, R.R. #6, TILLSONBURG, Ont. N4G 4G9
Great Lakes Scuba Divers, 24 Park Ave., INGERSOLL, Ont. N5C 1B5
Kent Divers Association, P.O. Box 493, CHATHAM, Ontario N7M 5K6
Kitchener-Waterloo Underwater Assoc. (C. Myaers), 291 Lourdes Cr., WATERLOO,
    Ont. N2L 1P6
London Skin & Scuba Club, 9 Weldon Ave., P.O. Box 23, ARVA, Ont. N0M 1C0
London Sub-Aqua Scuba Club, c/o 29 Beatty Street, LONDON, Ontario N5W 2N9
Long Point Divers, 54 Robinson St.,SIMCOE, Ont. N3Y 1W6
Orca Divers Scuba Club, c/o K. McRae, 1262 Victoria St., LONDON, Ontario N5Y
    4E4
Prevost Scuba Club (J. Collins), 59 August Cres., LONDON, Ont. N6E 2C9
South Shore Scuba Club, P.O. Box 384, LEAMINGTON, Ontario N8H 3W3
Underwater Club of Canada, 78 Icomm Dr., BRANTFORD, Ontario N3S 2X5
University of Guelph Dive Club (D. Dodd), Dept. of Athletics, U. of Guelph,
    GUELPH, Ont. N1S 2W1
Western Ontario Seastangs Scuba Club, c/o Rm. 212, U.C.C., Univ. of W. Ontario
    LONDON, Ontario N6H 4S3

DETROIT RIVER
Windsor Skin & Scuba Club, P.O. Box 26009, RPO Langlois, WINDSOR, Ontario
    N9A 7E9

ST. CLAIR RIVER
Sarnia Underwater Club, c/o John Gill, 1268 Lakeshore Rd., SARNIA, Ontario N7S
    2L4

LOWER LAKE HURON
Bluewater Scuba Club, 3-633 Harbour St., Bos 1893, PORT ELGIN, Ontario N0H 2C0

SOUTH OF TOBERMORY
Mary Ward Dive Club, MTSC Meaford, R.R. #1, MEAFORD, Ont. N4L 1W5

LAKE SIMCOE/MUSKOKA AREA
Aquaducks Diving, Inc., P.O. Box 1762, PETERBOROUGH, Ontario K9J 6X7
Barrie Sub-Aquians, c/o 53 Roslyn Rd., BARRIE, Ontario L4M 1L8
Huronia Aqua Descenders, 166 Gunn St., BARRIE, Ontario L4M 2H9
Poseidon Circle Scuba Club, 203 London St., PETERBOROUGH, Ont. K9H 2Y8
Trident Underwater Club, Inc., P.O. Box 656, PETERBOROUGH, Ontario K9J 6Z8
Twin Lake Divers, Box 203, ORILLIA, Ontario L3V 6H9

NORTH GEORGIAN BAY
Chapleau Dive Club, P.O. Box 805, CHAPLEAU, Ontario P0M 1K0
Dolphin Aquatic Club, P.O. Box 424, Station "B", SUDBURY, OntarioP3E 4P6
Elliot Lake Bottomtimers, 301 Rear Mississauga Ave., ELLIOT LAKE, Ontario P5A
          1E8
Espanola Dive Club (G. Shaler), P.O. Box 1944, ESPANOLA, Ontario P0P 1C0
North Bay Scuba Club, P.O. Box 831, NORTH BAY, Ontario P1B 8K1
North Muskoka Diving Club (B. McDonald), 10 Crestview Dr., HUNTSVILLE,
          Ontario P0A 1K0
Waterways Dive Team, c/o 485 Frood Rd., SUDBURY, Ontario P3C 5A2

ST. MARY'S RIVER
Lake Superior Tridents (H. Wyatt), P.O. Box 20102, 150 Churchill Blvd, SAULT STE
          MARIE, Ontario P6A 6W3

LAKE SUPERIOR
Kenogamisis Diving Club (B. Mascotto), P.O. Box 219, GERALDTON, Ontario P0T
          1M0
Lake of the Woods Depthfinders, c/o Bruce Hansen, R. R. #1, KENORA, Ontario P9N
          3W7
North Shore Dive Club, P.O. Box 954, TERRACE BAY, Ontario P0T 2W0
Patricia Pelicans Scuba Club, P.O. Box 455, SIOUX LOOKOUT, Ontario P0V 2T0
Red Lake Divers (J. Sinnons), Box 676, RED LAKE, Ont. P0V 2M0
Thunder Country Dive Club, 448 May St. North, THUNDER BAY, Ontario P7C 3R5

APPENDIX F: Marine Museums in Ontario

(For more detailed information, see *Dive Ontario Two!*, pp. 275-300.)

Wheelhouse Maritime Museum, Box 518, Ottawa, Ontario K1N 9H1.

Marine Museum of the Great Lakes at Kingston, 55 Ontario Street, Kingston, Ontario K7L 2Y2, (613) 542-2261.

Mariner's Park Museum Lighthouse Park, South Bay, Ontario, south via Highways 9 and 13, (May-October), (613) 476-4695.

Marine Museum of Upper Canada, Exhibition Place, west of the Princes' Gates entrance at Lakeshore Blvd. West and Strachan Ave., Toronto. (416) 392-6827.

Port Colborne Historical & Marine Museum, (April-November). Contact the Port Colborne Chamber of Commerce, 76 Main St. West, Port Colborne, Ontario

Sombra Township Museum, St. Clair Parkway, south of Sarnia, (April-October),

Moore Township Museum, Mooretown, (south of Sarnia) Ontario, (March-November), (519) 867-2020.

Huron County Marine Museum, (May-September), Harbour Road, Goderich, Ontario, (519) 524-9091. Information can also be obtained from the Huron County Museum, Goderich, Ontario, (519) 524-2628.

Bruce County Museum and Archives, one block north and one block east of Highway 21, Southampton, Ontario, (519) 797-2080.

St. Edmund's Township Museum, (May-October), Highway 6 south of Tobermory, Ontario, (519) 596-2479.

Owen Sound Marine-Rail Museum, 1165 1st Ave. West, Owen Sound, Ontario N4K 4K8. (519) 371-3333.

Meaford Museum, Bayfield, St., Meaford, Ontario. (519) 538-1060.

H.M.S. *Nancy,* Ministry of Natural Resources, Wasaga Beach Provincial Park, Box 183, Wasaga Beach, Ontario L0L 2P0, (705) 429-2516.

Collingwood Museum, St. Paul Street, Collingwood, Ontario, (705) 445-4811.

Historic Naval & Military Establishments, 1817-1856, (May-September), Penetanguishene, Ontario. Mailing address: Discovery Harbour, P.O. Box 1800, Penetanguishene, Ontario L0K 1P0. (705) 549-8064.

R.M.S. *Segwun,* historic steamboat cruises, as well as Friends of the *Segwun,* Box 68, Gravenhurst, Ontario P0C 1G0, (705) 687-6667.

North Bay Area Museum, Riverbend Road off Lakeshore Drive, North Bay, Ontario, (705) 476-2323.

S. S. *Norisle,* Museum ship, (July-August) Manitowaning, Ont. (705) 859-3977.

Gore Bay Museum, (June-Sept.) Dawson St., Gore Bay, Ontario.

Net Shed Museum, (June-Sept.), Meldrum Bay, Manitoulin Island.

Mississagi Lighthouse Heritage Park, Western Manitoulin Island, (May-Sept.); summer (705) 283-3444, winter (705) 866-2682.

M. S. *Norgoma* Museum Ship, (June-September) downtown waterfront, Norgoma Dock at Foster Drive, Sault Ste. Marie, Ontario. (705) 253-9850.

APPENDIX G

Eleven Fish a Diver Might Encounter in Ontario

BASS -- this popular game fish is often seen by divers in streams, ponds, and rocky lake areas.

BLUEGILL -- This fish is commonly seen by scuba divers on wrecks and especially in quarries. They are usually no larger than 8 inches (20 cms.) and weigh 0.5 pound.

BURBOT -- Also called ling, lingcod, or "lawyer fish", the burbot is seen on most Great Lakes shipwrecks and is easily recognized by a barbel at the tip of the jaw and its "eel-like" tail. Shunned as a food-fish due to its appearance and texture, it predaciously feeds upon smaller fish and may reach 4 feet (1.2 metres) in length.

CARP -- Considered a delicacy by some who know how to prepare it, this fish is also a bottom feeder. It can grow to a maximum length of 3 feet (almost 1 metre) and a weight of 50 pounds.

CATFISH -- Considered an active game fish and, by some, fine eating, in spite of the fact that they are bottom feeders. The maximum length is 4 feet (1.2 metres) and 55 pounds the maximum weight, but they are usually much smaller.

MUSKY -- This fierce game fish, which has teeth like a small barracuda and sometimes the temper to match, is rarely seen or caught today. Large ones could reach 6 feet (1.8 metres) in length and weigh 90 pounds.

PERCH -- Its white flesh is valued as one of the best food fish in the Great Lakes, and many people enjoy it as a sport fish. Although the record perch weighed over 4 pounds, most are just under one pound, with an average length of about 10 inches (25 cms.)

PIKE -- Although usually found in the northern Great Lakes regions, pike are occasionally seen and caught in Southwestern Ontario. They reach a length of 3.5 feet (one metre).

SMELT -- Smelt runs in the spring (usually late April) are very popular with net fishermen wearing waders. The average length of this fish is 6 to 9 inches (15 to 22 cms.)

STURGEON -- This migratory fish has occasionally been caught by sportsfishermen; recently a five-footer (1.5 metres long) was "captured" by a young man when he saw it basking near the surface of the St. Clair River. He jumped in and dragged it, alive and kicking, ashore.

WALLEYE -- This fish, like the perch, is one of the most important game and food fish in the Great Lakes. The large ones will be 2 feet (0.6 metre) in length and weigh as much as 14 pounds. Also called "pickerel" in some regions.

BIBLIOGRAPHY

BOOKS

Amos, Art. *Rudders, A Comparison Study.* Midland, Ontario: Ontario Marine Heritage Committee, 1993.

Amos, Art, and Patrick Folkes. *A Diver's Guide to Georgian Bay.* Toronto: Ontario Underwater Council, 1979.

Barcus, Frank. *Freshwater Fury.* Detroit: Wayne State University Press, 1960.

Barry, James P. *Wrecks and Rescues of the Great Lakes, A Photographic History.* LaJolla, California: Howell-North Books, 1981.

Bowen, Dana T. *Lore of the Lakes.* Cleveland: Freshwater Press, 1940.

------------*Memories of the Lakes.* Daytona Beach, Florida: Dana Thomas Bowen, publisher, 1946.

------------*Shipwrecks of the Lakes.* Cleveland: Freshwater Press, 1952.

Boyer, Dwight. *Ghost Ships of the Great Lakes.* New York: Dodd, Mead & Co., 1968.

------------*Great Stories of the Great Lakes.* New York: Dodd, Mead & Co., 1966.

------------*True Tales of the Great Lakes.* New York: Dodd, Mead & Co., 1971.

Charlebois, Peter. *Sternwheelers and Sidewheelers, the Romance of Steamdriven Paddleboats in Canada.* Toronto: NC Press Ltd., 1978.

Club Poseidon. *The St. Clair River...a sport diver's guide.* Port Huron, Michigan, June 1983.

Dolan, Tom. *Know Your Fish.* New York: Sports Afield Collection, The Hearst Corporation, 1960.

Folkes, Patrick. *Shipwrecks of the Saugeen, 1828 - 1938.* 1970.

Fox, W. Sherwood. *The Bruce Beckons, The Story of Lake Huron's Great Peninsula.* Toronto: University of Toronto Press, 1952, rev. 1962.

Gatis, Sheila, ed. *Days of the "Mud Hen" and other Memories of Colpoy's Bay Village, Ontario.* Wiarton, Ontario: printed by Echo Graphics, 1986.

Greenwood, John O. *Namesakes 1900-1909.* Cleveland: Freshwater Press, Inc., 1987.

------------*Namesakes 1910-1919.* Cleveland: Freshwater Press, Inc., 1986.

------------*Namesakes 1920-1929.* Cleveland: Freshwater Press, Inc., 1984.

------------*Namesakes 1930-1955,* Cleveland: Freshwater Press, Inc., 1978.

------------*Namesakes 1956-1980,* Cleveland: Freshwater Press, Inc., 1981.

Hatcher, Harlan. *The Great Lakes.* London, New York, Toronto: Oxford University Press, 1944.

------------*Lake Erie.* Indianapolis and New York: Bobbs-Merrill Co., 1945.

------------and Erich A. Walter. *A Pictorial History of the Great Lakes.* New York: Bonanza Books, 1963.

Heden, Karl E. *Directory of Shipwrecks of the Great Lakes.* Boston: Bruce Humphries Pubs., 1966.

Heyl, Eric. *Early American Steamers, Vols. I-VI.* Buffalo, New York: published by the author at 136 West Oakwood Place, 1961-1969.

Humphries, William. *Great Fury.* London, Ontario: Concept Printing (self-published), 1975.

Investigating...Canada's Deep South. A 1980 reprint of an informal Parks Canada publication entitled *Insite and Information, Point Pelee National Park,* originally produced in 1975.

Kohl, Cris. *Dive Southwestern Ontario!* Chatham, Ontario: self-published, 1985; revised ed., 1988.

------------*Shipwreck Tales: The St. Clair River (to 1900)*. Chatham, Ontario: self-published, 1987.

------------*Dive Ontario Two! More Ontario Shipwreck Stories*. Chatham, Ontario: self-published, 1994.

Landon, Fred. *Lake Huron*. Indianapolis & New York: Bobbs-Merrill Company, 1944.

Lockery, Andy. *Marine Archaeology and the Diver*. Toronto: Atlantic Publishing, 1985.

Mansfield, J. B., ed. *History of the Great Lakes*, Two volumes. Chicago: J. H. Beers & Co., 1899; reprint edition, Cleveland: Freshwater Press, 1972.

McKenney, Jack. *Dive to Adventure*. Vancouver: Panorama Publications Inc., 1983.

Metcalfe, Willis. *Marine Memories*. Picton, Ontario: The Picton Gazette, 1975.

------------*Canvas & Steam on Quinte Waters*. South Bay, Ontario: The South Marysburgh Marine Society, 1979.

Mills, John M. *Canadian Coastal and Inland Steam Vessels, 1809-1930*. Providence, Rhode Island: The Steamship Historical Society of America, Inc., 1979.

Nute, Grace Lee. *Lake Superior*. Indianapolis & New York: Bobbs-Merrill Company, 1944.

Pound, Arthur. *Lake Ontario*. Indianapolis & New York: Bobbs-Merrill Company, 1945.

Prothero, Frank & Nancy. *Tales of the North Shore*. Port Stanley,Ont.: Nan-Sea Publications, 1987.

Ratigan, W. *Great Lakes Shipwrecks and Survivals*. New York: Galahad Books, 1960.

Salen, Rick. *The Tobermory Shipwrecks*. Tobermory, Ontario: The Mariner Chart Shop, 1985.

Stone, Dave. *Long Point, Last Port of Call*. Erin, Ontario: Boston Mills Press, 1988.

Tatley, Richard. *The Steamboat Era in the Muskokas, Volume II -- The Golden Years to Present*. Erin, Ontario: Boston Mills Press, 1984.

Unitt, Peter, and Anne Worrall. *Unitt's Bottles Book & Price Guide*. Peterborough, Ontario: Clock House Publications, 1985.

Vanden Hazel, Bessel J. *The John Fraser Story*. North Bay, Ont.: Nipissing Univ. College, 1985.

Van der Linden, Rev. Peter J., ed., and the Marine Historical Society of Detroit. *Great Lakes Ships We Remember*. Cleveland: Freshwater Press, 1979; revised 1984.

------------*Great Lakes Ships We Remember II*. Cleveland: Freshwater Press, 1984.

------------*Great Lakes Ships We Remember III*. Cleveland: Freshwater Press, 1994.

Weir, Stephen. *Sinking of the Mayflower, lost November 12, 1912*. Burnstown, Ontario: General Store Publishing House, Inc., 1990.

Wolf, Julius F., Jr. *Lake Superior Shipwrecks*. Duluth, Minnesota: Lake Superior Port Cities, Inc., 1990.

Wrigley, Ronald. *Shipwrecked, Vessels that met tragedy on Northern Lake Superior*. Cobalt, Ontario: Highway Book Shop, 1985.

Young, Anna G. *Great Lakes Saga*. Owen Sound: Richardson, Bond & Wright Ltd., 1965.

PERIODICALS

Alford, Terry. "Kingston's Newest Wreck Dive" *Diver Magazine.* Vol.12, No.1. March,1986, p.18-21

------------"Time Capsule in Kingston, Queen of Kingston's Wrecks." *Diver Magazine.* Vol. 14, No. 1. March, 1988, pp. 19-20.

Bellefeuille, Monique J."Wreck Facts: The St. Lawrence River's *Conestoga.*" *Skin Diver Magazine.* Vol. 39, No. 8. August, 1990, pp. 18, 48, 57

Bellefeuille, Monique and Mike. *"Lillie Parsons." Diver Magazine.* Vol. 16, No. 7. Nov., 1990, pp. 18-19.

Eden, Glenda. "Ghost Towns of the St. Lawrence." *Diver Magazine.* Vol. 14, No. 3. May, 1988, pp. 18-22.

------------"Lost Villages." Diver Magazine, Vol. 17, No. 6, Sept., 1991, pp. 30-32.

Fell, John. "Bottle Diving Pays Off." *Diver Magazine.* Vol. 5, No. 6. Aug./Sept., 1979, pp. 18-20.

Fountain, Norah. "Waome Wetsuit Tribute. *Diver Magazine,* Vol. 21, No. 3. May, 1995, pp.20-21.

Gilchrist, David. "Diving Weekend at Port Colborne, Ontario (Wreck of the Steamer *Raleigh)." Diver Magazine,* Vol. 20, No. 5, Aug., 1994, pp. 14-15.

Golding, Peter. "Fathom Five Park." *Diver Magazine.* Vol. 5, No. 6. Aug./Sept., 1979, pp. 24-27.

------------"Inner Space Adventure, *Comet* in Lake Ontario." *Diver Magazine.* Vol. 5, No. 4. June, 1979, pp. 21-24.

------------"Innerkip Quarry, An Unusual Experience." *Diver Magazine.* Vol. 5, No. 2. February/March, 1979, pp. 22-23, 44, 45.

------------"Lady of Muskoka, The *Woame." Diver Magazine.* Vol. 6, No. 4, June, 1980, pp. 20-21.

------------*"Maple Dawn." Diver Magazine.* Vol. 6, No. 3, April/May, 1980, pp. 36-37.

------------*"Michigan's* Muscle Machines." *Diver Magazine,* Vol. 5, No. 4. June, 1979, pp.20-21.

------------"The *Price* Adventure." *Diver Magazine.* Vol. 4, No. 8. Nov./Dec., 1978, pp. 34-38.

------------"Tale of Two Wrecks, *Sweepstakes --- City of Grand Rapids." Diver Magazine.* Vol. 6, No. 1, January/February, 1980, pp. 24-25.

------------"Tobermory Tug." *Diver Magazine.* Vol. 7, No. 2. March, 1981, pp. 38-39.

------------"Tobermory's Limestone Grottos." *Diver Magazine.* Vol.5, No.3. Ap/May, 1979, p.28-31

------------"The Wreck of the *George A. Marsh." Diver Magazine.* Vol. 5, No. 8. Nov./Dec., 1979, pp. 38-40.

Hector, Bruce. "Kingston Wrecks." *Diver Magazine,* Vol. 17, No. 1, March, 1991, pp. 32-33.

Kemp, Bruce. "Lake Huron Mystery." *Diver Magazine.* Vol. 8, No. 2. March, 1982, pp. 17-20.

------------"Shipwrecks of the St. Clair River." *Diver Magazine.* Vol. 9, No.8. Dec., 1983, p.18-20.

Kohl, Cris. "Backwoods Secret." *Diver Magazine,* Vol. 17, No. 5, Aug., 1991, pp. 33-35.

------------"Lake Erie Shipwreck Discovery!" *Diver Magazine.* Vol.15, No.8. Dec., 1989, pp.18-22.

------------"Shipwrecks Threatened by Freshwater Barnacles." *Diving Times.* Vol. 12, No. 2, Summer, 1989.

------------"The Wreck of the *William H. Wolf.*" *Ontario Diver's Digest.* August, 1990.

Kohl, Cris, & Sharon Hamilton. "City of Genoa." *Diving Times.* Vol.10, #4. Winter,1987-88, p.14

Kozmik, Jim."*Arabia,* Fathom Five's Deep Lady."*Diver Magazine.* Vol.7, No.2. Mar.,1981, p. 28-29

------------"Diving the Flowerpots of Georgian Bay." *Diver Magazine.* Vol. 8, No. 3. April/May, 1982, pp. 34-35.`

------------"Stokes Bay for Wreck Diving enthusiasts." *Diver Magazine.* Vol. 6, No. 2. March, 1980, pp. 14-15.

Kuss, Dan. "Wreck of the *Rappahannock.*" *Diver Magazine,* Vol. 16, No. 8, Dec., 1990, pp. 19-21.

"Lake Erie Wreck Draws U.S. Divers to Canadian Waters." *Underwater U.S.A.* Vol. 4, No. 11. March, 1988, p. 35.

Mack, Robert. "Ten Dives in Eastern Ontario." *Diver Magazine.* Vol.16, No.3. May, 1990, p.14-15.

Mackie, Dan. "88 under the Ice." *Diver Magazine.* Vol. 8, No. 6. September, 1982, pp. 16-17.

McDaniel, Neil. "Fathom Five's Deep Treasure, The Barque *Arabia.*" *Diver Magazine.* Vol. 13, No. 3. May, 1987, pp. 22-23.

------------"Tobermory, Ontario's Wreck Diving Capital." *Diver Magazine.* Vol. 12, No. 8, December, 1986, pp. 24-31.

------------"Tobermory's Wreck of the Steam Barge *Wetmore.*" *Diver Magazine.* Vol. 13, No. 5. July/August, 1987, pp. 14-15.

------------"Wreck Diving at the Tip of the Bruce in Canada's First National Marine Park: Fathom Five." *Diver Magazine.* Vol. 15, No. 5. July/August, 1989, pp. 26-29.

McGrath, Vern. "Ice Floe Frolic." *Diver Magazine.* Vol. 6, No. 5, July/August, 1980, pp. 14-15.

McMaster, Robert W. "The Prize of Chippawa Creek." *Diver Magazine.* Vol. 5, No. 5. July, 1979, pp. 34-37.

Moran, Tim. "The *William H. Wolf,* A St. Clair River Wreck." *Canadian Diving Journal.* Number 2, 1985, pp. 32-33.

Mullings, Ken. "The Fate of the *Falconer.*" *Diver Magazine,* Vol. 18, No. 6, Sept., 1992, pp. 18-19.

Orr, Dan. "The Barque *Arabia:* 1853-1884." *Diver Magazine.* Vol. 11, No. 6. Sept., 1985, pp. 30-32.

Orth, Darryl, with Rick Skoryk. "Flagship of the Muskokas." *Diver Magazine,* Vol. 19, No. 9, Feb., 1994, pp. 30-32.

Soegtrop, Michael. "Bruce Peninsula National Park." *Diver Magazine.* Vol. 14, No. 2. April 1988, pp. 14-17.

------------"Canada's Archaeological Treasures." *Diver Magazine.* Vol.16, No.4. June,1990, p.24-29.

------------"Deep or Shallow, Tobermory Has It All." *Diver Magazine,* Vol. 19, No. 1, March, 1993. pp. 26-29.

------------"Killarney, Ontario." *Diver Magazine.* Vol. 14, No. 3. May, 1988, pp. 28-31.

------------"Killarney, Diving Georgian Bay's North Shore." *Diver Magazine.* Vol. 11, No. 4. June, 1985, pp. 20-21.

------------"Killarney Wrecks." *Diver Magazine,* Vol. 17, No. 1, March, 1991, pp. 25-27.

------------"Mapledawn, Wreck in Southern Georgian Bay." *Diver Magazine,* Vol. 18, No. 4, June, 1992, pp. 20-21.

------------"Shipwreck on the Move." *Diver Magazine,* Vol. 8, No. 8. December, 1982, p. 12.

------------"The *Mayflower.*" *Diver Magazine,* Vol. 17, No. 3, May, 1991, pp. 36-37.

------------"Tobermory's Classic Shipwreck, *City of Cleveland.*" *Diver Magazine.* Vol. 13, No. 1. March, 1987, pp. 24-29.

------------"Twice Lost by Fire (the *Atlantic),*" *Diver Magazine.* Vol.7, No.3. April`/May, 1981, p.27-29

Soegtrop, Michael, and Eva Woloszczuk. "Kingston." *Diver Magazine.* Vol. 7, No. 1, January/February, 1981, pp. 23-24.

VandenHazel, Bessel. "History in Glass, The Story Behind our Medicine Bottles." *Diver Magazine.* Vol. 9, No. 6. September, 1983, pp. 14-15.

------------"Lake Nipissing Shipwreck, The Story of the *John Fraser.*" *Diver Magazine.* Vol. 8, No. 7. October/November, 1982, pp. 26-27.

------------"Steam Tug of lake Nipissing, Life and Death of the *Screamer.*" *Diver Magazine.* Vol. 10, No. 5. July/August, 1984, pp. 19-20.

Weir, Stephen. "Bottle Mania, The Collecting Bottle Story: Ten Tips for Beginners." *Diver Magazine.* Vol. 16, No. 3. May, 1990, pp. 30-32.

------------"Dyer Bay". *Diver Magazine.* Vol. 9, No. 2. March, 1983, pp. 20-22.

------------"Hunting for Bottles." *Diver Magazine.* Vol. 7, No. 6. September, 1981, pp. 35-39.

MISCELLANEOUS

Diving Industry Index '95-'96. Ontario Underwater Council, 1185 Eglinton Avenue East, NORTH YORK, Ontario M2C 3C6, telephone: (416) 426-7033.

Hilton, Nancy, ed. *A 10 Year Summary of Sport Diving Fatalities in Ontario, 1979-1988.* Ontario Underwater Council, 1185 Eglinton Avenue East, NORTH YORK, Ontario M2C 3C6, telephone: (416) 426-7033.

"Master Sheets." Institute for Great Lakes Research. Bowling Green State University, Ohio. For the following vessels: Alexandria, Aloha, Ann Maria, Armenia, Atlantic, Avalon Voyager, Belle Sheridan, Chicago, City of Cleveland, City of Genoa, City of Grand Rapids, City of Sheboygan, Columbus, Comet, Conemaugh, Conestoga, Thomas Cranage, Henry C. Daryaw, Eastcliffe Hall, Ella Ross, Emma, Erie Stewart, Annie Falconer, Florence, Forest City, Gargantua, Gladstone, Goudreau, Jay Gould, Grand Traverse, India, Wm. Jamieson, Juno, Keystorm, Lycoming, Majestic, Mapledawn, George A. Marsh, Mary E. McLachlan, Fred Mercur, Julia B. Merrill, F. A. Meyer, Merida, Metamora, Michigan, Midland, Midland City, Charles P. Minch, Monarch, Monkshaven, Neebing, Newaygo, Northern Belle, Ontario, Charles B. Packard, Charles S. Price, Quinte, Rappahannock, Reliever, Robert K., Rothesay, St. Andrews, Sarah, Seattle, Singapore, Sligo, Specular, George Stone, Horace L. Taber, Tasmania, Frank E. Vigor, Mary Ward, Waubuna, W. L. Wetmore, Willis, William H. Wolf.

Reports from the Ontario Underwater Council Concerning Ontario Diving Fatalities, 1989, 1990, 1991, 1992, 1993, 1994. Ontario Underwater Council, 1185 Eglinton Avenue East, NORTH YORK, Ontario M2C 3C6, telephone: (416) 426-7033.

INDEX

An asterisk [*] denotes a photograph.
Ships' names are in *italics.*

Discarded Titles

If you feel that the title of this book, *Dive Ontario!* is misleading, I offer the rejected titles for your approval:

Favourite Dive Sites of Jacques Cousteau
Decompression to Conquer Loneliness
Huckleberry Fins
How to Impress Your Friends with Your Weightbelt (or How to Throw Your Weight Around)
Gone With the Current
No Man Is an Island
Advanced Dive Sites for the Simple-Minded
Canada's Top 250 Dive Sites
How to Find Gold and Silver Coins on Shipwrecks and Get Rich Quick
10,000 Loran-C Numbers for Great Lakes Shipwrecks
It Wasa Night To Remember Raising the Titanic
How to Retire After Four Dives
How to Change Your Drysuit into a Wetsuit
Everything You Always Wanted to Know about Snorkels --- But Were Afraid to Ask
Freshwater Sharks of Georgian Bay
Bottle Diving: My Shattering Experiences
400 Projects for Used CO2 Cartridges
Fear of Diving
My Wicked, Wicked Weights
Deep Float
The Impact of French Colonialism on Sixteenth Century Llama Routes in Peru
Real Women Don't Pump Air
Scuba Politicians are from Mars, Shipwreck Divers are from Venus
The Second-Last Frontier
Mid-Continent Oceanic Explorations
Raise the Hamilton, the Scourge, and the Edmund Fitzgerald Now!

HOW TO ORDER ADDITIONAL COPIES

Additional copies of *Dive Ontario!*, *Dive Ontario Two!*, and other shipwreck books by Cris Kohl may be ordered directly from the author at 16 Stanley Avenue, Chatham, Ontario, Canada, N7M 3J2. Telephone (519) 351-1966 or fax (519) 351-1753 for availability and prices.

HAPPY READING and *SAFE DIVING!*

EMERGENCY TELEPHONE NUMBERS

Ambulance:

Ontario Provincial Ambulance Service.
Dial "0" and request ZENITH 90,000.

State immediately that it is a scuba diving emergency.

Police:

Ontario Provincial Police.
Dial "0" and request ZENITH 50,000.

State immediately that it is a scuba diving emergency.

Hyperbaric Chambers:

Toronto (Ontario) General Hyperbaric: **(416) 340-4131**
After hours locating service: **(416) 340-3155**

Tobermory (Ontario) Hyperbaric Facility,
(519) 596-2305

A chamber is presently being established in Ottawa, but finalized information was not available at press time for this edition of *Dive Ontario!*.

D. A. N. (Diver Alert Network):
(919) 684-8111

This telephone number is in North Carolina. D.A.N. specializes in scuba diving emergencies in the United States. In the event of a scuba diving emergency in Ontario, D.A.N. will direct the victim to get him/herself to the Toronto chamber immediately because it is likely closer, as well as considerably cheaper, than going to a chamber in the United States.